# RENDERING
## UNTO
## CAESAR

# RENDERING
## UNTO
## CAESAR

*The Catholic Church
and the State
in Latin America*

ANTHONY GILL

*The University of Chicago Press*
*Chicago and London*

Anthony Gill is assistant professor of political science at the University of Washington. His articles have appeared in the *International Journal of Social Economics* and the *American Journal of Political Science*.

The University of Chicago Press, Chicago 60637
The University of Chicago Press, Ltd., London
© 1998 by The University of Chicago
All rights reserved. Published 1998
Printed in the United States of America
07 06 05 04 03 02 01 00 99 98    1 2 3 4 5
ISBN: 0-226-29383-1 (cloth)
ISBN: 0-226-29385-8 (paper)

Library of Congress Cataloging-in-Publication Data

Gill, Anthony James.
    Rendering unto Caesar : the Catholic Church and the state in Latin
America / Anthony J. Gill.
        p.   cm.
    Includes bibliographical references and index.
    ISBN 0-226-29383-1 (alk. paper).—ISBN 0-226-29385-8 (pbk. :
alk. paper)
    1. Church and state—Catholic Church—History—20th century.
2. Church and state—Latin America—History—20th century.
3. Catholic Church—Latin America—History—1965–  .   4. Latin
America—Church history—20th century.   I. Title.
BR660.G55   1998
261.7'098—dc21                                                            97-19432
                                                                                    CIP

♾ The paper used in this publication meets the minimum requirements of the American National Standard for Information Sciences—Permanence of Paper for Printed Library Materials, ANSI Z39.48-1984.

*To Becky,*
*who said she would never marry an academic,*
*but who did anyway.*

*By the side of every religion is to be found a political opinion,*
*which is connected with it by affinity.*
Alexis de Tocqueville, *Democracy in America*

# Contents

# Acknowledgments

When I was much younger, someone told me that polite people never discussed religion or politics at public gatherings. Given my stubborn nature, it was inevitable that from that moment on I would make these two topics the focus of my professional career. Whoever that person was, I owe my initial thanks. However, confining my field of study to only two contentious issues would never satisfy me; I had to add a third, that being economics. From the inception of this project, I realized that combining religion and politics with economic analysis would be highly controversial. Along the way, I ran into many naysayers who told me that it could not, or should not, be done. Striking out on this path of "greatest resistance" was difficult but rewarding. Over time, as I uncovered empirical evidence that confirmed my deductive hypotheses, I became assured that this line of research was worth pursuing. I know that there will continue to be skeptics who doubt the utility of my "rational choice" approach, but I am satisfied that I have added to the general academic debate on church-state relations by telling a story that has not been told previously.

Amid all the controversy this project has generated, a number of highly respected scholars and friends provided encouragement and sage academic counsel. On the academic front, my greatest debt is owed to Barbara Geddes and Jeff Frieden. Both provided detailed and extremely helpful comments at the early stages of this project, often under unrealistic time constraints. Michael Wallerstein and David López also offered their expert suggestions while this book was a dissertation at UCLA. A number of other scholars contributed helpful comments after having read either the entire manuscript or significant portions. They include Gretchen Casper, Mark Chaves, Dave Dixon, Carol Ann Drogus, Anne Hallum, Larry Iannaccone, Dan O'Neil, Rod Stark, Hannah Stewart-Gambino, and Ernest Sweeney. Youssef Cohen and an anonymous person read my manuscript for the University of Chicago Press. Their comments were incredibly supportive and useful; I could only wish for all my critics to be as open-minded and as understanding as they were. John Tryneski has lived up to his reputation as being one of the best editors in the business by supplying critical advice at some crucial moments. Michael Koplow, as copyeditor, did a great job wrestling with my convoluted prose.

I cannot forget to thank my good friends and peers at UCLA—Glen Biglaiser, Dave Brown, Dave D'Lugo, Carlos Juarez, and Nancy Lapp. They were willing to listen to my unformed ideas about religion and politics, and helped to give those ideas shape through various lunch discussions at North Campus and elsewhere around Los Angeles. My new colleagues at the University of Washington also have proven to be immensely helpful. I am especially grateful to Margaret Levi, Lance Bennett, and Michael McCann, who helped to promote the ideas of this relatively untested scholar. Lou Cabrera, Norma Rodriquez, and Dennis Palmieri provided excellent research assistance during the later stages of this project. The UW students in my winter 1995 seminar on religion and politics served as test readers for an earlier version of this book. As I asked their opinions of the manuscript prior to handing out final grades, I was not surprised to find that everyone liked it. Nonetheless, many of them did provide some very insightful critiques that I incorporated into the present version. Peter Bradley, Ron Brown, and Jay Gumbiner deserve special mention. My good friend Rob Pickering helped to proofread the entire manuscript as it neared completion and also contributed some helpful commentary on the theoretical and substantive material contained herein. Lars and Quinn never let me forget the need for relaxation during this long process.

Field research in Latin America would not have been possible without the help of various people and organizations. In Chile, I benefited from the assistance of Jaime Vatter, who secured my affiliation with the Department of Economics at the University of Chile (Santiago). I also owe thanks to the director of El Centro Bellarmino, Gabriel Valdivieso, and his staff. Oscar Godoy arranged access to the library at the Pontificia Universidad de Católica and Monsignor Christian Precht helped in establishing important contacts in Chile. The Bastías family—Magdalena and Manuel—were gracious hosts throughout my stay. Manolo Aburto Cofre was a great friend and guide while I was in Chile. I truly believe he represents an optimistic future for Latin America. Special thanks go out to Father Ernest Sweeney for arranging contacts for me in Argentina. Padre Fernando Storni and the other

Jesuits at the Centro de Investigación y Acción Social (CIAS) were superb hosts in Buenos Aires. Funding for research in Latin America came courtesy of the National Science Foundation (Grant No. SES 9223018) and UCLA's Latin American Center.

Finally, I reserve my greatest appreciation for my wife, Becky, who stuck with me through the often tedious, often harrowing process of writing a book. Becky served as expert typist, proofreader, and critic. But most of all, she gave me her love and understanding throughout the process. Thanks.

# ONE

# Introduction

## Caesar and the Church

*And when they were come, they say unto him, Master, we know that thou art true, and carest for no man: for thou regardest not the person of men, but teachest the way of God's truth: Is it lawful to give tribute to Caesar, or not? Shall we give, or shall we not give? But he, knowing their hypocrisy, said unto them, Why tempt ye me? Bring me a penny, that I may see it. And they brought it. And he saith unto them, Whose is this image and superscription? And they say unto him, Caesar's. And Jesus answering said unto them, Render to Caesar the things that are Caesar's, and to God the things that are God's.*

Mark 12:14–17

Conflict between church and state is nothing new. Tension arises from the fact that each institution draws its fundamental authority from a different source—religion from some divine mandate, governments from the secular need to maintain order and ensure economic growth. Although attempts have been made to separate the two realms as the biblical passage above indicates, the nature of each makes separation difficult to obtain in practice. States frequently enter the domain of personal morality and seek transcendental justification for their actions. And, for religions, the moral proclamations of spiritual leaders often have the effect of either legitimating or challenging power relations in secular society.

During times of rapid political and socioeconomic change (e.g., military coups), citizens frequently rely upon trusted public figures to provide guidance concerning political and social action. Even under "normal" political situations containing considerable uncertainty and imperfect information (e.g., voting), trusted public figures can provide indications to the public about appropriate behavior. In many societies, members of the clergy are

1

uniquely situated to perform these tasks, given their advanced level of education, supposed moral integrity, and relative independence from the secular work of politics.[1] Therefore, the content and tenor of their statements and actions regarding political matters may significantly influence the public's perception of any given policy, politician, or regime, in turn affecting the outcome of various political actions. Even when the clergy wish to avoid political entanglement, the public may interpret their silence as implying acceptance of certain policies, politicians, or regimes. As Dan Levine notes, "For religion and politics, whether the individual choice be neutrality or activism, the result is equally political: neutrality in effect commits one to work within the status quo; activism may require a commitment to change. Both are political positions" (1974, 498). For this reason, "rendering unto Caesar the things that are Caesar's" is not resolved easily for many religious elite. Their position as moral leaders in society almost inevitably leads them to pass judgment on political realities. Even in the United States, the constitutional separation of church and state cannot keep the religious and political realms apart. From the civil rights movement of the 1960s to the Christian Coalition in the 1990s, a high level of religious involvement in contemporary politics has been a fact of life. The intertwining of religion and politics is even more pronounced in Latin America—the focus of this study—where the issue of church-state separation remains far more ambiguous.

Without doubt, church-state relations have historically been complex and in constant flux. Throughout most of history—from King David to contemporary Iran—religious authority served to justify political regimes. In extreme cases, religious and political authority fused into one. More commonly, however, religious institutions would maintain a fair degree of autonomy from secular authority while simultaneously pursuing a close alliance with government officials; religious legitimation of a regime would be traded for financial assistance or other special privileges. On the other hand, spiritual leaders and organizations have been known to oppose governing bodies with great ferocity: The teachings of Jewish prophets and early Christian communities challenged Roman hegemony in Palestine; religious imagery played a crucial role in the Taiping Rebellion in China; Ayatollah Khomeini orchestrated the collapse of a secular dictator in Iran; and Christian base communities throughout Latin America frustrated the attempts of military regimes to silence criticism. Religious institutions, movements, and leaders always have been present in the political arena. Clearly, how and why religious leaders choose strategies of cooperation or conflict with secular authorities is an important topic for social science and historical research.

Unfortunately, for most of the twentieth century, the study of church-state relations was considered anachronistic. The common assumption among social scientists was that as society modernized, religion would fade eventually into the background, completely divorcing itself from public (and possibly even private) life.[2] "Secularization theory," as this line of analysis became known, was perhaps the least questioned school of thought in academia. However, the tremendous resurgence of religious movements around the world over the past three decades has challenged this thesis.[3] Religion wreaked savage revenge on the "inevitable" march of secularization. Even the aggressive atheism of communism could not stamp out spiritual beliefs and practices among those exposed to its message (Greeley 1994). As would be expected, the resurgence of religion did not escape scholarly attention and studies of church-state relations took on a new importance.[4] For the political scientist, the relationship between religious institutions and government raises a number of interesting questions: Why do religious authorities, at any given time, choose to oppose or support government policies or even a political regime? How do institutional reforms in one sphere affect activities in the other? What effects do large-scale social changes (e.g., urbanization, economic chaos, rise of new ideologies) have upon church-state relations?

Since the late 1960s, Latin America has become a major focus for the study of these questions, and appropriately so; given the wide variation in church-state relations in a region possessing a reasonably uniform religious culture, Latin America offers a unique historical laboratory from which to pursue rigorous social-scientific research. Nowhere else has the relationship between church and state been more volatile in recent decades. For the interested scholar, cases of both cooperation and conflict abound. Traditionally, Catholic Church officials forged tight links with the antidemocratic elite in each country, often using spiritual authority to legitimate repressive rule in exchange for a protected status. Despite occasional squabbles with specific governments, usually initiated by secular politicians, the norm for Catholic bishops and clergy was to seek accommodation with the political elite. However, beginning with Brazil in the late 1960s, several national episcopacies began actively opposing not only the brutal tactics of autocratic regimes, *but the underlying legitimacy of authoritarianism as well*. This represented a notable shift in Church-state relations. The Catholic Church moved "beyond condemnation of specific rulers or regimes to challenge whole economic, cultural and political systems as unjust and sinful" (Levine 1987, 93). Moreover, where in the past it was government officials who typically provoked hostility with the Church, the most recent wave of Church-state conflict was initiated by the clergy. This represented a significant change in political strategy for the Church, whose leaders typically criticized governments only *after* being attacked.

From a pastoral standpoint, this new strategy took the form of a "preferential option for the poor" and became apparent in several countries prior to the onset of the most recent wave of Latin American authoritarianism (roughly 1964–89). Bishops, arguing that the Church's primary concern should be to serve the long-neglected underclass, saw authoritarian rule as incompatible with the Church's pastoral mission. Not only were specific human rights violations denounced, but the deeper structural relations underlying state repression were questioned. Because of this stance, many bishops, clergy, and lay activists suffered at the hands of the state (see Lernoux 1980). The assassination of Salvadoran archbishop Oscar Romero in 1979 dramatically revealed the risk that the Church ran in opposing the powers that be.

However, not all national episcopacies elected to challenge the legitimacy of newly imposed or long-standing dictatorships in the 1960s,'70s, and '80s. Several national episcopal conferences, enunciating the *official* policy of the institutional Church, actively endorsed military regimes (as in Argentina) or remained silent (as in Uruguay, Bolivia, and Honduras). For the latter group, silence indicated a certain degree of acceptance of the status quo, legitimating dictatorship in a passive, yet nonetheless real way. Although progressive grassroots organizations arose in several of these countries to speak against political repression, such groups generally operated without the consent of the hierarchy and remained isolated (Mainwaring and Wilde 1989, 14). In other countries, such as Paraguay, the right of the regime to exist was never seriously questioned despite occasional denunciations by the episcopacy regarding the more flagrant abuses of power (Carter 1990).

## The Question at Hand

While examining the dimensions of church-state relations in general, the principal goal of this book is to answer the following question: Why did some national Catholic episcopacies in Latin America actively oppose dictatorial rule, while others did not? The focus is on the Catholic Church's *official* political strategy during the 1960s and '70s. "Official" implies that the primary unit of analysis is the national Catholic episcopacy. Bishops represent a vital intersection between the Church's pastoral agents (e.g., parish priests, lay activists) and the state. Frequently, they must choose between the often contradictory goals of supporting progressive pastoral agents who work in radically politicized settings and promoting the institutional interests of the Church in the political arena. The choice is neither easy nor automatic since carrying out the Church's evangelical mission and preserving its institutional strength may entail some rather unholy alliances with unsavory political actors. If and when the Church's pastoral interests clash with the ambitions of the political elite, the episcopacy must make a strategic choice between carrying out its evangelical mission and maintaining an alliance with the ruling class. This conflict is most apparent under right-wing authoritarianism since pastoral efforts among the poor frequently threaten the raison d'être of the regime.

The Catholic Church is a diverse and complex organization, and bishops are not the only Catholics who impact the political arena. The rise of grassroots religious movements over the past three decades has played an enormous role in shaping the identity of Latin American Catholicism. Although these movements require official sanction at a minimal level to survive, many have secured a fair degree of autonomy from their local bishops (see Levine 1992). Christian base communities and other organizations at the lower levels of society have weighed into the episcopacy's overall political calculus, but are not solely determinative of Church policy. Despite the many changes in Catholicism since Vatican II, the Church remains a very hierarchical organization and power still flows from the top down.

I define "opposition" as sustained public denunciations of the regime by a majority of the bishops within the country. *Not all bishops are of like mind on this issue,* but the increasing use of national bishops' conferences since the mid-1950s as a vehicle for enunciating Church policy makes identification of the Church's *institutional* position easier. To borrow Mainwaring and Wilde's terminology, we are looking for the Church's "center of gravity" (1989, 5). Proclamations against the legitimacy of a regime must be maintained over a substantial period of the regime's tenure to be considered antiauthoritarian. Even the most antidemocratic bishops must occasionally question blatant disregard for human rights. However, unless such denunciations are sustained over time, it is not reasonable to assert that the episcopacy is pursuing a political strategy of opposition. Furthermore, when gauging episcopal support or opposition toward dictatorship, one should note that Church leaders frequently keep a low profile during the first year of military rule. Rather than representing complicity, such silence is more akin to a "wait-and-see" strategy. The episcopacy's official position toward authoritarianism typically becomes clear after twelve months of autocratic governance.

Focusing on the episcopacy's official position toward authoritarianism has three attractive analytical qualities. First, it is a matter of increasing political importance in Latin America. Opposition to authoritarianism has important implications for democratic stabilization in the region. Admittedly, the Church by itself will not determine the fate of any given regime, but the presence of an enduring institution that provides moral justification and legitimation for more open systems of government certainly strengthens the prospects for stable democracy to some degree. Many social scientists are rediscovering that strong community values, such as trust, are a necessary, though not sufficient, condition for democratic stability and effective governance (Putnam 1993; Fukuyama 1995). Religious organizations serve as one primary source for generating such values. Knowing why religious leaders champion certain sets of values over others becomes an important topic to social scientists.[5]

Second, official opposition to authoritarianism is sufficiently narrow to constitute a manageable topic of study. The range of religious influence on political life is extensive. Not only does it encompass formal links between church and state, but religious belief frequently informs how individuals and groups view themselves in the political realm. Studying all of the political aspects of religious change could easily envelop one's entire academic life. The goal here is much more humble. This work represents one small piece of an infinitely large puzzle: what accounts for shifts in the political strategy of the Catholic elite? From this perspective, it is important to realize that the analysis presented here cannot explain all religious-political interaction, nor is it meant to.

Finally, the hierarchy's attitude toward a regime can be identified through the actions of any given episcopacy. This should avoid some of the definitional problems that make the study of religious change a difficult subject. Although inherently interesting, explaining the rise of Catholic "progressivism" often leads to difficulty in defining what one means by "progressive." Obviously, progressivism is subjectively determined by where one stands on the ideological spectrum. As Daudelin and Hewitt have observed, excessively subjective scholarship has led to an exaggeration of the strength of progressive Catholicism in the past (1995, 177). By narrowing the topic to the Church's official stance toward authoritarianism the degree of scholarly objectivity should increase and a more accurate picture of Catholic political strategy should emerge. While no study is completely detached from the researcher's worldview, it is possible to augment the degree of scholarly objectivity by constructing increasingly stricter definitional categories (Riker 1990, 168–69). Given these definitional issues, the term "progressive" is still useful when describing the *general ideological direction* of the Catholic Church from support for authoritarian methods of rule toward critical opposition.

Over the past two decades, scholars have devoted substantial energy to examining the growth of grassroots Catholicism in Latin America. Although much of this research addresses itself to the *consequences* of the Church's new orientation toward serving the poor, there has been ample speculation about the causes for this change. Three general explanations for the rise of Catholic "progressivism" and (more specifically) opposition to authoritarianism can be identified throughout the literature: a growing awareness on the part of the Church of the increasing "structural" poverty resulting from industrialization; an awakening to the rise in repression associated with authoritarian regimes; and reform within the international Church. Very few scholars attribute change to a single cause. Rather, some combination of these three factors is advanced as the general explanation for the Church's changing position. However, the greatest emphasis is placed on changes occurring within the Church as a result of the Second Vatican Council (1962–65) and its Latin American manifestations—the 1968 Medellín Conference, the 1979 Puebla Conference, and the advent of liberation theology. This study tests these hypotheses of Church change on a comparative basis.

In addition to testing these previous hypotheses, I advance a new explanation. This hypothesis concerns the effects religious competition has had on the Catholic Church. This competition has come most notably from evangelical Protestants, Spiritist movements, and Marxist organizations. I argue that religious competition increases the importance of obtaining active followers among nominal Catholics. Such Catholics are found predominantly among the rural and urban poor, where Catholic pastoral care has historically been weak. Shifting attention toward the lower classes risks conflict with military regimes that seek to suppress "subversive" activities among these social sectors. Church officials are then faced with a choice between scaling back pastoral work among the poor to appease the military and continuing with such efforts and risking a repressive response from the government. Moreover, a credible commitment to serve the poor, so long neglected by the Church, requires strong public statements in their defense. Where the Church faces greater competition for members, bishops will be under pressure to defend the interests of the poor, thereby breaking their traditional alliance with the elite. Not doing so would lead to a greater loss of poor parishioners to competing groups (e.g., evangelical Protestants). Where competition is weak or nonexistent, bishops can continue an alliance with the military without much fear of losing parishioners to other denominations.

## *Methodological Considerations*

How does one study church-state relations? The methods are nearly as numerous as the number of scholars studying the subject. Nonetheless, some broad methodological categories—including definitional issues, theoretical framework, and data-analytic techniques—can be delineated. As the manner in which one studies a subject can often affect the results, especially in the social sciences, it is appropriate to make one's methodology as explicit as possible. What follows is a general description of the methodology used in this work; it will help the reader understand how I derived the conclusions put forth in subsequent chapters.

### Concepts and Definitions

This study is primarily concerned with "church and state," as opposed to "religion and politics." The latter category alludes to a wide variety of behavior that exists outside of the confines of formal institutions—e.g., construction of personal and social identities, power relations between different levels of an organization, etc. On the other hand, *church and state* refers to the formal interactions between two institutional entities or, to be more precise, the official representatives of those institutions (Levine 1987). Given my interest in the general political strategy of the Catholic episcopate, I adopt an institutionalist perspective and consider organizational interests and procedures more relevant than the idiosyncratic actions of specific individuals. This is *not* to say that individuals are unimportant. Bishops such as Oscar Romero and Dom Hélder Câmara played historic roles in shaping the struggle for justice in Latin America. However, institutional prerogatives generally weigh heavily on individual bishops forcing their interests and actions to conform to those of the Church at large.

What does one mean by the terms *church* and *state?* To this point, these terms have been used quite loosely. In part, this merely reflects customary academic usage. Scholars in the subfield of church-state relations commonly assume that readers understand these concepts. For the most part, their assumption is warranted. But since I am attempting to bring a more rigorous methodological approach to bear on the subject, explicit definitions are in order.

For present purposes, *church* refers to an organization that professes a belief in some transcendental being and codifies behavioral norms that presumably are in accordance with this belief. The level of formal organization can vary quite considerably among churches and is not at issue here. Sociologists of religion typically differentiate churches from sects and cults. The terms *sect* and *cult* generally indicate religious organizations in tension with their social environment, with cults being the more deviant form (Stark and Bainbridge 1985, 19–37; 1987, 124–26). While helpful to studies of religion, the distinction between churches, sects, and cults is of minor relevance here. Hence, all religious organizations and movements will be considered churches. The primary exception to this rule occurs when one religious organization identifies another as a sect, since this reveals an important value judgment relevant to this study. (For example, Catholic statements about the "invasion of the sects" in Latin America indicate strongly that Catholic bishops consider Protestant denominations new to the region to be a serious, competitive, and unwelcome threat to Catholicism's traditional hegemony.) To clarify the definition further, where it is said that a "church" decides to undertake some action, "church" refers to the leaders of that institution. I wish to avoid the tendency to reify institutional entities; although institutions may impose significant constraints on individual actors, institutions do not make decisions—people do. Use of "church" to signify a set of clerical leaders merely represents a rhetorical simplification.

Related to this point, each national Catholic Church (as represented by its episcopal leaders) will be considered as a unitary actor, unless otherwise noted. This may seem a controversial assumption to some. After all, an organization as large as the Catholic Church inevitably possesses individuals with differing goals and ideological perceptions, and these differences may indeed play a significant role in shaping Church policy. I do not doubt this. Furthermore, I do not claim that all bishops think alike nor that the Church is a monolithic entity. However, as partially noted above, there are a number of justifiable reasons for assuming that the Church can be studied as a unitary actor. First, the hierarchical nature of the Catholic Church tends to mute internal conflict. While there may be ongoing debate within the Church regarding the direction of policy, there is a general deference to authority when it comes to taking action. For instance, certain bishops may disagree with the decision to maintain a celibate clergy, but rarely do they start ordaining married priests in their diocese. Second, leaders of the Catholic Church have a strong interest in presenting a unified front, especially as pertains to major policy decisions. A divided Church is a Church that lacks bargaining power and moral authority. Significant policy positions (e.g., publicly opposing a military government) will surely be debated among the hierarchy, but when action is taken bishops typically put aside differences and support the final decision.

Finally, there is an established practice in the social sciences of treating groups (e.g., political parties, labor unions, economic classes, and even nation-states) as individual actors. This is done for analytical simplicity: to control for intraorganizational power struggles so as to center attention on other significant variables external to the group itself. Of course, scholars must proceed cautiously when using such levels of aggregation and recognize that some of the behavior not explained by exogenous variables may be the result of internal group dynamics.[6] If the exogenous variables fail to account for any of the variation in the dependent variable, it then would be appropriate to place greater emphasis on intraorganizational factors.[7] As will be demonstrated below, assuming the Catholic episcopacy to be a unitary actor does not diminish the explanatory power of my central thesis that religious competition forced bishops to reevaluate their pastoral strategy among the poor and make a credible commitment to this social sector by opposing right-wing dictatorships. We certainly could improve our understanding of Catholic Church policy by examining the detailed interactions of specific prelates, but the unitary-actor assumption still yields some very interesting empirical findings. Moving away from particular historical individuals allows us to make a number of generalizations about church-state relations across time and space. My explicit intention here is to provide such generalizations with the hope that scholars studying different regions or epochs will be able to gain some insight into church-state relations by adopting (and modifying) the analytical framework advanced here.

The term *state* also requires definition. Unfortunately, since little consensus exists as to what the state is, a firm definition is hard to come by. I do not intend to resolve the debate, especially given that the main topic under investigation is the Catholic Church's political strategy toward the state. The definition adopted here borrows from the Weberian tradition as presented in Rueschemeyer and Evans. For them, the state is "a set of organizations invested with the authority to make binding decisions for people and organizations juridically located in a particular territory and to implement these decisions using, if necessary, force" (1985, 46–47). This definition avoids the Marxist inclination to view the state simply as the tool of the dominant class and the pluralist tendency to see the state as a neutral arbitrator of interest groups. State actors possess reasonably autonomous interests and varying degrees of capacity to act upon those interests. While Rueschemeyer and Evans (1985) help to delimit the boundaries of state authority, they tend to ignore the role of the individual. It is important to recognize that the organizations that they talk about are inhabited by rational individuals with interests shaped, but not necessarily predetermined, by their institutional surroundings (Geddes 1994, 7–14; Levi 1988, 185–204). This study examines only the highest executive decision makers (e.g., presidents, dictators, juntas) within the state. The word *state* will refer to these individuals.

## Theoretical Framework

In terms of a paradigmatic approach, my analysis relies on a rational-actor (i.e., microeconomic) model of behavior. On the surface, such an approach would appear misplaced. After all, most religious experiences and decisions are considered "nonrational," proceeding not from rational calculation of costs and benefits but from faith. However, although religious belief per se may be placed outside the realm of rationality, leaders of religious institutions are subject to the many of the same concerns and constraints as their secular counterparts (e.g., politicians, labor leaders). Primary among these concerns is the need for their church to survive and expand—i.e., to preserve the institution and increase membership. In addition to proclaiming the Word of God, bishops are also bureaucrats. They devote much of their time and energy to deciding how to distribute scarce resources so as to serve their basic goals. No matter how divinely inspired the clergy may be, a church exists in a world of scarcity and can thrive only to the extent that its leaders use resources efficiently. The conditions that cause secular actors to modify their behavior in defense of their institutionally determined goals will likewise apply to leaders of religious institutions; clergy who act irrespective of their church's institutional health will find that they are presiding over a weak and irrelevant organization with few believers in tow. A more extensive justification of the use of rational choice to examine religiously based behavior can be found in the appendix.

## Data Analysis

A unique blend of methodological techniques is used to test the thesis advanced here. I rely on both cross-national comparisons and detailed case studies, as well as quantitative and qualitative data analysis. Methodological diversity allows for one given technique to correct for the weaknesses of another. To begin, this study is explicitly comparative in nature. This approach differs from the majority of previous scholarship on Latin American church-state relations, which undertook detailed single-case studies of progressive Catholic Churches. Although contributing greatly to our empirical understanding of progressive Catholicism in Latin America, single-case studies are limited by their lack of variation on the dependent variable. Furthermore, given that the number of independent variables typically exceeds one, it becomes impossible to determine the relative importance of each explanatory factor. Not surprisingly, it is difficult to extend the findings of these studies to explain phenomena in other countries, specifically those with conservative episcopacies.

Using a comparative methodology, I examine both anti- and proauthoritarian Churches to test my theoretical propositions of Church behavior in Latin America. Obviously, much of the detailed richness unique to individual case studies will be lost by this approach. However, I believe the theoretical gains from broad comparisons adequately balance such costs. Barrington Moore reminded us of these benefits. "Comparisons can serve as a rough negative check on accepted historical explanations. And a comparative approach may lead to new historical generalizations. In practice these features constitute a single intellectual process and make such a study more than a disparate collection of interesting cases" (1966, xiii). Examining the histories of several countries, I seek to identify the larger historical processes underlying church-state relations in Latin America and elsewhere.

The comparative nature of this study is complemented by the use of two detailed case studies—Argentina and Chile. These specific case studies serve as a check on the cross-national statistical comparisons and shed light on the causal linkages in a way that "large *n*" studies cannot.[8] Argentina and Chile were chosen based upon their similarities and differences. In comparison with the rest of Latin America, both countries have relatively "Europeanized" cultures, similar economic histories, and significant middle classes and labor movements. Furthermore, each country has experienced reasonably successful and competitive electoral democracy for some extended period during the twentieth century. On this front, Chile scores better than Argentina, but the latter has seen the rise of institutionalized party structures and the alternation of opposing civilian factions in power. In this respect, one cannot say that liberal democracy was a practice unfamiliar to either country.

The principal difference between these two countries is how their respective Catholic episcopacies responded to the military regimes of both countries during the 1970s. In Chile, the Church became an outspoken critic of the military dictatorship and publicly demanded greater social justice and a return to democratic rule. The Argentine Catholic hierarchy, on the other hand, actively supported the two military regimes between 1966 and 1983. As will be seen in later chapters, these two countries also differed significantly with respect to the intensity of religious competition each Catholic Church faced. Presenting these cases side by side reveals the important causal link between Protestant expansion among the poor and Catholic political strategy.

The period under investigation is roughly the years between 1930 and 1979. This time frame encompasses the significant development of Protestant missionary activity, the expansion of indigenous, non-Catholic religious movements, and the presence of Marxism as a serious regional threat (real or perceived). It also marks the high point of Catholic opposition to military rule. The ascension of Pope John Paul II in 1978, the 1979 Nicaraguan revolution, and the gradual democratization of the region tempered much of the Church's opposition to authoritarianism, though it did not end it. The new pope asserted greater control over radical theologians and bishops in Latin America, fearing division within the Church. Sandinista victory in Nicaragua renewed the fear of communism among Church officials. Remembering the decimation of the Cuban Church under Fidel Castro two decades earlier, right-wing authoritarianism was temporarily preferable to left-wing dictatorship. Moreover, as military governments began yielding power to civilian rulers, the Church felt it best to ease its criticism in order to facilitate a more conciliatory transition to civilian rule. This is not to say that the progressive dynamics that began in the 1950s and 1960s ended. The 1979 meeting of the Latin American Bishops' Conference (CELAM) in Puebla, Mexico, reaffirmed the Church's "preferential option for the poor." However, the transitory political situation during the 1980s and '90s has increased the complexity of Catholicism's role in society many times over. While Church leaders remain concerned about the plight of the poor, they have been less willing to criticize often fragile democratic governments so as not to jeopardize their legitimacy.

With respect to the specific data used to test the hypotheses, quantitative and qualitative indicators are used. Statistical data are gathered on religious competition to test the central hypothesis of this work. Social and economic data are used to test rival hypotheses.[9] Statistical analysis, however, can only indicate correlation between variables, not causation. To establish causal linkages, I refer to a number of primary sources of qualitative data, including Catholic and Protestant documentation of events that transpired between the 1930s and '70s. Much of this information reveals the reasoning behind decisions made by Catholic bishops and clergy. Nonetheless, many of the clergy's public statements are cloaked in religious metaphors leaving their motivations ambiguous. To correct for this, secondary sources documenting the actual historical conduct of Catholic bishops and Protestant clergy are examined in light of their stated intentions. After all, actions frequently speak louder than words. Fortunately, a wealth of case histories exists on church-state relations in Latin America during the 1960s and '70s, especially for countries with progressive Catholic episcopacies. Secondary sources on more conservative Catholic Churches were more difficult to obtain, but sufficient information existed from which to make reasoned inferences.

I also conducted personal interviews with both Catholic and Protestant officials. These interviews served to substantiate what was in the written historical record. The selection of interviewees was based primarily upon availability. Many of the principal actors of the events I examined are no longer living. Locating people willing to speak about their experiences often meant relying upon references from past interviewees. In short, no random sample was taken. The interviews themselves were open-ended, allowing me to explore experiences unique to a given respondent. The general line of questioning centered around Catholic-Protestant and church-state relations, although there was no exact replication of questions across respondents. Given these methodological limitations, interviews were used only to corroborate other forms of evidence and not as a systematic source of data in their own right.

All told, this methodological diversity provides a multifaceted array of empirical checks on the theoretical assertions put forth in this study. While cross-national statistical comparisons tested the generalizability of my central thesis against competing explanations, the detailed case studies of Argentina and Chile fleshed out the specific causal linkages between religious competition and Catholic political strategy. Quantitative evidence, in turn, was held accountable to the historical record using more qualitative methods of analysis. Primary sources documenting the personal motivations of religious officials and descriptions of their own actions were cross-referenced with secondary sources and personal interviews. From all of this, some rather interesting findings linking the growth of Protestantism in Latin America to changes in the behavior of the Catholic Church emerge.

## Plan of the Book

History and theory are interwoven throughout the text. Chapter 2 examines relations between the Catholic Church and various Latin American governments on a general level from the Conquest to the mid–twentieth century. While focusing on the dominant pattern of church-state cooperation, I draw attention to two key periods of conflict, the early 1500s and the mid-1800s. The first period represents the only major pre-1965 example of *church-initiated* conflict and provides a number of interesting parallels with contemporary church-state conflict. State-initiated conflict during the mid-1800s is discussed, since this provides the historical basis for the rise in religious competition in the twentieth century.

Chapter 3 develops the primary hypothesis that Church opposition to authoritarianism is a function of religious competition. This hypothesis is set in the context of a more general model of church-state relations. The goal here is to provide a coherent theory that explains both church-state cooperation and conflict. This theory rests upon an argument about the relative costs and benefits leaders in each institutional sphere receive from cooperation versus conflict. Following this theoretical discussion of relations between church and state, chapter 4 surveys the growth of evangelical Protestantism in Latin America and the Catholic reaction to religious competition. Historical and statistical evidence is brought to bear on the primary hypothesis in order to answer several critical questions: Was Protestantism a significant threat to the Catholic Church? When did this threat occur? Is there a correlation between competitive threat and the Catholic Church's opposition to authoritarianism? If so, what was the specific causal path that led to Church opposition? Brief historical sketches of the twelve selected cases will be used to support the contention that a causal relationship exists. Other explanations for the rise of Catholic progressivism also are tested on a comparative basis.

Having demonstrated the efficacy of the religious-competition hypothesis on a regional basis, chapters 5 and 6 single out Chile and Argentina for detailed examination. These two countries represent polar opposites with respect to the support Church officials lent to military dictators. Evangelical Protestantism, especially the Pentecostal derivative, made its earliest and most significant gains in Chile. The influence of communism and socialism, in the form of agrarian unions and organized political parties, also played an important role in determining the political strategy of the Chilean episcopacy. As a result of these competitive pressures, this country developed one of the most innovative Catholic episcopacies in the world, initiating progressive pastoral reforms well before Vatican II. Following a relatively short and tense accommodation period with the Pinochet regime, the Chilean Church became one of the most vociferous proponents of a return to democracy. The Argentine Church, on the other hand, faced little competition from proselytizing denominations and remained a staunch ally of the numerous military regimes that came to power after 1930. Threats from communists were dealt with first by Juan Perón's corporatist policies, and later on by brutal military dictatorships. In both instances, the Church found that supporting the state was the best means of dealing with communism, the eventual conflict with Perón notwithstanding. Not surprisingly, the Catholic hierarchy in Argentina has been one of the most consistent supporters of authoritarianism in the region.

Given that the astonishing growth of Protestantism has continued throughout the 1980s and 1990s, chapter 7 projects the political implications of religious change into the near future. The return to democratic forms of government in Latin America raises an interesting question for the study of religion and politics: What are the institutional limits on Catholic political action? While advocating political democracy, the Catholic Church appears to be having difficulty instituting liberal reforms within its own organization. Furthermore, the Church has shown a tendency to return to elite-based political strategies under democracy. Does this "conservative retrenchment" reflect the political beliefs of Pope John Paul II, or is such behavior consistent with the underlying political strategies that led the Church to oppose authoritarianism? While recognizing the importance of the former, I argue a case for the latter.

The postscript reconsiders an economic interpretation of church-state relations in light of evidence from other parts of the world. Special attention is given to the former Soviet-bloc countries. The reintroduction of religious liberty in these countries has created some interesting church-state dynamics consistent with the general model proposed here. Recent research on the Middle East is then considered with an eye to seeing whether the argument could apply to religious traditions other than Christianity.

# TWO

# A Brief History of Church-State Relations in Latin America

*[W]ith what swords and cannons did Christ arm his disciples when he sent them to preach the gospel? Devastating provinces and exterminating natives or putting them to flight, is this freely sharing the faith? How blind are men's minds! What a truly deplorable calamity! When Christ sent his disciples to preach the gospel, he recommended meekness among them. "Remember," he says, "I am sending you out like sheep among wolves."*

Bartolomé de las Casas, *In Defense of the Indians*

Understanding the present means, in large part, understanding the past. Despite the fact that church-state conflict dates back to the initial period of colonization, most scholarship on this subject has focused on contemporary times (circa 1965–present). It is interesting to consider why conflict prior to 1965 garnered so little attention compared to the most recent wave of conflict. First, the sequence of events as played out in Latin America until the 1960s appeared to confirm the predictions of secularization theory. According to this theory, as society became increasingly modernized, religion would gradually fade from the public arena (Wallis and Bruce 1992). Even in the private sphere, religion would become less important and participation in organized religion would decline. With the advance of liberalism among the Latin American intellectual elite, the separation of church from state seemed inevitable. That "separation"[1] became a contentious affair was not surprising. After all, an institution the size of the Catholic Church could not be expected to relinquish its political privileges without a fight.

Second, despite sometimes tumultuous relations between Church and state following Independence, the Catholic Church remained a static institution. As Daniel Levine points out, "It is not surprising . . . that the role of religion in politics was long taken for granted by observers of Latin America.

Everyone knew that 'the Church' was a pillar of the traditional order, and there really was not much to add, aside from circumstantial detail" (1974, 497). Society changed, the Church did not. The Catholic episcopacy continued its policy of accommodating the political elite and resisted efforts to reform the status quo. Most of the conflict that arose occurred in the first several decades of colonial rule and the period of independent state building in the mid-nineteenth century. Furthermore, it was typically government officials that initiated hostility, not the bishops or clergy. As scholarship tends to be biased toward examining the most dynamic sectors of society, researchers naturally turned their attention to what was changing (e.g., the sociopolitical environment), rather than what was not (e.g., the Catholic Church).

The most recent bout of Church-state conflict has drawn greater attention because it is qualitatively different from that of the past. To begin, the predictions of secularization theory have proven inaccurate, to say the least (Stark and Bainbridge 1985; Finke and Stark 1992; Warner 1993; Casanova 1994). Today, organized religion plays a greater role (both politically and spiritually) in Latin American society than at any time in the recent past. The rapid growth in Protestantism since 1930 and the subsequent revitalization of the Catholic Church have increased participation in religious activities (Berryman 1994; Klaiber 1970). Furthermore, the Catholic Church, at least in several countries, is now a source of innovation and social change, often at the expense of alienating traditional allies. Whereas secular authorities had initiated conflict between church and state in the past, it is now the Catholic Church that has challenged governmental authority. All of these events were surprising to an academic community that predicted the dwindling influence of religious organizations.

To better understand the uniqueness of the current situation, we must examine the historical context under which the Latin American episcopacy has operated. While the central argument of this study is not strictly path dependent, I am aware of and sensitive to the fact that historical events influence the set of strategic choices available to social actors. As will be discussed later, events that appeared to have little impact at the time proved to be critical further down the road. For example, the implementation of laws guaranteeing religious freedom in the late 1800s opened the gates to a surge in competition when Protestant missionary groups began to take advantage of this situation in the 1930s. For the time being, it is enough to define the historical domain that Catholic bishops find themselves in during the latter half of the twentieth century.

## Church-State Relations in Historical Context

Latin America is a large and diverse region with each country experiencing its own particular historical sequence. Nonetheless, four general phases of church-state relations can be identified for the region as a whole: the colonial era, the period of Christendom (1493 to early 1800s), characterized by close relations between church and state; Independence and the breakdown of Christendom (early to late 1800s), wherein hostility between Church and state was generally initiated by the secular government; neo-Christendom (late 1800s to 1950s), a period when the Church built its institutional strength and tried regaining the privileges lost in the previous phase; and the period of the progressive Church (1960s to present), wherein Church officials in some, *but not all,* countries, initiated a break with traditional political allies. I am primarily concerned with explaining the shift in Church policy during the last period, keeping in mind the historical background that led to those changes.

An additional phase—the Church under democracy (mid-1980s to present)—potentially could be added. This current period is characterized by a return to Catholic conservatism and greater accommodation with the political and economic elite. Nonetheless, progressive reforms still survive and it is too early to tell what direction the Church will take. Discussion of the Church under democracy can be found in chapter 7. The historical antecedents leading up to the progressive Church will be considered briefly here.

### Colonial Period: Christendom (1493 to Early 1800s)

The Catholic Church and secular governing authority were intimately intertwined in colonial Latin America from the beginning. A letter written by Queen Isabella of Spain to the governor of Hispaniola in 1503 indicates how economic and spiritual conquest were part and parcel of one another:

> [W]e are informed that because of the excessive liberty enjoyed by the said Indians they avoid contact and community with the Spaniards to such an extent that they will not even work for wages, but wander about idle, and cannot be had by the Christians to convert to the Holy Catholic faith; and in order that the Christians of the said island . . . may not lack people to work their holdings for their maintenance, and may be able to take out what gold there is on the island; . . . and because this can better be done by having the Indians living in community with the Christians of the island, and by having them go among them and associate with them, by which

means they will help each other to cultivate and settle and increase the fruits of the island and take the gold which may be there and bring profit to my kingdom and subjects . . . beginning from the day you receive my letter you will compel and force the said Indians to associate with the Christians of the island to work on their buildings . . . and so that on feast days and such days as you think proper they may be gathered to hear and be taught in matters of the Faith. (Goodpasture 1989, 7–8)

This was the period of Latin American Christendom when the Church functioned as an integral part of the state apparatus (Dussel 1981, 37–46).[2] Christianity provided colonial rulers with an ideology capable of pacifying the indigenous population and the moral legitimation to carry out their political and economic goals. In exchange, the state guaranteed the Catholic Church unlimited and protected access to a new source of souls. At a time when various heresies and the Protestant Reformation chiseled away at Catholic dominance in Europe, protecting the Church from unwanted competitors in the Americas became a high priority for the Vatican (Prien 1985, 75).

Although this relationship provided substantial gains to both Church and state, the Church paid a significantly higher price by giving up most of its institutional autonomy. The series of agreements that formally encapsulated the costs and benefits of the relationship was known as *el patronato real* (the royal patronage system), which actually developed prior to the colonization of the Americas but was immediately applied to the colonial situation. Through the *patronato* the Vatican yielded to the Spanish and Portuguese crowns "the selection of all persons for ecclesiastical office and the right to collect all ecclesiastical tithes throughout its dominions in the New World" (Wood 1966, 174).[3] In the colonies, the agreement was expanded to include the state's prerogative to determine "the establishment of new dioceses together with determining their geographical boundaries, as well as the sending of all missionaries and religious"[4] (Dussel 1981, 39). Obviously, what the Church received in access to the Americas, it relinquished in autonomy.

The crucial question is why the pope would ever surrender autonomous control over the Church's nominations and finances. Although there clearly were benefits to be gained from a relationship with the Spanish crown—e.g., access to a vast territory full of unevangelized souls—in the joint partnership of cross and sword, the crown held the greater bargaining leverage and extracted substantial concessions from the Church. First, the Vatican simply lacked the resources needed to undertake a massive missionizing effort overseas. It was either agree to the conditions of the Iberian monarchs and "piggyback" on their efforts or not go at all. Second, the Protestant Reformation exacerbated the resource problems the sixteenth-century pontiffs faced. Not only did the need to combat the spread of religious competitors strain the treasury and personnel of the Holy See, but it intensified the Church's dependence on the goodwill of those who controlled power and resources in Europe. Spain and Portugal were more valuable as allies to the Church in the sixteenth and seventeenth centuries than vice versa.

Besides having a relatively weak bargaining position against the crown, Catholic prelates actually had an interest in allowing the state to run the Church's affairs, especially with regard to finances. As do most religious organizations, the Catholic Church requires financial resources to carry out its ultimate mission—the evangelization of society. However, without any sizable coercive apparatus to ensure the collection of tithes, parishioners are likely to contribute substantially less than what the organization needs to survive. In the colonial period, the solution to this dilemma was to rely upon the state's coercive capacity to collect the *diezmo*, a 10 percent religious tax on income. The colonial government would turn this money over to the episcopacy or use the funds to construct church buildings, seminaries, etc. While colonial officials and the crown often skimmed finances from this source of funds, the revenue gathered forcibly by the state would have undoubtedly exceeded the amount gathered by the Church had it been left to its own devices. In addition to benefiting from state revenue collection, the Church was also granted large *encomiendas* (landed estates) which provided another source of revenue. In terms of the benefits of enhanced revenue collection then, Catholic officials had a strong incentive to allow themselves to be "subordinated" to the power of the secular governing apparatus.

Even considering the Church's weaker bargaining position and financial interests in being "subordinate" to the state, the Catholic episcopacy did not lose nearly as much autonomy as a superficial reading of the various legal documents of the time would imply. Despite ideas that religions in general are easily subordinated by economic and political powers (Miliband 1969, 198–205) and that colonial Catholicism was particularly subservient (Wood 1966; Dussel 1972), ecclesiastical leaders exercised considerable autonomy and opposed secular rulers when their institutional interests were at stake. Dedication to the Church's principal mission—evangelization—provides a case in point. Many Catholic bishops and religious orders took their missionizing task quite seriously during the first century of colonialism (Poblete 1970, 39–41). In order to achieve their fundamental objective of converting the native population to Christianity, Catholic missionaries needed to win their trust. Often this meant defending them against ill treatment by the secular colonizers, an activity that frequently generated conflict with the colonial government.

The peak of the Church's defense of the Amerindians, and ensuing conflict with secular authorities in the colonies, occurred between 1542 and 1568, when several bishops were able to convince the Spanish crown to enact legislation easing exploitative conditions. "The passing of the *Leyes Nuevas* (New Laws) in 1542, which partly suppressed the *encomienda* system and prohibited the enslavement of Indians, led to intense conflicts between civil and religious authorities" (Rodríguez León 1992, 42). Notable among the early defenders of the native populations were bishops Bartolomé de las Casas (Chiapas), Juan de Zumárraga (Mexico City), Vasco de Quiroga (Michoacán), and Antonio de Valdivieso (Nicaragua). Protecting the indigenous peoples from abuse reinforced the caring image the Church wished to cultivate, thereby making conversion to the faith more likely (Dussel 1972, 114–15; de las Casas 1992). The logic is simple. If you want people to join and contribute to an organization, you must provide them with some selective (i.e., individualized) benefits (Olson 1965). Protection from enslavement and abuse was an attractive incentive for Amerindians during colonial times.

This is not to say that abuses did not occur, nor is it to absolve the Church of blame for its share of exploitation. Catholic missionizing efforts were linked with the repressive *encomienda* system, which virtually enslaved the native populations for the economic benefit of colonial landlords (and the Church itself). As *encomenderos* controlled access to their workers, missionaries were unlikely to criticize them. Religious orders possessing *encomiendas* (also known as *reducciones*) of their own may have been slightly more merciful than their secular counterparts, but hardly enough to qualify for any humanitarian awards (Goodpasture 1989, 43–48; Durán Estragó 1992). Rather, the defense of the Amerindians by key bishops and clergy merely illustrates that when the interests of the Church (e.g., evangelization) conflicted with the objectives of colonial officials, Church leaders did not mechanically opt for the state because of their privileged or controlled status.

The crown also possessed an incentive to grant the Church a substantial degree of autonomous power. This stemmed from the fact that the monarchy faced a difficult principal-agent problem in the colonies. Conquistadors and colonizers were sent to the Americas to extract wealth for the mother country. However, those same settlers had an incentive to keep as much as they could of the wealth they created (or stole) for themselves. To counter this, the monarchy created a limited system of checks and balances. Viceroys and governors were rotated frequently and required to return to Spain or Portugal at the end of their tenure. Regular judicial reviews (*residencias*) and random audits (*visitas*) were also used to ensure that the colonial administration was not cheating the crown. The Church was also an indispensable part of the crown's strategy to control the colonists. The clergy were granted the power of the Inquisition. While this institution was meant to address spiritual heresy in theory, in practice "the Inquisition came to be used more and more for political ends. In particular it was used to keep liberal ideas out of America by placing a strict surveillance over the importation of books" (Mecham 1966, 35). The Inquisition further acted as the Church's principal means of countering potential threats to its privileged position in society. Not surprisingly, when Latin America finally broke from Spain in the 1820s, one of the first actions on the part of independent governments was to abolish the Inquisition lest it be used against them in an effort to reestablish royal control over the Americas.

Several other means existed for the ecclesiastical hierarchy to assert its autonomy against the constraints imposed by the *patronato*. First and foremost was its control over religious education. Although monarchs (or designated agents) were allowed to nominate bishops, the pool of nominees was rather small and the Vatican closely supervised the education of potential candidates (Mecham 1966, 28). Bishops owed as much to the Church for their training and ideological formation as they did to the favoritism of civil authorities, albeit the latter influence was much more immediate at the time of appointment. Second, lifetime tenure for bishops meant they could potentially outlast their secular patrons. In such instances, they did not necessarily owe allegiance to the ruler's successor. Finally, the episcopal power of excommunication represented a sizable deterrent for those afraid of burning in hell. The Church did indeed have power autonomous of civil authorities; it was not a simple lackey of the state.

Church autonomy frequently manifested itself in the colonial period.

> [M]embers of the hierarchy and . . . representatives of the crown often clashed theoretically and even physically, much to the dismay of those looking for an harmonious existence of the two powers. . . . Colonial records are full of personal altercations between civil and ecclesiastical authorities over issues which today appear childish but which then were full of symbolic meaning to the participants. (Bialek 1963, 13)

This is an important observation for the contemporary period and bears repeating: Despite the presence of extraecclesial regulation, bishops are capable of acting autonomously in defense of their institution. Whenever the government hampers the Church's ability to recruit and retain members, the episcopacy is more likely to oppose the government even at the risk of jeopardizing its privileged political status. This was as much the lesson of Bartolomé de las Casas in the colonial period as it is for the case of Mexican bishop Samuel Ruíz today.

Throughout the colonial period, Church officials continually sought to renegotiate the terms of the *patronato* to their advantage. Citing an earlier study of Argentine political thought, Pike observes that "although the Church recognized the right of royal patronage, 'in fact, it aspired to override political authority each time it could, and it was accustomed to make use not only of the prestige it enjoyed with the people, but also of the influence it possessed at Court and the threats of the Inquisition'" (1964, 7).[5] Thus, despite the numerous concessions made by the Vatican, the colonial Church enjoyed a reasonable degree of autonomy. Because prelates chose not to exercise their autonomy at certain times did not imply that such autonomy was missing, only that it was not exercised. Certainly, the Church was disadvantaged by its dependence on the crown to guarantee access to the colonies, but bishops were far from powerless.

Conflict over Indian rights eventually subsided as the evangelization efforts of the Church wound down. By the early 1600s, the Church had secured the religious "commitment" of the entire settled continent. Some missionary work continued, mostly at the behest of religious orders that sought to bolster their own power within the Church by gaining the allegiance and revenue associated with new followers. The Jesuits, in particular, were aggressive proselytizers setting up their own *reducciones*—settlements similar to *encomiendas*, though with a missionizing purpose (Durán Estragó 1992). However, support for these orders by the episcopacy was minimal, as they were not directly under the control of diocesan bishops. This fact was revealed in the next major conflict between the state and a religious organization—the expulsion of the Jesuits from Brazil in 1759 and from Spanish America eight years later.

The Jesuits were the most successful religious order in the colonies, and one of the most autonomous. At a time when Iberian influences were waning, the "extensive labors and undeniably powerful influence of the Jesuits provoked the jealousy of civil authorities both in Spain and Latin America" (Poblete 1970, 43). Actually, the Jesuits' *reluctance to share* the fruits of their success provoked more jealousy than their success per se. "A central reason for the expulsion of the Jesuits was not their economic pursuits . . . but the fact that the Jesuits refused to pay tithes on their large land holdings and capitalistic enterprises thus diminishing the shares of King and Pope" (Bialek 1963, 14). Once it was decided to rid the continent of their influence, colonial officials acted rapidly. Their expulsion was accomplished forcibly in a matter of hours, with Jesuits being taken away in the middle of the night and put on ships bound for Spain and Portugal.

This conflict did not dramatically affect government relations with the episcopacy, "the Church being as glad to be rid of them as the civil authorities, landowners, and merchants" (Vallier 1970, 26; see also Bidegain 1992, 84). It is important to note that the loss of the Jesuits left the evangelizing arm of the Church largely incapacitated (Poblete 1965, 18–19), a fact that did not cause grave concern among the colonial bishops. Since nearly all of the Latin American population was at least nominally Catholic by this time, evangelization took a back seat to preserving the legal and financial status of the institutional Church. The Wars of Independence and advance of liberalism a few decades later further reduced the bishops' concern for evangelization. Their immediate task became defending the Church from the onslaught of a new political and intellectual elite that attempted to redesign society in ways that threatened the Church's traditional influence.

## Independence and the Breakdown of Christendom (Early to Late 1800s)

Although religious motivations were not a principal cause of the revolt against colonial powers, the Church became a significant player in the immediate events leading up to, and following, Independence (Mecham 1966, 60). Indeed, the "religious question"—i.e., determining the sociopolitical status of the institutional Church—became a central issue in the political battles waged to define the new Latin American republics. The Church represented the largest and most important institution held over from colonial times. Combined with its control over religious symbolism, a potent mobilizing force in Latin American society, this institutional presence meant the Church was the primary obstacle to the political consolidation of the newly independent regimes. For this reason, it became imperative for the liberation forces to control the Church either by continuing to manipulate the internal workings of the Catholic hierarchy via the *patronato* or destroying its external sources of power, mainly its wealth and ideological linkages to the population. On the other hand, the Catholic episcopacy's primary interest was to augment Church autonomy and rebuild itself following the flight of substantial numbers of clergy and prelates in the latter stages of the struggle for independence. Given the opportunity to appeal to the mass of the population for support and immerse itself in a "new evangelization" of the continent, prelates instead chose to focus on "high politics" to either restore or preserve colonial privileges (sans *patronato*).

Having been closely associated with the colonial elite, the sympathies of the bishops lay with the royalist forces in the early stages of Independence (Mecham 1966, 51). Although a break with the colonial order created the opportunity to renegotiate the *patronato* on terms more favorable to the Church (Casiello 1948, 57; Aguilar-Monsalve 1984, 206), changing the status quo posed considerable risks:

> The Church was cognizant of Gallicanism in France, of Josefism in Austria, and of the wave of rationalism which had washed up "dangerous ideas" upon the shores of America. The teachings of Adam Smith, Locke, and Luther struck at the foundations of religio-political domination in the Spanish dominions. . . . [There is] little evidence to indicate that the Church was eager to trade Papal recognition of the republics at the outset of the Revolution in return for a guarantee of the restoration of Church liberty in the New World. . . . This is not to say that such a trade would have been a natural or timely development at that time. (Bialek 1963, 15)[6]

Material concerns also played a role in the bishops' calculus. While the Spanish and Portuguese monarchies had become weak by the latter half of the eighteenth century, the Church still fared well financially under colonial rule. Emancipation offered no guarantees about the financial security of the Church. Indeed, it was reasonable to expect that newly independent governments would be revenue starved and would have to reduce payments made to the Church, at best, or expropriate Church wealth, at worst.

Episcopal support for the royalist position also was influenced by a leadership vacuum in the Church at the time. Overall, the Latin American episcopacy lacked the bargaining power needed to guarantee the Church a better position after independence than it currently enjoyed under colonial rule. First, a sizable proportion of the prelatures remained vacant during this time (Dussel 1981, 89). France's occupation of Spain created political confusion, both in Spain and Latin America, as to who had the power to appoint bishops. Vacated sees went unfilled, often for years. Second, with Pope Pius VII imprisoned by Napoleon from 1810 to 1814, there was no unified actor to negotiate new terms (Prien 1985, 367–68). In short, both the uncertainty associated with early demands for independence and the organizational disunity of the Church affected the proroyalist response of the hierarchy in the early stages of the struggle for independence.

In contrast to the Church's upper leadership, parish priests generally supported the patriot cause from the outset (Wood 1966, 179; Bidegain 1992, 87).[7] They faced the same problem as the predominantly creole insurgents: rising expectations coupled with a lack of social mobility. Bishops were typically recruited from the mother country, not from clergy that had lived their entire lives on the western side of the Atlantic (Coleman 1958, 14). For creole priests, the end of colonialism meant rewriting the rules so that ecclesiastic appointments would be determined in Rome or in their American homeland. Either arrangement worked to their benefit. If the *patronato* were maintained under a liberated America (as it would be for a half century following Independence), national governments would be more likely to draw bishops from a local pool of candidates than to select foreigners, a situation working to the benefit of lower-level clergy. Alternatively, appointments made by the Vatican were prone to take account of relations with the independent states and to privilege locals. When the *patronato* finally was abolished and the Vatican gained control over episcopal appointments, locals were preferred over foreigners with few exceptions. Moreover, coincident with colonial tax reforms, the monarchy had engaged in "religious reforms, which were designed to assure fidelity to the monarch and his officers" (Bidegain 1992, 87). As most bishops were already loyal to the crown, it was the pastoral agents of the Church who bore the brunt of this additional interference. Resentment built easily among those who rarely received the benefits, but suffered the costs, of the *patronato real* system. A *patronato nacional*, the probable result of independence, would be less overbearing on the indigenous clergy. Not surprisingly, then, priests were often found among the ranks of the most influential liberators (e.g., padres Miguel Hidalgo y Costilla and José María Morelos in Mexico).

After 1815, independence appeared inevitable. A regime change in Spain finally convinced the bishops that it was time to reevaluate their political loyalties. With the Holy See resistant to the idea of giving the right of patronage to the liberal Spanish government (1820–23), the allegiance the bishops owed to Spain diminished significantly. There were two episcopal responses to the coming independence. First, those bishops who were most vocal in their support for the royal cause feared for their lives and fled the

Americas shortly after Ferdinand VII was restored to the Spanish throne in 1814. The second response reveals the opportunistic behavior of the bishops who remained. Mecham noted that

> a reasonable regard for their temporalities induced many high ecclesiastics to manifest sympathy for the party which was destined to exercise power in the new State. These clerics, fearing the vengeance of the patriots when independence should be established, decided wisely to ward off this danger by joining the independentists. (1966, 59)

This political strategy of accommodating *potentially* hostile rulers[8] became the norm over the century to come. Rather than engaging opponents in prolonged battles that civil authorities were always more likely to win, bishops found it more expedient to coopt, or be coopted by, potential enemies. Defeat following a stubborn battle with the patriots meant the possible loss of all ecclesiastical privileges, whereas an early surrender and accommodation with the opposition meant some privileges could be retained. So long as government action did not impinge upon the Church's hegemony over its flock, prelates were willing to compromise some of their material interests and autonomy in order to maintain Catholicism's preeminent status in society.

All in all, Church support for the rebellion remained tepid, certain pockets of lower clergy excepted. As the independence movement progressed, it became clear that the sociopolitical landscape would be altered. "Neither the revolution nor the counter-revolution could gain a decisive victory without mobilizing the lower classes, and no victory so gained could be without social consequences" (Halperín Donghi 1993, 58). Fearing these potential consequences, the remaining prelates opportunistically cheered the rebels but did nothing to stir up popular support, hoping instead to preserve the colonial social order intact. Their political strategy remained elite based, allying them with the most conservative social sector—the landed elite. Church interests were naturally aligned with those of this sector due to the Church's extensive landholdings. The urban elite adopted a more radical posture on social change, their future lying in a more modernized economy.

In part, the bishops got what they wanted. Society remained essentially unchanged for the majority of the population and the Church continued to be the dominant cultural actor. However, changes began taking place at the elite level that had profound effects on Church-state relations. These changes manifested themselves in anticlerical ideas, movements, and policies, which had the effect of redefining the relationship between Church and state, *but not the political strategy of the episcopacy.* Despite a tendency to favor conservative (proclerical) parties over liberal (anticlerical) ones, bishops continued to accommodate the dominant political actors, even those that diminished clerical influence in society. Temporary resistance to politicians who attacked Church privileges inevitably gave way to accommodation, followed by intensive lobbying efforts to restore the Church's position.

From 1825 until about 1850, the Church retained its pre-Independence status in the polity, including subjugation to the restrictive conditions of the *patronato* (now called *patronato nacional*). The difficulties usually associated with consolidating a new regime required that the newly independent republics avoid alienating the institutional influence of Catholicism. Nevertheless, such an attitude did not prevent these governments from seeking to control the Church. Thus, shortly after Independence, the primary source of tension became the status of the *patronato*. The Church attempted to retain all the trappings of its colonial privilege, but without state interference in its internal affairs (Aguilar-Monsalve 1988, 236). The independent governments, on the other hand, considered the *patronato* a right of sovereignty. Turmoil resulted when the government's attempt to preserve the *patronato* clashed with the Church's desire to gain autonomy:

> The new republics, liberal as they considered themselves to be, were anxious to take to themselves the old privilege of patronage. The Spanish crown had enjoyed the right to name and appoint new bishops; but Rome, suspicious of all liberal governments, was unwilling to renew the privilege. Prolonged and complex negotiations left the entire continent in a state of ecclesiastical disorder. (Poblete 1970, 44)

When it became apparent that all forces—Conservative and Liberal—wanted to exert control over the Church, the episcopacy opted for the Conservatives. At least under the Conservatives the Church would be guaranteed all the privileges of the *patronato* in addition to the costs. A Liberal regime promised all cost and no benefit. Nonetheless, in the turbulent decades immediately following Independence, few alterations in Church-state relations were made. For the governments concerned, ecclesiastical relations took a back seat to political consolidation.

The situation changed with the success of Liberal parties in the latter half of the nineteenth century. Wanting to free Latin America from all vestiges of colonial rule, which Liberal politicians felt were an impediment to modernization, the process of Church-state separation began. Given the natural alliance between the religious hierarchy and conservative rural interests, the Church became a prime target of Liberal administrations seeking to consolidate the rule of the urban commercial elite (Pike 1964, 20). Liberal governments wanted to break the power of the Conservatives. One way of accomplishing this was to further weaken their strongest ally—the Catholic episcopacy.

Perhaps more important, Liberal actions against the Church also served to strengthen the financial status of the state. The mid-1800s saw several Latin American countries fall into bankruptcy and default on foreign loans. Political survival meant gaining revenue quickly since unpaid soldiers were quick to lead coups. The extensive landed estates owned by the Church proved to be an easy target for regimes wanting to raise revenue fast. Under clerical ownership, fertile land often went fallow for extended periods. Even when in use, the agricultural output typically was not geared toward the export market, where it could easily be taxed by the government. By expropriating these lands and turning them over to commercial interests, the state not only received the immediate revenue from the actual sale of Church lands to commercial farmers but also captured a steady income stream in the form of duties on agricultural exports. Moreover, land sold at favorable prices netted the government important rural allies at a time when its hold on power was rather tenuous.

Liberal governments also expropriated other sources of Church revenue by secularizing cemeteries and marriages, each of which was associated with user fees. The end result was to fill the coffers of secular authorities while financially weakening the Church. A final target of the state's assault on the Church was the registry. Expropriating the power to keep records on births, deaths, and property provided the government with the basic administrative capacity to tax the population.[9] State building implies that politicians build an efficient bureaucratic structure capable of extracting revenue from society (Levi 1988). For the new states of the Americas facing immediate financial and political pressure, the easiest way to develop a bureaucratic infrastructure was to take over the functions of one that was currently in existence—i.e., the Catholic Church.

By focusing on the ideological confrontation between liberalism and Catholicism, scholars frequently overlooked these material incentives underlying church-state conflict in the latter half of the nineteenth century. Such ideological battles did play a role at this time. The Liberal program of modernizing Latin American society along the lines of the United States and Europe ran headlong into opposition with the antiquated traditionalism of Catholic doctrine. Vatican policy at this time, under the influence of the ultramontane Pope Pius IX (1846–78),[10] centered around combating the supposedly harmful ideas of the English Enlightenment and French Revolution. These ideas shaped much of the thinking of Latin America modernizers and put them on an ideological crash course with the Roman pontiff and his subordinates. Thus, the battle between Liberals and the Church was forged both of interests and ideas.

In the end, the modernizing forces typically won. Liberal victories entailed reducing financial support for the Church, removing its constitutional status as the state religion, expropriating some Church properties and landholdings, secularizing education, marriage, and the civil registry, and implementing the freedom of worship. Each reform sought to reduce the political and economic influence of the Church and free the way for the more modern sectors of society to evolve. Of greatest concern for this study was the last condition—the introduction of religious toleration. Constitutional guarantees of religious freedom were implemented not only to punish the Church for supporting Conservatives, but out of economic necessity. With the expansion of economic relations with Protestant North America and Europe, it became imperative to provide an appropriate religious climate for foreign traders. This opening never was meant to radically transform the region's religious landscape. The thought among government officials at the time was that Latin America was firmly Catholic. Little did they realize how tenuous a hold Catholicism had over the majority of the population, a fact that would be exposed several decades later when Protestant missionaries began to devote serious attention to proselytizing.

Initially, Church leaders responded to these encroachments by supporting the Conservative adversaries of the Liberals. Bishops threatened to excommunicate uncooperative government officials, and priests led public protests (Pike 1964, 15). The Church's unwillingness to yield to the desires of the Liberal rulers only fueled the fires of anticlericalism, especially among the urban elite. But once bishops realized that the Liberals were a permanent fixture of the Latin American polity, they accepted and accommodated Liberal rule, a tactical retreat that placed the well-being of their institution over highminded, ideological principles (Aguilar-Monsalve 1988, 245). This action was only reinforced when it also became apparent that even the Conservatives were unwilling to reverse many Liberal reforms (Mecham 1966, 330). In exchange for its lost privileges, the Church generally received a greater degree of control over its internal affairs: the *patronato* was either abolished or substantially modified in favor of the Church.[11] To the extent Catholicism remained culturally hegemonic, the prelates could tolerate the loss of some state-based privileges so long as they gained autonomy over their institution.

By the early 1900s, Church-state conflict had subsided and relations remained reasonably amicable until the latest wave of conflict in the 1960s. Although the meaning of the phrase "separation of church and state" is too ambiguous to be of much use in the Latin American context, it is possible to identify specific years in which the religious question was sufficiently resolved.[12] Resolution meant that laws regulating the institutional Church were no longer central to political debate and, at least for present purposes, religious freedom was legally mandated though not always practiced. Table 2.1 presents a list of dates when Christendom (i.e., the direct association of Church and state) ended in Latin America.

## Neo-Christendom (Late 1800s to 1950s)

Freed from its moorings as a state-sponsored institution, the Church found itself looking for new methods of ensuring its status in society. Above all, the Church's political experiences in the nineteenth century taught bishops the dangers of tying their institutional interests too closely to any single party (as they had done with the Conservatives). When this group fell from power, so did the privileges of the Church. But did such a lesson necessarily imply breaking relations with the elite altogether? No. Quite the opposite, in fact. During the first half of the twentieth century, bishops in various countries broadened their relations with the political and economic elite, coming to terms with the Liberal parties that they had once fought so bitterly. The period of neo-Christendom was one wherein Church leaders disassociated themselves from a single set of elites and learned to accommodate whatever

Table 2.1   Dates of "Effective" Religious Disestablishment*

| | |
|---|---|
| Colombia (1848, 1853)[†] | Chile (1884, 1925) |
| Argentina (1853, 1884)[‡] | Brazil (1889) |
| Mexico (1857, 1910) | Nicaragua (1894) |
| Costa Rica (1860, 1871) | Cuba (1902) |
| Paraguay (1870) | Panama (1904) |
| Guatemala (1871) | Ecuador (1906, 1937) |
| El Salvador (1871) | Bolivia (1906) |
| Honduras (1880) | Uruguay (1917) |

*Sources:* Edelmann 1965, 159–60; Mecham 1966; and Dussel 1981, 101–3.

* "Effective" disestablishment is defined by the date when laws regulating the Church were no longer central to the political debate and when religious liberty was legally mandated. Religious regulations still remain hotly contested in many Latin American countries to this day. Multiple dates represent successive stages in the process, with the later date representing the greatest degree of disestablishment.

†During the Conservative's rule from 1886 to 1930, many of the Liberal reforms implemented in 1853 were reversed. In 1930, however, freedom of worship was reestablished (Dussel 1981, 102).

‡The *patronato* was not eliminated officially in Argentina until 1966, but the government rarely exercised its authority over episcopal nominations after 1884. See chapter 6.

regime held political power, be it liberal or conservative, democratic or despotic. The institutional survival of Catholicism dictated a flexible response to changes in the political elite.

A more flexible response in dealing with the state meant that Church leaders would have to rely more heavily upon lobbying and bargaining than in the past. While bishops always were conditioned to bargain with the state, they no longer had the legal guarantees granted to them during the Christendom period. In effect, this loss of legal privileges (and financial power) meant a loss of bargaining power. Effective representation in the political arena now meant that the episcopacy would have to strengthen its bargaining power in other ways. The initial years of the neo-Christendom period became a time of institution building for the Catholic Church. More dioceses were created and more clergy recruited indigenously as well as being brought in from overseas. This movement toward strengthening the organizational infrastructure of the Church was fueled by an ultramontanist papacy. Three decades after the First Vatican Council (1869–70) rallied Catholic forces against the advancing attacks of Liberalism in Europe, the Vatican convened the Latin American Plenary Council (1899), marking the first time Latin American bishops gathered to discuss a unified pastoral and political strategy, albeit one dictated by the Holy See. As Beozzo remarks, the "Council's intention was not to get inside the Latin American situation, but to refashion it in accordance with the new model Church entirely centered on Rome" (1992, 133). Despite its ultramontanist leanings and relative insensitivity to the Latin American context, the Plenary Council enhanced the political bargaining position of the Church. Instead of dealing with a fractured institution, politicians now faced a more unified national, and international, episcopacy.

Following several decades of institutional (re)building, the Church improved its bargaining position in relation to the government. Furthermore, as time wore on, rabid anticlericalism tended to wane. In this new environment, many national episcopacies attempted to renew their political influence in a number of ways. Lobbying government officials was the preferred method of restoring the Church's former privileges. In essence, this tactic represented a continuation of earlier methods used to influence the elite. But now, without official representation in the polity,[13] it became even more imperative to establish and maintain informal links with public leaders (Vallier 1970, 56). Among the two most important issues for the Church were education and public funding of Church organizations and projects. As for the former, bishops pushed for mandatory religious education in public schools (to which, of course, they would happily supply the priests to teach Catholic values) and subsidies for parochial schools. Church leaders also asked the state to finance the construction and maintenance of churches and seminaries, various Catholic youth programs, and other pastoral projects.

In Brazil, Cardinal Sebastião Leme mastered the techniques of political manipulation to the point of convincing a former opponent of religious establishment, Getúlio Vargas, to reinstate a number of perquisites the Church had enjoyed prior to 1889 (Todaro Williams 1976). Similarly, the Argentine and Colombian Churches won back many of the privileges they had lost earlier. Success for the Argentine Church came with the 1943 military coup that paved the way for the populist presidency of Juan Perón. In Colombia, the Church sided with the Conservative party during the chaotic period known as La Violencia (1948–57). Afterwards, a constitutional reform restored the Church's protected status as the state religion (de Roux 1992, 278). Elsewhere in the region, bishops lobbied intensively to recapture their political influence with varying degrees of success (Prien 1985, 516). All told, the energies exerted by bishops led to a revitalization of the Catholic episcopacy, as seen in the further strengthening of hierarchical organizations. Continuing the trend toward formulating a coherent episcopal strategy that began with the Latin American Plenary Council (1899), national bishops' conferences were created during the 1930s and '40s. This gave the Church the organizational strength it needed to engage in future pastoral projects (Mecham 1966). A transnational bishops' conference—the Conferencia Episcopal Latinoamericana (CELAM)—was created in 1955 to coordinate the policies of the Church at the regional level.

Another method of wielding political influence was to sway the electorate by endorsing certain political platforms. Occasionally, some bishops supported a specific party or candidate outright.[14] However, such blatant politicking was risky; in the event the bishops' choice lost, it was unlikely that the Church would receive the support of the winning candidate. Papal prohibitions on direct political activity also made it difficult for the Church to openly back specific candidates or parties. Instead, the episcopacy opted for a more circuitous route.[15] Knowing what political parties stood for ahead of time, the episcopate could ask "good" Catholics to vote only for those candidates that did not harm Church interests. The effect was the same as directly endorsing a specific party, but the vagueness of episcopal statements allowed for working relations in the event the opposition won.

What defined the neo-Christendom period more than anything else was the Church's efforts to combat "alien" ideological influences with organizations aimed at strengthening the faithfulness of key segments of the populace. The hallmark movement of this period was Acción Católica[16]. The sectors of the population targeted were university students, middle-class youth, urban professionals, and urban workers. The first two groups ranked high on the Church's priority list because they would eventually produce the country's future leaders. They were also highly vulnerable to anti-Catholic ideological movements such as liberalism, Masonry, and Marxism. Priority was also given to urban workers due to their vulnerability to socialism. It was not uncommon for the Catholic Church to establish competing unions—or *círculos obreros* (workers' circles)—to forestall the possibility of socialist unionization. Catholic unions were not as confrontational as their socialist brethren, largely due to the fact that Church leaders were not interested in alienating the elite at this time. The motivation behind *círculos obreros* came not from a passion for workers' interests per se, but instead from a concern for preserving Catholicism's ideological hegemony. Not surprisingly, Catholic efforts among labor focused on those workers who were most easily unionized—i.e., workers in large-scale industry. Noticeably missing was a commitment to workers who were relatively immune from socialist unionizing and the rural and urban poor. With only a limited amount of financial resources and personnel, bishops concentrated their pastoral effort where the threat to Catholicism was greatest at the time. It would take a new threat—Protestantism—to awaken the clergy to the plight of the lowest strata in society. While Protestantism began making inroads by the early 1900s in some areas of Latin America, thanks largely to religious liberty laws enacted under Liberal governments, it would take another several decades before they became a visible threat to episcopal leaders (see chapter 4).

Despite programs encouraging greater lay participation in the Church, the episcopacy's political strategy remained essentially elitist. Writing of the lay organizations created during the first half of the twentieth century, Goodpasture argues that "for the most part, their activities were restricted to the small middle and upper classes, and this mainly in the countries that were already most open to new ideas, countries where the traditional church faced the most serious challenges—Mexico, Chile, Argentina, and Brazil" (1989, 202). The hope was to repair the damage done by liberal policies of the late 1800s. Bishops rarely provoked conflict with the ruling elite and the few instances where conflict did erupt (e.g., Argentina 1954–55, Guatemala 1954), it was generally initiated by the government.

Overall, relations between Church and state improved during the first half of the twentieth century. However, beginning in the 1950s, signs appeared that the Church, in some countries, was shifting attention away from the elite and toward the popular classes. Pastoral letters began addressing the "social question," a broad term used to address poverty and poor working conditions. With this concern came a shift away from short-term charity, the previously favored method of dealing with poverty. Increasingly, bishops started to concern themselves with the long-term causes, consequences, and solutions to the problems of the popular classes.

### The Emergence of the Progressive Church (1960s to Present)

Most scholars view the appearance of progressive Catholicism as a dramatic break with the past. Considering the Latin American Church's five hundred–year history, the transition from an elitist Church to a "Church of the poor" within the span of roughly two decades provides just cause for characterizing the change as dramatic. However, the seeds of progressivism were planted during the neo-Christendom period when lay participation gained in importance. Although designed mostly with the elite in mind, many episcopacies expanded these earlier programs to cover the popular sectors long neglected by the Church. This shift in attention toward solving the economic and political problems of the poor defines progressive Catholicism.[17] However, it should be noted that although the Churches of most Latin American countries established pastoral outreach programs (e.g., Acción Católica) during the period of neo-Christendom, only a handful later translated these projects into a preferential option for the poor.

Catholic progressivism in Latin America is typically dated from the Second Vatican Council (1962–65). It was at this historic conference (originally designed to meet the challenges of modernization in Europe) that "democratic" reforms were first introduced and sanctioned by the papacy (O'Dea 1972). Mass was to be said in the vernacular, Church members were to practice toleration for alternative ideas, and greater attention was to be paid to social justice. But, in reality, a few Latin American Churches anticipated these reforms by at least a decade, especially with regard to social justice. Brazil and Chile led the way. During the 1950s, bishops in these two countries expressed interest in land reform, literacy campaigns, and rural cooperatives.[18] These efforts went beyond the traditional alms giving favored in the past; instead, they represented a sincere desire to improve the long-term living conditions of the lower classes. Even before the convocation of Vatican II, attention also was given to promoting greater lay involvement in religious services in these countries.

Three years after the closing of Vatican II, progressive Catholicism received another boost. In fact, no event in Latin America crystallized the progressive movement more than the Second General Conference of CELAM, held in Medellín, Colombia, in 1968.[19] The purpose for gathering bishops from throughout the region was to apply the reforms and recommendations of Vatican II to the Latin American context. Under the leadership of progressive bishops such as Hélder Câmara (Brazil) and Raúl Silva Henríquez (Chile), this conference was celebrated for its declaration in favor of social justice, later called the "preferential option for the poor." Supposedly, the poor always possessed a special place in Catholic doctrine. Nevertheless, the Latin American bishops thought it necessary to publicly declare support for this social group. Given the tarnished past of the Church when it came to serving the poor, this was the least they could do. While Medellín was truly a defining moment for the Latin American Church, its regional impact should not be overemphasized. As Crahan (1975) points out, this conference was dominated by a handful of progressive bishops who had the foresight to set the conference agenda. When it came to applying this preferential option in their home countries, several episcopacies, including that of the host country, Colombia, were less than responsive to the needs of the popular classes. Thus, although Medellín may appear to represent a change in the entire Latin American Church, a definite gap existed between the more progressive episcopacies (e.g., Chile, Brazil) and those hanging on to their more traditional past (e.g., Argentina, Paraguay). Explaining this variation is the central concern of this book.

To put the preferential option into action, the participants at the Medellín conference advocated the development of *comunidades eclesiales de base* (CEBs), known in English as ecclesial base communities.[20] Purportedly born in Brazil, CEBs encompass a wide array of organizations.[21] Typically, base communities contain anywhere from fifteen to thirty people who share some common interest (e.g., they live on the same block, work at the same factory, enjoy weaving, etc.). These people gather together on a regular basis (often weekly) to read passages from the Bible and discuss how the readings apply to their everyday lives. Lay leaders often moderate the discussions, although it is also common to find priests acting as CEB leaders. In addition to the religious aspect of these groups, members frequently organize and participate in community projects or activities geared toward self-improvement. Community projects could include improving irrigation channels in rural areas, attending community meetings to press the government for public services, and clothing drives for the desperately poor. As for self-improvement, some base communities teach participants crafts or job skills or serve as Alcoholics

Anonymous groups. Overall, the range of CEB activity is quite broad. In some instances, notably in Nicaragua and El Salvador, these groups have served as cover for guerrilla forces. Despite their notoriety for radical political activity, no presupposition should be made regarding their ideological content. Most people participate in base communities primarily for their religious content and often ignore the political messages propagated by their progressive leaders (Burdick 1993). Even in Nicaragua and El Salvador, most CEBs were not engaged directly in revolutionary activity. They developed a "subversive" reputation mainly because they taught the poor how to empower themselves, an activity not encouraged normally by military dictatorships.

The intellectual engine driving Catholic progressivism during the 1960s and 1970s was liberation theology.[22] As defined by one of its founding fathers, Gustavo Gutiérrez, liberation theology

> attempts to reflect on the experience and meaning of the faith based on the commitment to abolish injustice and to build a new society; this theology must be verified by the practice of that commitment, by active, effective participation in the struggle which the exploited social classes have undertaken against their oppressors. (1973, 307)

Two elements stand out in this philosophy. The first is its reliance on Marxist methodology. More accurately, liberation theologians base their understanding of Latin American poverty on dependency theory, a perspective that views poverty and repression in the Third World as a direct function of the world capitalist economy dominated by Western Europe and the United States.[23] Central to the solutions for persistent underdevelopment offered by many dependency theorists and liberation theologians is the concept of class struggle. This provided radical Catholics the intellectual justification they needed to join revolutionary movements during the 1970s. Second, liberation theologians emphasize *praxis*, or putting the liberating words of the Gospel to work. For this reason, liberation theologians have been the most fervent advocates of CEBs, giving the base-community movement its reputation for political radicalism. Although both CEBs and liberation theology have had a significant qualitative impact on Catholic thought and action, these movements remain quantitatively small (Daudelin and Hewitt 1995). Their primary influence has been to challenge nonliberationist priests and bishops to think more carefully about the plight of their poorest parishioners. Many bishops were receptive to this challenge, others not.

In terms of Church-state relations, Catholic progressivism manifested itself as opposition to authoritarian rule. Not only did several episcopacies denounce their respective military rulers, but they rejected authoritarianism as a method of rule per se. This represented a significant break with the Church's traditional preference for elite-based politics. In the past, whenever the Church felt its interests were somehow threatened by a given government, it would simply throw its support to those elites who opposed the sitting governors. Beginning in the 1960s, this strategy changed. Espousing a preferential option for the poor implied defending the interests of the popular classes against dictatorial abuses. The policies adopted by military governments during the 1970s had the effect of distributing income upward, away from the lower classes. In order to accomplish this task with a minimal amount of social resistance, dictators resorted to previously unseen levels of repression. Labor movements and other popular-class organizations bore the brunt of this assault. To show solidarity with the popular sectors, bishops publicly denounced both the economic policies and repressive tactics associated with military regimes. In addition, these bishops also attacked the philosophical underpinnings of authoritarian rule as being inherently unjust.

In Brazil, the episcopacy responded to the dictatorship (1964–85) by consolidating a number of progressive elements that were already developing in several dioceses. Base communities were expanded, though they still reached only a small fraction of the country's Catholic population. Episcopal criticisms of human rights abuses and economic injustice grew increasingly common beginning in the late 1960s with the appointment of Dom Aloísio Lorscheider as general secretary of the Church's episcopal conference and with the ascension of Dom Paulo Arns to the archbishopric of São Paulo in 1970 (Bruneau 1974; Mainwaring 1986). In Chile, the episcopacy, under the guidance of Cardinal Raúl Silva Henríquez (a bishop previously considered conservative), organized several institutions to monitor the human rights abuses of General Augusto Pinochet's military regime (Lowden 1996). These organizations frequently came under attack from the government, yet both the episcopacy and clergy stood firm in their criticism. During the 1980s, the Catholic hierarchy played a crucial role in Chile's return to democracy by mediating between Pinochet and opposition groups throughout the 1980s (Fleet 1995). Two Catholic Churches in Central America stand out for their opposition to dictatorship—El Salvador and Nicaragua. In the latter case, traditionally close relations between the Catholic Church and the Somoza family dynasty began to sour in the 1970s as the regime fell into obscene corruption and lost the support of almost all sectors of society. This only catalyzed a progressive Catholic movement that had been growing throughout the 1960s in the poorer sections of the country (Foroohar 1989; Dodson and O'Shaughnessy 1990). The Salvadoran Church experienced a similar trend with a grassroots progressive sector growing in strength in the 1960s. The bishops became emboldened to speak out about political abuses following massive electoral fraud in the 1972 presidential elections. As the Salvadoran state became increasingly militarized during the 1970s, the episcopacy felt the need to speak out against political repression and policies that kept the majority of the population in poverty (Cáceres Prendes 1989). Sadly, the most outspoken critic of the government, Archbishop Oscar Romero, was assassinated while saying Mass in 1980. His martyrdom gained international attention, but unfortunately he was not the only religious figure to suffer at the hands of despots; hundreds of clergy and lay Catholics were tortured and killed for their actions in defense of democracy and the poor (Lernoux 1980; Whitfield 1995). Choosing to oppose repressive governments came at a great cost for the Catholic Church, and it was a decision that was never made lightly.

Not all national Catholic episcopacies opposed military rule. Bishops in Bolivia and Paraguay acquiesced to the military's demands to tone down progressive activities. The Honduran and Uruguayan episcopacies largely remained silent. And in Argentina, the episcopal conference actively endorsed the military juntas that came to power in 1966 and 1976. Although bishops in these countries promoted limited pastoral reforms, their commitment to these projects and the interests of the popular classes was not enough to alter the episcopacy's traditional attitude toward the conservative dictatorships. Granted, in all of these countries there were isolated pockets of Catholic resistance, particularly among the lower-level clergy, but these groups never won the public support of the hierarchy. The presence of both antiauthoritarian and proauthoritarian (or "neutral") Churches in Latin America during the 1970s raises an interesting question: What factors caused some national episcopal conferences to oppose dictatorship, while others supported authoritarianism? We now turn attention to previous explanations for this question.

## Previous Explanations for Catholic Opposition to Authoritarianism

To date, there have been very few generalized theories proposed of why certain Latin American Churches broke with tradition and opposed the political elite. This is true for a number of reasons. First, most work done on this subject has been inductive. While inductive reasoning can lead to theoretical propositions, the general tendency in the literature has been toward a reliance on description over explanation. Obviously, certain theoretical principles inform the selection and presentation of historical "fact," but these principles are often left unstated and are not immediately apparent to the reader (and perhaps even the author). Admittedly, any complete analysis must take into account the historical context in which a phenomenon takes place. On the other hand, an excessive reliance on "context" (i.e., historical detail) results in a loss of generalizability, as each observed event results from a set of historic circumstances so specific that it will never be repeated. Furthermore, these descriptive analyses emphasize the specific actions of individuals to the point of ignoring the systemic and institutional forces that condition the decisions these individuals make.

Second, and coincident with the first reason, there has been a preponderance of single-case studies. While greatly enhancing our detailed knowledge of a particular country or event, these single-case studies provide little in the way of comparative analysis. The most evident limitation of this approach is that with more explanatory variables than cases, it is difficult to determine which factors are more important than others.[24] To sift out which factors are most important in determining an outcome, the problem should be viewed in comparative perspective and cases chosen to show variation on the dependent variable (Geddes 1990).[25]

Finally, many studies of religion and politics in Latin America have dealt with the consequences of progressive Catholicism, rather than its causes. The causes (as presented below) commonly are taken as given, thus adequate attention has not been devoted to which factors may have played a more decisive role in determining the episcopacy's choice of political strategies. This is largely an artifact of the aforementioned considerations; when one looks at a single case, the causes for the political shift in the Church may seem obvious, so a more interesting study naturally focuses on the social impacts of this change. Unfortunately, this leaves us without a rigorous examination of the assumed causes. With these restrictions in mind, it is possible to pull from the literature three variables often used to explain Church opposition to authoritarian rule: poverty, repression, and internal Church reform. Rarely are these explanations presented in isolation; scholars typically present all three in conjunction with one another. However, for purposes of spelling out the hypothesized relationships between these variables and change in the Catholic Church, they will be separated below.

## Poverty

Chronic poverty has long been a problem in Latin America. Following World War II, the problem became more noticeable due to rapid population growth, the capitalization of agriculture (which forced large numbers of peasants from their livelihood), declining terms of trade with the industrialized North, and misguided economic policies. The story of how this affected the Church's political strategy is relatively straightforward. As poverty worsened,

> [t]he marginalized popular masses increasingly pressed for a greater economic, political and cultural share in social life, and to create at last a new egalitarian society in which the people could be the subjects or enactors of their own history. It was this context of social crisis and conflict that *saw the awakening*, first, of small Christian groups and later of ever-growing sectors of the Church. (Castillo 1979, 86; emphasis added)

Gustavo Gutiérrez lays out the connection between poverty and the episcopacy's position more clearly:

> The new and serious problems which face the Latin American Church and which shape the conflictual and changing reality find many bishops ill-prepared for their function. There is among them, nevertheless, an *awakening to the social dimension* of the presence of the Church and a corresponding rediscovery of its prophetic mission. The bishops in the most poverty-stricken and exploited areas are the ones who have denounced most energetically the injustices they witness. But in exposing the deep causes of these injustices, they have had to confront the great economic and political forces of their countries. (1973, 106; emphasis added)

Simply put, bishops and clergy become more aware of their social responsibility as poverty spreads. Numerous passages in the Bible (e.g., the Sermon on the Mount) show that Christianity has an outright concern for the poor—not just the "poor in spirit," but the economically poor and politically disenfranchised as well.[26] Several papal documents, including *Rerum Novarum* (1891), *Mater et Magistra* (1961), and *Populorum Progressio* (1967) also provide a justification for defending workers and the poor against exploitation. Given that these social teachings provide a guide for episcopal action, the poverty hypothesis implies that all bishops need to do is become conscious of the economic destitution around them. Accordingly, we should see the most progressive bishops in the most impoverished countries (and dioceses). Furthermore, as military rule was widely considered the political means whereby the rich guaranteed their economic exploitation of the masses, opposition to dictatorship went hand in hand with the Church's preferential option for the poor.

Despite the aesthetically appealing logic of this hypothesis, it cannot adequately explain the variation in episcopal support or opposition to authoritarianism. As Mainwaring and Wilde argue:

> Recent increases in poverty were not so dramatic as to move the Church from its historical conservatism. Moreover, social inequalities and injustice were not notably greater in the countries where Church progressives have exercised great sway and [sic] those where they have been relatively marginal to the overall ecclesiastical enterprise. (1989, 14)

Surely, many of Latin America's progressive bishops truly were concerned about the plight of the impoverished popular classes. This concern undoubtedly affected most bishops in the region. (Indeed, it is hard to find a bishop who admits he cares little for the poor.) However, the scattering of pro- and antiauthoritarian episcopacies in comparatively rich and poor countries alike prods us to look elsewhere for a determinative cause of this variation.

### Repression

Closely linked to the logic of the poverty explanation, the increase in political repression during the 1960s and 1970s also led the bishops to hear the "cry of the people." As Brian Smith maintains:

> [C]hurch programs for human rights are basically reactive strategies, responding to unforeseen crises in secular society. The policy of promoting human rights (although legitimized in the Medellín documents of 1968) did not become a conscious priority of any of the national hierarchies until they were stimulated to act by pressures from below in their own churches or from outside the ecclesiastical institutions. In some cases the killing of clergy moved the bishops to set up emergency programs; in others, direct attacks on already existing church programs benefiting the poor moved them. In many situations, however, the response came from general public pressure, as many people had nowhere else to go for help and the churches were the last remaining organizations with any relative degree of freedom to act. (1979, 182)

According to the implicit logic of this explanation, the evident connection between increased repression and authoritarianism left the bishops no choice but to denounce the method of rule that promoted such atrocities. As with Catholic social teaching on economic conditions prompting action on poverty, prelates could refer to *Pacem in Terris* (1963), a papal encyclical on human rights, to prod them into taking a stand against brutal dictatorships.

Like the poverty hypothesis, this explanation suffers when placed in comparative perspective. In the two countries where human rights violations were worst—Chile and Argentina—episcopal responses differed dramatically. Arguably, the Argentine military was the more brutal of the two and public demands were made on the Church to take action. Despite this, the Argentine episcopacy remained intimately attached to the authoritarian rulers (see chapter 6). It is possible that the hierarchy responds to repression only when it is directed specifically at Church personnel or lay workers. Two problems immediately arise with this modified hypothesis. First, Churches that oppose a dictatorship are more likely to face government reprisals than those that offer support or remain silent. Militaries rarely attack dominant cultural institutions for no reason. Thus, the hypothesized relationship is reversed. In order to be attacked, the Church must first be doing something that antagonizes the regime. Second, even when clergy are targets of abuse, there is no guarantee that the episcopacy will come to their defense. In countries such as Argentina, Uruguay, and Honduras, attacks on progressive priests were largely ignored by the episcopacy. Again, it is not so much that these bishops condone torture; most prelates are men of high moral character who would find military abuses reprehensible. Rather, a better explanation for the variation in political strategies across national Churches lies elsewhere.

### Internal Church Reform

By far, the most common explanation for episcopal opposition to authoritarianism relates to changes taking place within the Church. Both Mainwaring (1986) and Levine (1992) contend that changes in how the Church envisions its spiritual mission in society (i.e., its "worldview") affects its general political strategy. As Mainwaring states, "the starting point for understanding the Church's politics must be its conception of its mission. The way the Church intervenes in politics depends fundamentally on the way it perceives its religious mission" (1986, 7).[27] According to this idea, "traditional images of the Church (Church as institution and Church as perfect society) have in recent years been challenged by a rapid succession of new images of the Church: as people of God, as servant, and as sign of salvation in the world" (Mainwaring 1986, 9). While this change from a hierarchical-authoritative definition of the Church to a more democratic view obviously leads to changes in the political strategy of the Church, we are left wondering what provoked these changes in the first place. In Latin America, three major interrelated events were responsible for these changes: Vatican II, the 1968 Medellín conference, and the advent of liberation theology.

Almost all recent discussions of the Church in Latin America assign Vatican II a crucial role in explaining the growth of progressivism. As mentioned earlier, this conference promoted a new concern for social justice and subsequently shifted the episcopacy's political preferences away from authoritarian rule. The following passage is representative of the literature at large:

> The most important single influence to modernize and galvanize the Latin American church was the Second Vatican Council. . . . [F]rom October 1962 until December 1965, almost the entire Latin American hierarchy—600 in all—met in the last three months of each year in Rome as participants in the Council's sessions. They held their own annual CELAM assemblies there, and were advised by several hundred Latin American *periti* (experts) and younger clergy, many of them students or recent graduates of the theological faculties of Europe. The updating and opening that were taking place at the council had a particularly strong effect on the Latin American bishops. They discussed with each other common problems, thought about the application to Latin America of the Council's teachings, and returned resolved to apply these teachings in their own national conferences. (Sigmund 1990, 23)

Likewise, the Medellín conference and liberation theology expanded upon and disseminated the ideas presented at Vatican II. Shepherd argues that a "crucial transformation in the Church's thinking took place during Vatican II and Medellín. Priests taking part in Vatican II dwelled at great length on 'immense inequalities,' while advocating an 'option for the poor' in combating them" (1995, 124). Shepherd suggests that "the preexisting relationship between the Church and the states" (1995, 124) helped determine a progressive or conservative outcome, but the predominant weight of his explanation falls upon changes in episcopal ideology prompted by these major gatherings.

Liberation theology also is credited for shaping the mindset of the Latin American episcopacy. Even if many bishops did not agree with the Marxist methodology of liberation theologians, they could not but help to reflect upon their critiques of Latin American society and perhaps arrive at less radical, but still progressive, conclusions regarding military rule. Each of these events—the Medellín conference and rise of liberation theology—promoted a new understanding (or worldview) of the Church's role in society. In other words, they focus on shifting preferences and attitudes as compared to the long-standing, institutional interests of the episcopacy.

Unfortunately, this explanation fails to account for the differences in political strategies of various Latin American episcopal conferences. If all Latin American bishops were exposed to the progressive ideas of Vatican II, Medellín, and liberation theology, and if these ideas were of central importance in determining the Church's new political strategy, then change should have occurred uniformly across the region. This was hardly the case. Even Mainwaring and Wilde admit that

> [i]f changes in the international Church were an adequate explanation for the character of ecclesiastical change, then we would not expect sharp differences across national borders. The Church is an international institution, but it is one in which considerable diversity and crossnational differences exist. These crossnational differences are explained in part by the differing contexts the Church faces. (1989, 12)

Vatican II undeniably played a role in shaping episcopal political attitudes, but that role was more a catalyst than a determining factor; bishops who were in some way predisposed to denounce injustice found that Conciliar reforms gave them the added institutional latitude to pursue their own programs. Bishops who were not so inclined could simply drag their feet or ignore the Council's recommendations altogether.

Overall, most scholars studying the progressive Church combine some variation of the poverty, repression, and internal Church reform arguments in their own analyses. Vatican II and subsequent intellectual gatherings and movements are believed to have raised the consciousness of Latin American bishops, who then could not help but notice the increasing economic and political misery around them. For the most part, this line of reasoning goes unquestioned, and when proposed as a cause for the rise of progressivism in any one case (e.g., Brazil), such an analysis seems reasonable; poverty and repression were rampant in Brazil during the 1970s and all the bishops were aware of the various Church social writings proliferated at and after Vatican II. However, when placed in comparative perspective, this type of analysis loses its appeal. With the limitations of these previous explanations in mind, the following chapter constructs a deductive model of Church-state relations that seeks to better account for the presence of both pro- and antiauthoritarian episcopacies in Latin America.

# THREE

# An Economic Model of Church-State Relations

*[T]he clergy, reposing themselves upon their benefices, had neglected to keep up the fervour of faith and devotion in the great body of the people; and having given themselves up to indolence, were becoming altogether incapable of making any vigorous exertion in defence even of their own establishment. The clergy of an established and well-endowed religion frequently become men of learning and elegance, who possess all the virtues of gentlemen . . . but they are apt gradually to lose the qualities, both good and bad, which gave them authority and influence with the inferior ranks of people. . . . Such a clergy . . . have commonly no other resource than to call upon the civil magistrate to persecute, destroy, or drive out their adversaries, as disturbers of the public peace. It was thus that the Roman catholic clergy called upon the civil magistrate to persecute the protestants.*

Adam Smith, *The Wealth of Nations*

The previous chapter briefly discussed some of the inadequacies that current explanations for Catholic progressivism face when considered in comparative perspective.[1] Variables such as international Church reform, increasing poverty, and growing repression cannot adequately account for the persistence of proauthoritarian Catholic episcopacies in Argentina, Guatemala, or Bolivia. An alternative hypothesis is needed to answer the question of why certain Catholic hierarchies opposed military rule while others embraced it (or remained passive supporters). Here, I argue that religious competition from below presented Latin American bishops with the difficult choice of either maintaining ties to an authoritarian elite, thereby risking further membership losses among the poor, or defending the rights of the poor in an effort to win (or regain) their allegiance at the risk of alienating the government and losing state-guaranteed privileges.

Rather than viewing Catholic political action from the "demand side"—i.e., an increasing desire for social justice and religion among the poor that bishops respond to (see Gutiérrez 1973; Lernoux 1980)[2]—I hypothesize that the Church's new stance is a strategic response to an increasing supply of religious and ideological alternatives, namely Protestantism, Spiritism, and Marxism. There has always been a relatively high demand for both social justice and religion in Latin America.[3] What has recently changed, though, is the supply of religious goods and services. A change in the religious market structure towards greater competition pressures the clergy to be more responsive to the needs of their neglected parishioners. To the extent that this competition affects a segment of the population that is hurt by the military regime's social and economic policies, the Church will have an incentive to defend the interests of its parishioners against the state. Lacking any competition, an episcopacy can ignore parishioner complaints (to a large extent) and continue an alliance with the political elite.

This hypothesis is framed in a more general model of church-state relations that not only explains religious opposition to authoritarianism, but also underlines the strong incentives for church-state cooperation, a topic commonly neglected in the religion-and-politics literature. Only by understanding the motives that both church and state have to ally with one another—the historical norm in Latin America—can one explain why certain national episcopacies decided to oppose authoritarian rule, while others continued the traditional strategy of accommodation. Furthermore, exposing these underlying incentives for cooperation provides insight into the Church's apparent "conservative retrenchment" under democracy, wherein many bishops have returned to currying favor with political elites.[4]

I will present the general theory of church-state relations as a series of axioms and propositions culminating in the central hypothesis explaining why only certain Catholic Churches in Latin America opposed the military. Axioms are simply statements that are taken as self-evident for the purpose of constructing theory. While each axiom presented in this study could be held to the light of rigorous empirical verification, I will simply take them as given. A brief discussion follows each axiom to provide a certain level of justification. Likewise, the general propositions presented below serve as building blocks for the central hypothesis of this book, that religious competition led to a reevaluation of the Catholic Church's political strategy in several Latin American countries. Although I do not test them directly, I provide brief anecdotal evidence for each proposition, suggesting its plausibility. Furthermore, as each proposition is critical for the final hypothesis, a test of the central hypothesis serves to validate indirectly the preceding propositions. With this in mind, we now turn attention to the economic model of church-state relations.

## The Church-State Bargain: Incentives for Cooperation

Since church-state accommodation has been the norm throughout history, it seems appropriate to begin a study of church-state relations by examining the underlying incentives each entity has to cooperate. A cooperative church-state arrangement will be conceived here as "establishment," wherein a given religious organization receives special financial or legal privileges from the state. These privileges could include, among other things: designation as the official state religion; subsidies for clerical salaries; religious education in public schools; state assistance in the construction and maintenance of church buildings; lower tariffs for goods imported by the church; favorable communications rights; preferential tax status; direct subsidies for religious programs; or prohibitions on alternative religious movements.[5] Although "establishment" often connotes a dichotomous situation, it is best considered a continuum where the amount of governmental assistance a church receives can vary over time and space. In other words, churches can be more or less established. Religious leaders seeking the various privileges associated with establishment are considered to be pursuing a political strategy for church-state cooperation. Likewise, political leaders offering such privileges solicit greater church-state cooperation.

Conceptualize establishment as a bargain wherein two autonomous institutions strike a deal to cooperate. Neoclassical economics, the foundation for rational choice theory, posits that economic exchanges occur under the expectation of mutual benefit. If one actor benefits only at the expense of another, the losing partner has no incentive to participate in the exchange.[6] When either partner in the bargain believes that the costs of the bargain outweigh the benefits, defection (in this case disestablishment) occurs. For this study, the crucial issue becomes what both the church and state gain from establishment and what conditions would place strain on this bargain. Rational choice explanations require specification of the actors, their preferences (or goals), and the constraints they face. With this in mind we now examine the goals of both church and state leaders, the inherent obstacles they encounter in achieving those goals, and how cooperation can alleviate the problems caused by these constraints.

## Church-State Cooperation: The View from the State

*Axiom 1: States Attempt to Minimize the Cost of Ruling*
State actors—politicians and bureaucrats—want to minimize the costs of ruling. In other words, they desire an obedient citizenry at the lowest possible cost. This is a reasonable assertion for two interrelated reasons. First, a compliant or supportive population increases the probability of surviving in office, and political survival must be the foremost goal of any state leader (Mayhew 1974; Geddes 1994). As Barry Ames observes, "political leaders cannot attain their substantive goals unless they hold onto their jobs" (1987, 7). This is true for democratic as well as authoritarian rulers. Even the most repressive military regime needs some minimal degree of citizen compliance. High and consistent levels of civil unrest can inspire internal countercoups, revolutions, or foreign invasions.

Second, as politicians are assumed to have substantive goals (ranging anywhere from amassing a personal fortune to building a just society), they will want to minimize the costs of securing a compliant population so as to free up more resources for their favored policy objectives. Since all politicians act under budgetary constraints, the more they spend on ensuring political survival, the less they devote to realizing their policies. Although leaders retain the option of raising taxes to fund their policies, there exists some upper limit of taxation where long-term revenue extraction begins to decline or the population becomes actively resistant to the ruler (hence threatening political survival). Given this threshold, state actors prefer to maximize the revenue available to them to enact policies by minimizing the cost of gaining citizen compliance and increasing the efficiency of tax collection (Levi 1988).[7]

*Axiom 2: Ideology Is the Least Expensive Method of Obtaining Citizen Compliance*
There are three basic means of gaining citizen compliance: coercion; patronage; and ideology. State actors will try to minimize the cost of ruling by seeking an optimal mix of these options. Coercion and patronage affect the material incentives that citizens have in obeying the government by altering the costs and benefits associated with compliance (Taylor 1982, 11–20).[8] Both are relatively costly because significant amounts of resources need to be devoted to policing, monitoring, or "paying off" politically important groups. Moreover, these costs tend to increase over time. Coercion is costly not only in terms of paying a police force, but it may create popular animos-

ity towards a government, making disobedience—either active or passive—more likely, thereby requiring more coercion. Patronage has a similar spiraling effect: Once a group is paid off, it has an incentive to ask for more patronage to guarantee continuing support. Other groups have an incentive to make their own demands. Given that the resources used for coercion and patronage are relatively high and could be used for satisfying other policy objectives, politicians will seek to minimize the use of these instruments of rule.

Ideology, on the other hand, is a relatively cost-effective form of control since people obey out of the belief that what the government does is right. By creating a system of values and norms, a strong ideology regulates citizens' behavior by providing an internal guide to acceptable and unacceptable activity. As noted by Taylor, ideological persuasion is

> [a]nother process by which a person may get another to do something he would not otherwise have done . . . by changing his mind so that he now wants to do it, not by exercising power [i.e., coercion and patronage], but by altering his attitude to the alternative courses of action themselves and in such a way that he is aware of what is being done. This would typically be done by providing information and arguments about the nature of the choice alternatives, about the consequences of adopting different courses of action and the costs and benefits attached to them. (1982, 20)

To the extent that politicians successfully propagate norms and values that emphasize obedience to the government, they enhance their political survival while simultaneously lowering the amount of resources needed for coercion and patronage. Moreover, ideological values and norms tend to reinforce themselves, thereby providing a relatively long-term source of compliance.

Put another way, a believable ideology legitimates a government, and legitimacy lowers the costs of ruling. In his discussion about the importance of ideology, Douglass North argues that the

> costs of maintenance of an existing order are inversely related to the perceived legitimacy of the existing system. To the extent that the participants believe the system fair, the costs of enforcing the rules and property rights are enormously reduced by the simple fact that the individuals will not disobey the rules or violate property rights even when a private cost/benefit calculus would make such action worthwhile. (1981, 53)

Thus, creating legitimacy vis-à-vis the creation of certain ideological norms and values is the most cost-effective method of ruling. A state can create such an ideology itself, or it can rely upon the norms and values created by other institutions to legitimate its rule. It is this latter observation that provides state leaders the incentive to seek cooperative relations with religious organizations.

### Axiom 3: *Churches Specialize in the Production of Ideological Norms and Values*

Religion offers the state a readily available source of ideological support. Churches specialize in the production and dissemination of norms and values. Considering that one of the central activities of religious organizations is teaching people what constitutes proper behavior, religious organizations have a comparative advantage in the creation of ideological norms and values relative to the state. This is not to equate religion with secular ideology as is the tendency of Durkheim (1965). Religion possesses a supernatural component that defies empirical verification whereas secular ideologies do not (Stark and Bainbridge 1985). However, it is important to note that norms and values are essential components of both secular ideology and religion and that both can be used to alter behavioral preferences of individuals thereby affecting the political choices they make. In this respect, religious norms and values can be used to legitimate political authority. Church leaders "can offer supernatural sanctions of the state's authority. Thus, all challenges to the state will be classified as sins—political dissent will be identified with sacrilege, for the state rules with divine right" (Stark and Bainbridge 1985, 508). While the latter part of Stark and Bainbridge's claim may overstate the case for modern polities, any level of positive association with a religious organization should enhance a government's legitimacy and ensure greater compliance from the population, at least among the religious. Therefore, the endorsement of religious leaders helps reduce the cost of rule. How is this so? How can religious leaders effectively convince their parishioners that obeying the government is good?

Political situations often involve uncertainty. People frequently lack adequate information about the motivations of actors, the possible impact of various policies, etc. Given this, people find it difficult to make even basic political choices, such as whether or not to comply with the various demands of the government. Citizens reduce this uncertainty by seeking guidance from people they trust. In essence, citizens seek to minimize the "costs of citizenship" (e.g., gathering information). Deferring to the judgments of trusted officials—e.g., religious officials—reduces these costs.

Religious leaders have a strong incentive to remain trustworthy. The very nature of their job—providing answers to questions that often cannot be verified (see below)—requires them to invest heavily in their own trust-worthiness and credibility.[9] A religious organization has

> a strong incentive to protect its primary capital asset—its claim to being the sole institution representing God on earth. All of the spiritual services the church [offers] to its "consumers" (including aid in securing salvation, prayers, the interpretation of Scripture, etc.) [are] ultimately based on the credibility of this one central claim. In fact, these services [are] essentially pure credence goods; the quality and reliability of the church's output could not be determined even after "purchase", but presumably only after death. . . . Consequently, any threat to the credibility of the church's relationship to God [is] potentially a huge capital loss. New entrants in the "market for religion" who could inspire greater credibility on the part of consumers would rapidly compete with [that church] and drive it out of existence. (Anderson et al. 1992, 344)

In large part, this explains why clergy, especially those in competitive religious markets, typically rank as the most trustworthy profession in opinion surveys. Religious leaders can transfer the trust that their parishioners have in them to a political leader or entire regime. Parishioners, realizing that the clergy want to preserve the trust of their followers, can rest assured their religious leaders are acting in their best interests. Priests who consistently make poor political endorsements will discover that their followers will question not only their political judgment, but the spiritual guidance they offer as well. Thus, if a religious leader endorses a government, and that religious leader is widely trusted, his or her parishioners will be more likely to offer their compliance to that government.[10] *This does not rule out the possibility of church officials consistently making political endorsements contrary to the interests of their parishioners.* The Catholic Church in Latin America has a long history of doing just that. As discussed below, religious monopoly shelters church leaders from the consequences of poor political decisions, reducing their incentive to remain trustworthy. Where parishioners have an option to exit to another denomination, religious leaders will be held more accountable for their actions.

Ideological legitimation is not the only benefit that churches bring to political actors. Churches also offer mobilization power in that members exist in close-knit communities with common beliefs and norms. Scholars have shown that such communities enhance collective action by reducing incentives to free ride (Taylor 1982; Lichbach 1995, 111–28). As free riding is the greatest obstacle to political mobilization (Olson 1965), churches become a central locus from which to launch political action. State actors could tap this source of mobilization to rally support for their political causes. Quite obviously, the ideological and mobilization power of churches could be used against the state. Indeed, this is what happened in several Latin American countries, such as Chile and El Salvador in the 1970s and '80s. This provides a further incentive for politicians to seek cooperative relations with churches so as to minimize any potential threat to their political survival.

From the above discussion, we can lay out explicitly our first proposition of church-state relations.

> **Proposition 1:** State Incentives for Church-State Cooperation
> Given that (1) states seek to minimize the costs of rule, (2) ideological legitimation is the cheapest form of rule, and (3) religious leaders have a comparative advantage in the production of norms and values, state actors will cultivate cooperative relations with religious leaders more often than not.

Although complete unification (i.e., theocracy) represents the strongest possible form of cooperation, a government can benefit from any positive level of association (i.e., establishment).[11] This is true, however, only to the extent that a government identifies with the *dominant* religion. Identification with a minority religion means that less than half of the population is susceptible to the legitimating proclamations of that religion's leaders. Where church-state establishment exists in religiously plural societies, and where such establishment significantly favors one religion, the likelihood that political conflict will be based on religious cleavages increases. At the bare minimum, rulers should avoid alienating churches; conflict should be the exception and not the rule. This hypothesis does not exclude the possibility of church-state conflict. As discussed below, certain circumstances may alter the calculus of politicians in such ways that cooperation yields few benefits relative to costs. Nonetheless, the basic logic stated in the above hypothesis goes a long way in accounting for the historical norm of church-state cooperation, at least from the side of the state. However, since cooperation is a two-way street, we must next address the incentives of religious leaders to affiliate with the state.

### Church-State Cooperation: The View from the Church
Despite images of state religions being mere puppets of the ruling class (Miliband 1969, 198-205; Marx 1975, 39), churches possess interests and goals autonomous from the state. Nonetheless, obtaining these objectives pushes the clergy in a direction that favors religious establishment. The in-

herent difficulties associated with producing religious goods provides religious leaders with a strong independent desire to be protected by the state. In order to understand this, it is necessary first to examine the basic preferences of religious leaders and then explore the structural constraints religious leaders face in obtaining their goals.

***Axiom 4:*** *Churches Maximize Parishioners and Resources*
Religious leaders, first and foremost, prefer more adherents to their faith than less. The strong version of this assumption—parishioner maximization—works well with proselytizing religions (e.g., Christianity, Islam); these religions actively seek to expand their religious market share with the ultimate goal being a religious monopoly.[12] If religious leaders truly believe that their spiritual message is correct, it is reasonable to assert that they would want as many other people to believe similarly. Even leaders of specific denominations that do not appear to be aggressively expansionary (e.g., Anglicanism) would prefer to have an entire population believe in their particular religious creed, given the choice.[13] This assumption can be relaxed to allow for non-proselytizing religions (e.g., Judaism, Confucianism, gnostic sects). Here religious leaders prefer to minimize parishioner losses. Since this study focuses primarily on Catholics and Protestants in Latin America, both proselytizing faiths, the stronger assumption will be used. In any event, membership acts as a measure of the religion's success and is often one of the only visible indications of how well the clergy are servicing their followers. Defections from one religious tradition to others indicate that parishioners are not satisfied with their former religion and that the church's leadership is doing something wrong (see Hirschman 1970). Clergy who fail to take remedial action run the risk of becoming socially irrelevant. At the level of individual interests, the career success of individual clergy may depend upon their ability to grow (or prevent losses from) their ministry. Catholic priests incapable of sustaining parish membership face the possibility of reassignment, whereas successful clergy are more likely to be promoted within the ranks. For Protestant pastors, especially those running independent ministries, loss of adherents might well mean loss of occupation and income.

Maximizing parishioners requires resources. As one economist observed, a "church need not make a conscious decision to maximize profit . . . [but] the long-run survival of a church in part depends on its ability to maintain non-negative wealth" (Hull 1989, 8). Ministers must be paid, churches must be built, schools must be staffed, charities must be funded, and so forth. Despite the images scholars paint of progressive clergy constantly fighting the forces of social evil, a substantial portion of a priest's time is devoted to managing the parish budget. Thus a related secondary goal of church officials will be raising revenue.

In their study of the medieval Roman Catholic Church, Ekelund, Hébert, and Tollison summarize these two basic objectives of religious organizations: "The chief monetary goal of the church [is] to increase its ability to finance its salvation effort [i.e., resource maximization]: its main nonmonetary goal [is] to preserve and extend its doctrinal hegemony—that is, to increase demand, and lower demand elasticity, for final output [i.e., parishioner maximization]" (1989, 322). To the extent that a given church can raise revenue and exclude competitors by itself, it can remain independent of the state.[14] If these goals are elusive, leaders of a religious institution will solicit state assistance—i.e., religious establishment. After all, the modern state's monopoly over coercion gives it a comparative advantage in resource extraction and ability to forbid certain activities.[15] As I will argue, churches have a strong incentive for religious establishment due to the peculiarities of producing religious goods, namely vulnerability to competition and tendency for consumers (i.e., parishioners) to free ride. The former threatens the ability of churches to maximize their parishioner base at a monopolistic level, while the latter inhibits their ability to maximize revenue. Before proceeding to these constraints, however, we must specify the nature of "religious goods."

Religions produce general compensators with supernatural content. Stark and Bainbridge define a compensator as "the belief that a reward will be obtained in the distant future or in some other context which cannot be immediately verified" (1985, 6). Compensators substitute immediate rewards for promises of future rewards, thus campaign promises qualify as compensators. What differentiates campaign promises from religious compensators is that the latter cannot be verified by any currently known means. Such nonverifiable promises and answers are *general* compensators; specific compensators are subject to empirical verification at some reasonable point in time. Religion provides

> general compensators that offer explanations for questions of ultimate meaning. . . . "Does life have purpose? Why are we here? What can we hope? Is death the end? Why do we suffer? Does justice exist?" . . . When we consider such questions it is self-evident that some of them require a supernatural answer. . . . [T]o answer certain common questions about ultimate meaning it is necessary to assume the existence of the supernatural. (Stark and Bainbridge 1987, 39–40)

Or, to quote a recent pontiff:

> Men *turn to various religions to solve mysteries of the human condition,* which today, as in earlier times, burden people's hearts: the nature of man; the meaning and purpose of life; good and evil; the origin and purpose of suffering; the way to true happiness; death; judgment and retribution after death; and finally, the ultimate ineffable mystery which is the origin and destiny of our existence. (John Paul II 1994, 78; emphasis in original)

Their supernatural content differentiates religious compensators from secular ideologies or promises. And this defines the unique social role of churches; they are the only organizations that specialize in the production of supernatural compensators. Granted, religious organizations also provide more tangible goods such as social insurance, codification of property rights, education, and fellowship, but these goods are not unique to religious organizations. They often, though not always, can be obtained more efficiently elsewhere.[16] The main reason most people practice religion is to consume these supernatural compensators.

## Axiom 5: *Religious Organizations Are Susceptible to Free Riding and Competition*

Unfortunately for religious producers, supernatural compensators are highly intangible—most do not have a verifiable payoff (at least in this life); thus their credibility potentially remains under constant doubt. The production of such intangible goods presents churches with two difficult problems: a high vulnerability to competition; and susceptibility to free riding. For the religious elite, the former makes it difficult to maintain the hegemonic (monopolistic) presence in society required by the church's mission of parishioner maximization. The latter limits the ability of clergy to collect revenue, which in turn inhibits their ability to service their parishioners. The easiest solution to both problems is reliance upon the coercive power of the state to limit competitors and extract revenue from society. To understand the church's incentive to cooperate with the state, let us examine these two constraints more closely.

First, given their intangible nature, compensators can be challenged easily. Theoretically, when two or more untestable explanations are offered for some phenomenon, the result is to cast doubt upon all explanations. Stark and Bainbridge explain that "[w]hen there is disagreement over the value of an explanation, the individual will tend to set a value that is a direct averaging function of the values set by others and communicated to him through exchanges, weighted by the value placed on such exchanges with each partner" (1987, 93).[17]

In essence, if several different religions propose to have the single "absolute truth," and if those "truths" differ, doubt arises as to which one is correct (Cox [1965] 1990, 1). Secularization theorists have argued that this would raise doubt as to the credibility of all religious compensators, leaving people less likely to contribute to, participate in, or believe in any religion (Durkheim 1951; Berger 1967). However, such has not been the case. Doubt about the credibility of religious compensators *has not diminished the demand* for such compensators, but it has made it easier for religious consumers to switch denominations in search of compensators they consider credible given their life circumstances.

> This arises because of the inherent inability of a single form of a product to satisfy divergent tastes. More specifically, pluralism arises in unregulated markets because of the inability of a single religious firm to be at once worldly and otherworldly, strict and permissive, exclusive and inclusive, expressive and reserved, whereas the market always will contain distinct consumer segments with strong preferences on each of these aspects of faith. (Stark 1992, 262)

In this manner, the intangible nature of religious goods increases the fluidity with which people can move between religious denominations. The greater the degree of religious pluralism, the more likely parishioners are to leave one religion for another that better meets their needs, ceteris paribus.[18] Preventing defection and maximizing parishioners implies maintaining a religious monopoly, thereby limiting the number of available religious options to one. It follows that religious leaders will try to restrict competition whenever possible. The experience of colonial North America supports this assertion.

> Despite nostalgic stories of early settlers migrating to the colonies for religious freedom, it was not the intent or the desire of these colonists to separate the authorities of church and state. . . . While it is true that some immigrants came to the colonies for religious freedom, few desired religious freedom for all. Politicians and preachers alike considered the idea of religious freedom, or even religious toleration, a dangerous and heathen notion that was sure to undermine the authority of the state and the very survival of the church. (Finke 1990, 610-11)

History brims with further examples of churches trying to maintain exclusive domain over a population.

How successful can parishioner-maximizing churches be in limiting competition without recourse to state assistance? The answer is, "not very." Related to the problem of intangibility, religious organizations are highly susceptible to competitive pressure because of low entry barriers into the religious market. Intangible goods (e.g., ideas, promises, etc.) are easy to produce. Compared to other industries (e.g., steel), it takes little capital to start a religion. Basically, one only needs some ideas and the ability to convince others that those ideas are correct. Low barriers to entry implies that unregulated religious economies will tend towards pluralistic competition. Such competition, when combined with the relative ease of switching denominations, means that no one religion will be able to establish a religious monopoly without the assistance of the state.[19] The state can issue laws that forbid the practice of other faiths or significantly raise the costs. Regulations that affect church property ownership, access to education and the media, and financial subsidies give an established church a significant advantage in winning (or maintaining) market share (Gill 1995). Thus, given the intangible nature of religious goods and the natural tendency towards religious competition, any religious organization wanting to monopolize the market will seek establishment. Official recognition as the state church and any other financial or legal assistance is thus highly desirable and leads religious leaders to court political favoritism and church-state cooperation.

The desire to maximize parishioners combined with low entry barriers and ease of denominational switching in pluralistic environments leads churches to seek establishment, ceteris paribus. However, this hypothesis needs to be qualified to account for the actual competitive positions of various churches in the religious market. Socially dominant and highly bureaucratized religions that find it costly to attract and maintain parishioners will naturally favor efforts to minimize religious freedom and competition, while cost-efficient and upstart religions will lobby for unconstrained religious markets. Evidence of this can be found by viewing the variations in pastoral strategy of the Catholic Church worldwide. In Asia, Russia, and parts of Africa, where Catholics are a minority and relatively unencumbered by established Church bureaucracies, clergy lobby heavily for religious freedom. In Latin America, on the other hand, where the Roman Church faces highly aggressive and cost-efficient Protestant denominations, the Catholic hierarchy has tried to limit religious freedom. This does not mean minority religions will turn down state assistance. It implies only that where religious establishment already favors one denomination, all other competitors will want a more level playing field so as to expand their own ministries with greater ease.

The second problem associated with religious production, and the one that pushes religious leaders to seek church-state cooperation, revolves around the inability of religions to prevent free riding. Because religions specialize in the production of ideas, and the dissemination of ideas is difficult to control, religious consumers can receive the benefits of religious compensators without having to pay for their provision. This is not a trivial problem for Catholic officials who constantly complain about declining revenues due to stingy parishioners (Harris 1993). Although clerics can, and do, charge fees for tangible benefits (e.g., marriage services), the fundamental objective of providing compensators is too difficult and elusive to price. If people desire religion to provide answers on the meaning of life, the nature of good and evil, etc., and those answers are aired publicly, there is no incentive for a religious consumer to continuously pay a cleric to provide that answer.[20] Moreover, religious organizations typically do not want to limit the spread of their ideas. If, as Mainwaring (1986, 4) contends, saving souls is central to religions such as the Catholic Church, then the "prophet motive" trumps the "profit motive."

Still, an organization needs resources to keep afloat; a bankrupt church is much less effective at spreading the word than a resource-rich one. No matter how altruistic the goals of an organization are, money matters. Religious organizations constantly attempt to address the problem of free riding by relying upon moral suasion and providing exclusive benefits to contributing parishioners where possible (Iannaccone 1992). This explains why the issues of civil marriage and funereal services have been so contentious during certain periods of Latin American history—marriage and burial provide the Catholic Church with one of its few sources of guaranteed income, since each had tangible qualities and could be denied to those who did not pay.

For a church, the most cost-effective way to ensure adequate and continuous levels of funding is to obtain direct state subsidization. With its coercive powers, the state can extract resources from the general population and direct some to religious organizations. This is not uncommon even in highly secularized states. Consider the tax-exempt status given to churches in the United States. Though not a direct subsidy, tax-exempt status does indicate preferential financial treatment. It comes as no surprise that in Latin America the salaries of bishops and other Catholic officials were paid directly by the state even after the breakdown of the *patronato*. Given the financial advantages that accrue from establishment, religious officials have a strong incentive to pursue such an arrangement. Even without official recognition, the desire for preferential treatment dictates that a church seek friendly relations with the government whenever possible. Recent historical work on church-state relations in Brazil supports this claim (Serbin 1995).

It is now possible to restate the church's desire for cooperation with the state in a more formal fashion:

> **Proposition 2:** Church Incentives for Church-State Cooperation
> Given that (1) religious leaders want to maximize parishioners, (2) religious leaders also want to maximize resources, (3) religious compensators are susceptible to competition, and (4) religious goods are susceptible to free riding, religious leaders will seek church-state cooperation more often than not.

Combining proposition 1 with proposition 2, it is reasonable to expect that church-state cooperation will be the historical norm. A natural trade-off exists between church and state. Religious leaders provide the state with the legitimation it needs to lower its costs of rule, while state actors protect the church from religious (and ideological) competitors and subsidize many of the church's activities. It should be noted that state officials have an incentive to subsidize the church only up to the point where they can guarantee the continued support of the clergy. Given that the state has other means of securing a compliant citizenry—coercion and patronage—while the church has limited options in dealing with competitors and free riders, the state is in the more advantageous position and will provide the church with fewer resources than religious officials would otherwise demand. Thus, monopoly churches that rely on state subsidization typically will not have adequate resources to minister to the entire population in a way that would guarantee that the needs of all religious consumers are satisfied. Monopoly religions will be weak not only because they cannot be all things to all people (Stark 1992), but because their reliance on state subsidies will leave them chronically underfunded for the task of ministering to the entire population.[21]

### Historical Evidence of Church-State Cooperation

A casual reading of history will reveal that church-state cooperation is quite common. Moreover, this cooperation takes the form of religious legitimation being exchanged for financial resources and exclusive religious dominion. States have frequently paid the salaries of clergy members, exempted churches from taxation, and declared heresy illegal. Likewise, officials of a state-sponsored church are commonly supportive of government officials. Consider the discussion of colonial Latin America found in the previous chapter. It is quite clear that the Catholic Church had a genuine interest in gaining access to new souls out of the reach of the Protestant Reformation at a time when this alternative source of religious compensators was spreading rapidly across Europe. The Spanish crown and colonial administration, on the other hand, used Catholicism as a means of pacifying the indigenous populations, thereby making the conquest a less costly task. The bargain was straightforward: The Church traded religious legitimation of the state for access to new souls, protection from Protestant competitors, and substantial material benefit in the form of vast landholdings and financial assistance. While the Church lost considerable (though not complete) autonomy, this cost was minor compared to what it received in return.[22]

A more contemporaneous example can be found in Brazil during the reign of populist dictator Getúlio Vargas (1930–45). Despite official "separation" of Church and state in 1891, the Catholic Church continued to lobby for the reinstatement of certain privileges throughout the early 1900s. Success came in 1930 when Cardinal Sebastião Leme da Silveira Cintra negotiated a substantial reestablishment bargain with leaders of the 1930 "revolution." Given that the new regime encountered numerous challenges to its legitimacy, including a serious revolt in São Paulo, President Vargas was willing to provide the Church with very favorable terms—terms presented by an admitted atheist who had previously voted against a similar measure of establishment as governor of Rio Grande do Sul (Todaro Williams 1976). A similar situation occurred in Argentina during the first reign of Juan Perón: a previously disestablished Catholic Church was able to negotiate significant terms of reestablishment during the regime's tenuous first years.[23] Finally, the weakening position of the Institutional Revolutionary Party in Mexico during the 1980s led President Carlos Salinas de Gortari to eliminate anticlerical laws contained in the country's constitution and enact new laws favorable to the Catholic Church. The Catholic Church responded, in part, by supporting various government programs and silencing critics of the government within the Church. Realizing the government's weak position meant a stronger bargaining position for the Church, and given the episcopacy's desire for institutional autonomy, the Mexican bishops were not as supportive as the government would have liked (Gill 1995).

## Church-State Conflict: Breakdown of the Bargain

Given that both church and state have strong interests in cooperation, the next logical question is why conflict should occur at all. If both parties to the establishment bargain appear to benefit from the exchange, why would one or the other choose to break the bargain and initiate hostilities? Economic theory suggests that conflict will occur when the opportunity costs of cooperation exceed the benefits one party receives. If either party could improve its situation by breaking the bargain, it will choose to do so. This leads to a rather straightforward and general proposition.

**Proposition 3:** General Conditions for Church-State Conflict
Church-state conflict occurs when the opportunity costs of cooperation for any one party exceeds the present or future benefits of cooperation.

As it stands, this proposition seems trivial. A more interesting explanation would specify why opportunity costs would exceed benefits. Opportunity costs are affected by exogenous changes. Because exogenous changes depend largely on historical circumstances, it will be difficult to generalize about the exact causes of church-state conflict. Below I suggest a number of potential causes as to why either the state or the church would *initiate* hostilities. (In order to understand church-state conflict, we need to isolate the provocateur. Either party could be expected to retaliate once attacked; this result is rather uninteresting.) Following that discussion I develop a specific hypothesis as to why several Roman Catholic episcopacies openly criticized authoritarian regimes in Latin America during the 1970s and early '80s. This situation embodies an empirical oddity since state-initiated breaks are historically more common than church-initiated hostility, largely because religious organizations bear the greater short-term costs of disestablishment.

### State-Initiated Conflict

There are two general categories of circumstances—i.e., changes in opportunity costs—that prompt the state to attack religious authority. The first concerns availability of alternative sources of legitimacy. The second relates to valuable assets held by the church that state officials would like to appropriate to bolster their own financial position. First, given that a regime benefits from religious establishment by receiving an "enduring" source of legitimation, state-initiated disestablishment can potentially result from the rise of alternative secular ideologies (e.g., nationalism, communism). If the state cultivates an independent source of ideological legitimacy, it loses the incentive to subsidize the predominant religion and can divert the resources set aside for church support to other uses. In other words, alternative ideologies controlled directly by the state provide a less expensive source of legitimacy; no autonomous group has to be paid off for use of that ideology, as do church officials who control religious symbolism. Such a scenario is unlikely since the direct costs of maintaining an established religion are relatively low and disestablishing a popular church runs the risk that the moral suasion of the church could be employed against the regime. Therefore, state officials must weigh the benefits gained from reducing church subsidies and adopting a secular ideology against the potential loss of legitimacy that occurs when religious officials condemn the regime. If religious officials command obedience over a significant portion of the population and use their clout to denounce the government, the regime will likely lose valuable support and may have to resort to coercion or patronage to regain control, both of which are costly endeavors.

This situation partially took place during the first reign of populist leader Juan Perón in Argentina (1946–55). Availing himself of European fascist thought supposedly combined with the social teachings of the Vatican, Perón's minister of planning, Raúl Mende, constructed a theory known as *justicialismo* to justify state policy and actions (Crassweller 1987, 227). This was followed by the replacement of Catholic with state holidays and the "secular beatification" of Perón's wife Evita. Episcopal protests were met with harassment of several Catholic organizations (Burdick 1995, 57-76). Although it is debatable whether Perón consciously sought to undermine the legitimating power of the Catholic Church, the result was to alienate the Argentine episcopacy. Naturally, such action provoked the episcopacy to mobilize opposition to the government with Perón responding by threatening church-state separation. While many other factors contributed to hostility between the bishops and government leaders, the regime's adoption of an alternative secular ideology clearly added to church-state hostility (Lubertino 1987, 81). It may very well be that the presence of alternative ideologies reduces the cost of separation for the state when other factors (discussed below) make disestablishment an attractive option.

As a version of this first condition, revolutionary turnover may also prompt state officials to attack religious organizations. If religion was used to legitimate the ancien régime, revolutionary leaders will find it difficult to coopt that source of legitimation prior to taking power. Typically, revolutionaries want to undermine every pillar of their opponent's strength. This means attacking the church. Once in power revolutionary leaders have an incentive to clamp down on the power of the church lest it be used for counter-revolutionary purposes. This was certainly the case in Mexico, where the Catholic Church paid a high price for supporting the conservative Victoriano Huerta in 1913 and the Cristero rebellion a decade later. Castro acted similarly to keep religious dissent to a minimum. In Nicaragua, the Catholic Church stood in opposition to the Somoza regime, allowing the Sandinistas to coopt the grassroots sectors of the Church. Nonetheless, tension erupted between the episcopacy and FSLN in the early 1980s, making it difficult for the government to rely upon religious legitimation.

A second and more likely scenario for state-initiated disestablishment relates to the indirect costs of maintaining an established religion. In terms of direct costs to the government (e.g., paying bishops' salaries, educational subsidies), religious establishment is relatively cheap. However, the indirect costs of subsidizing a church may not be as trivial. If a given church holds assets that are more beneficial to government officials than the ideological support it receives from that church, an incentive to expropriate those assets exists, especially if the church is not putting those assets to use for the benefit of the state. This situation is most likely to occur during the state-building process after governments have become sufficiently secure in their political survival, but are still in need of financial resources.[24] To justify expropriation, political leaders will turn to arguments legitimating the separation of church and state. Often these ideological justifications are taken at face value and separation of church and state is blamed on the clash between modern and traditional values.

In Latin America, the primary asset under contention between church and state was land. Considering the growing importance of export-oriented agriculture during the 1800s, many modernizing (primarily Liberal) governments saw the Church's unproductive use of its vast landholdings as harmful to future economic development.[25] The economic gains associated with expropriating Church lands outweighed the subsequent loss of political support from bishops that inevitably accompanied land seizures. The state also benefited from the expropriation of other Church revenue streams. Requiring civil marriages, secularizing cemeteries, and mandating public education diverted revenue from the Church to the state. Although the revenue generated by marriage licensing and burial fees was small, Latin American governments at this time were flat broke and defaulting on foreign loans. Expropriation of the registry was also a critical move in the state-building process in that it gave governments the record-keeping ability necessary to create a workable tax system. Conservatives, who were mostly the rural elite, stood to lose the most if taxation became more efficient; thus it was not surprising to find them siding with the Church on this issue. Conservative support for the Church probably owed as much to material interests as to philosophy, if not more so.

From a general perspective we can assert the following:

**Proposition 4:** State Incentives for Initiating Conflict
Given their desire to secure political survival and maximize revenue, state actors will initiate conflict with the church when the opportunity costs of church-state cooperation exceed the benefits of religious legitimation. This is most likely to occur when there are alternative secular ideologies to legitimate the state or when the church holds financial assets valuable to the state and expropriation is the only means of obtaining these assets.

Given the state's ability to secure rule through other means, namely coercion and patronage, and the church's strong dependence on state assistance to maintain a religious monopoly and adequate funding, the state is generally in a better position from which to launch the first salvo. Nonetheless, clergy have adequate incentive to attack the state should their interests be violated.

## Church-Initiated Conflict

As mentioned above, one of the primary goals of most religious organizations is maximization (or retention) of parishioners. Church officials keep this fundamental objective in mind when deciding whether to seek state assistance. If access to government patronage and other state support enables the church to retain or expand its membership, close cooperation with government officials will be desired, ceteris paribus. On the other hand, if the terms of establishment create a situation that promotes parishioner defections, cooperation is a poor strategic choice for church officials. Church-initiated conflict therefore results when government policies interfere with the church's ability to maximize its parishioner base. When association with a government or regime diminishes the credibility of the church among the segments of the population most hurt by government policies, parishioners are more likely to defect to other religious denominations. *This situation presents itself only under conditions of religious competition* since without other religious alternatives parishioners cannot adequately express dissatisfaction with church policy by exercising their exit option (see Hirschman 1970). Thus the first, and most important, factor that affects the church's opportunity costs for cooperating with the state is the presence of competing faiths. Under monopolistic conditions the parishioner base of the monopoly religion is artificially maximized and church officials have fewer incentives to respond to parishioner needs and desires. With the introduction of competition, however, church leaders cannot afford to make political decisions that adversely affect the welfare of their flock.

To demonstrate more clearly how monopoly religions adjust their political strategy in reaction to the introduction of religious competition, a brief digression on the economics of monopolized religion is in order. This discussion is important because the type of parishioner service resulting from a monopolized supply of religious compensators significantly affects where competition will arise and what the response of religious officials will be. In effect, an economic approach to church behavior predicts that the battleground for parishioners will be among the most disenfranchised in society.

As shown earlier, church officials desire religious monopoly because it guarantees the maximum parishioner base. However, religious monopoly brings with it a major social disadvantage: Like monopolized industries, religious monopolies devote fewer resources to customer satisfaction than would be the case under greater competition (Iannaccone 1991). This relationship between religious monopoly and inadequate attention to parishioners' needs was noted by one of the forefathers of neoclassical economics. Adam Smith (1986, 307–8) described the relationship between religious monopoly and an apathetic clergy,[26] as did another famous social theorist three centuries earlier: "[T]he nearer people are to the Church of Rome, which is the head of our religion, the less religious are they. . . . We Italians then owe to the Church of Rome and to her priests our having become irreligious and bad" (Machiavelli 1950, 151). In short, an economic model of religious monopoly predicts that less pastoral effort will be expended by churches possessing a monopolized religion.

If one assumes that church officials seek to maximize their parishioner base at the lowest possible cost, preserving scarce resources for other objectives, an economic model of religious organizations yields an additional prediction as to where pastoral resources will be concentrated. Since ministering to the faithful requires significant resources (in terms of personnel, time, and money), the most attractive group of people to receive pastoral attention will be those who are most capable of contributing resources to the provision of such services. For this reason, pastoral effort will likely be concentrated in wealthier neighborhoods. The poor, having little to donate to the church, have a greater tendency to free ride and thus will generally receive less attention under a religious monopoly.

Assuming that inadequate service does not affect the overall demand for religion (and there is no a priori reason to expect so), the lack of attention paid by church officials will do little to affect the *nominal* parishioner base under conditions of religious monopoly. Parishioners wanting religion will retain their nominal status in the church although consumption of such goods will be suboptimal given inadequate supply (both in terms of quantity and quality). In other words, countries served by monopoly religions should maintain relatively high nominal rates of association but exhibit unusually low rates of active participation, especially among the populations least able to provide the church a return on its efforts.

Prior to the rapid expansion of Protestantism, the portion of Latin Americans considering themselves Catholics was approximately 95 percent, if not greater. Nonetheless, only about 10 percent of this group were active participants in the faith. In comparison, roughly 50 to 70 percent of those considering themselves Catholic in the United States actively participate in the religion (Barrett 1982, 711–28; Finke and Stark 1992, 259–60; Finke and Stark provide the lower estimate). Lacking spiritual alternatives, someone who desires religious compensators would rather associate with a "corrupt" church than with no church at all, perhaps out of fear of punishment in the afterlife. Actually, these disaffected churchgoers may consider themselves "of the faith but not of the church" (i.e., they believe in the basic theological truths that the church promotes while disagreeing with institutional methods of disseminating those ideas). Many parishioners may invest in their own ritualistic behavior outside of the confines of the institutional church. "Folk Catholicism," the practice of the Catholic faith in a noninstitutional setting, is a clear example of this phenomenon.[27]

Although monopoly guarantees that religious consumers cannot defect to other faiths, a lack of pastoral attention to its parishioners will weaken the popularity and credibility of the church. Religious apathy and cynicism result. For example, if the clergy preach that the poor hold a special place in church teaching but consistently fail to provide them with adequate religious services, the lower classes will likely develop distrust toward their religious leaders. Recall also that religious authorities have a strong incentive to associate with the political elite in order to secure financial patronage and legislative support that otherwise would be unavailable. If government officials pursue policies contrary to the interests of a certain social group (e.g., the poor), and religious leaders avoid criticizing such policies for fear of alienating their *political* support, the credibility of the church will suffer among those who are hurt most by government policies. In Latin America, governments historically linked with the Catholic Church exhibited little regard for the interests of the poor, with the end result being a heightened distrust of Catholic prelates among members of the popular classes.

Once religious competition increases, the situation changes. As exit becomes an available option to parishioners, the objective of parishioner retention grows significantly more important for church leaders who heretofore could rely largely upon a lack of competitors to maintain artificially high membership. If competitors adequately meet the needs and desires of previously ignored religious consumers, there should be a general movement toward those substitute denominations resulting in a numerical decrease in the parishioner base of the formerly monopolistic church. In order to prevent or slow an erosion in membership, church leaders must alter their pastoral and political strategies to meet the new challenge. In terms of pastoral effort, the monopoly church will have to commit more resources to direct parishioner service, especially in areas of intense competition. If church leaders continue ignoring the needs of these segments of their (nominal) parishioner base, competitors will undoubtedly continue making substantial gains in these areas.

A second factor affecting the church's opportunity costs of continuing church-state cooperation is the popularity of the state. Association with an unpopular government or regime reduces the credibility of a religious organization. If parishioners see religious leaders acting against their political and economic interests, they are unlikely to believe those same leaders are concerned for their spiritual interests. In a competitive religious market, parishioners can express discontent by exiting to alternative faiths. Church leaders then are placed in a situation where they must weigh the benefits received from establishment against the costs that the church would incur if it continued to pursue cooperation with the government. These costs take the form of lost credibility for the church among adherents and an increase in defections. If government officials feel no pressing need to eliminate the competitors to the monopoly church, or if they are incapable, the church's strategy tilts toward political opposition. Furthermore, if church officials have a long-standing history of cooperation with unpopular governments, the only commitment likely to be credible is all-out public opposition to the policies of the government as they pertain to the population most adversely affected by them.

On the other hand, where parishioners lack an exit option, the incentive for religious leaders to oppose a regime is virtually nonexistent. Indeed, much more could be lost than gained by a decision voluntarily to break relations with the government, no matter how unpopular that government is.[28]

Church-initiated disestablishment would result in a reduction of government support with no subsequent expansion of the parishioner base, which remains artificially inflated by the lack of alternatives. True, active (as opposed to nominal) participation in the faith may rise, but such an increase also depends upon the willingness of the church to allocate resources directly to parishioner service. Given that disestablishment entails the loss of state resources and any increase in pastoral activity would require that additional church resources be expended, this would result in a net loss of resources to the church. Because of this, church-initiated disestablishment is highly unlikely under monopolistic conditions.

A final variable that influences the church's opportunity costs is the availability of nonstate funding. One of the principal motivations driving religious leaders into an alliance with the state is the need to finance their institution. However, in the process of obtaining state aid, the church usually loses a degree of autonomy. To the extent that church leaders can find resources independent of the state, they enhance their autonomy and are better positioned to oppose the government should they choose to do so. Again, this decision is contingent upon the level of religious competition and the popularity of the regime. Even with outside sources of revenue, the church still could benefit from any state subsidization. Nevertheless, religious organizations that are more efficient at collecting tithes from their parishioners will be less likely to lobby for government support than their less efficient counterparts, ceteris paribus.

While the exact reason for church-initiated hostility is determined by historical events, it is possible to draw some conclusions about the general circumstances that increase its probability.

> **Proposition 5:** Church Incentives for Initiating Conflict
> Religious leaders will initiate conflict when the opportunity costs
> of cooperation exceed the benefits, typically measured in the ability
> of the church to maximize its parishioner base. The church's
> opportunity costs of cooperation depend on three variables: the
> degree of religious competition, the popularity of the regime, and
> the availability of nonstate funding. The likelihood of conflict
> increases with a rise in competition and access to external funding
> and a decrease in the government's popularity.

I will now flesh out this final proposition in the Latin American context, paying particular attention to how different types of religious competition affect the Catholic Church's political strategy.

## Central Hypothesis: Origins of Church-State Conflict in Contemporary Latin America

We can now apply the economic reasoning underlying church-state cooperation and conflict to the specific historical context of Latin America to explain why several national Catholic episcopal conferences denounced authoritarian rule from the late 1960s onward while others did not. The basis for this hypothesis flows from the logic of the previous propositions and differs only by the addition of specific historical circumstances.

In Latin America, over four centuries of monopoly rule by the Roman Catholic Church resulted in a lack of attention to pastoral concerns and a strong desire to accommodate the political elite in return for patronage and legislative support for Church teachings. When religious competitors began making significant gains among the poorest sectors of society as early as the 1930s in some countries, Church leaders had to reevaluate their traditional pastoral and political strategies. Where competition for the souls the popular classes was fierce, a pastoral strategy of a preferential option for the poor was adopted. Under authoritarian regimes that pursued policies inimical to the poor, the Church's new pastoral strategy conflicted with the interests of the military government. In order to maintain a credible commitment to serving the poor in the face of growing religious competition, Church leaders broke their traditional alliance with the political elite and opposed authoritarianism as a system of rule. Often, this opposition attracted financial contributions from human-rights organizations, which reduced the episcopacy's reliance on the state. Where competition was minimal, bishops downplayed the preferential option for the poor and sought to maintain cordial relations with military rulers so as to preserve traditional perquisites.

As a final addendum to this hypothesis, we must consider how the government reacts to specific types of competition, as this will affect the political calculations of the episcopacy. Although an increase in religious competition among the popular classes refocuses the pastoral attention of Church leaders onto these segments of society, bishops can meet this challenge in either of two ways: state assistance or direct pastoral action. These options need not be mutually exclusive, although they may be under authoritarian regimes. If pastoral action implies mobilizing or defending the poor in order to win their trust, and if the military junta enacts policies that hurt the poor (e.g., austerity measures, demobilization of labor unions), pursuing pastoral action may damage relations with the government. The state assistance option is preferable because it does not require the use of scarce Church resources.[29] However, government officials may not be willing or able to undertake the actions necessary to rid society of non-Catholic religions and ideologies. If the cost of eliminating a competitor to the Church exceeds the benefits the state receives in return—either from a gain in national security or the provision of religious legitimation—then the government will not undertake the action. To be more precise, governments will eliminate the Church's competitors up to the point where the difference between marginal benefits and marginal costs is maximized. This means that "residual" competition will undoubtedly remain. For example, hunting down the country's last remaining Marxist would be more costly to the regime than any damage this person could do. Moreover, eliminating some groups may provide no benefits at all to the regime while imposing increasing marginal costs. Thus, the nature of the competition becomes an important factor. Of the three principal competitors to the Latin American Catholic Church—Marxism, Spiritism, and evangelical Protestantism—the latter two are more likely to induce Church-state conflict under authoritarianism. Marxism creates ambiguous incentives for Catholic bishops, who largely depend upon the government's capacity to eliminate it. Let us examine the incentives each of these challenges poses for Church-state relations in Latin America.

## Marxism

Throughout the 1950s and 1960s, Latin America was a strategic battleground in the Cold War. Fidel Castro's victory in Cuba and subsequent alliance with the Soviet Union reminded policy makers in the United States of the geopolitical significance of their southern neighbors. During this period and continuing well into the 1980s, U.S. foreign policy aimed to convince Latin American governments to combat leftist organizations and ideologies. From the Alliance for Progress to the arming of the contras in Nicaragua, anticommunism proved to be one of the hallmarks of the postwar political landscape.

This stance was no less true for the Catholic Church. Following World War II, the Vatican experienced a significant loss of influence in Eastern Europe. In the immediate aftermath of the Cuban revolution, the Church also witnessed a substantial decrease in its political and social clout (Kirk 1989, 103–5). The apparent hostility of communist parties to religion put fighting Marxism high on the list of Catholic priorities. Even democratically elected socialist parties were suspect. And, despite the opening of some Catholic theologians and clergy to class-analytic sociological methods (the basis for liberation theology), the Church hierarchy remained continually wary of left-wing ideologies.[30]

In Latin America, the Marxist challenge to Catholicism, be it real or perceived, provided a strong incentive for Church-state cooperation. Since most military regimes during the 1960s and 1970s were devoutly anticommunist, the Church had a natural ally against its Marxist competitors. Right-wing military regimes were essentially willing to invest a significant amount of resources in coercion to rid their countries of communists because the perceived benefits (i.e., enhanced national security and freedom to pursue economic policies without labor intervention) exceeded the costs. An alliance with the Catholic Church provided dictatorial rulers with a ready-made ideological justification for eradicating communist subversives—the defense of Christian society. Recognizing the potential power of religious belief in legitimating government actions, dictators often continued to justify their repressive actions as a defense of Christian civilization, long after Catholic bishops publicly rejected their legitimate claim to do so.

From the Church's vantage point, government policy directed at eliminating Marxist/socialist challengers does not hinder the Church's goal of parishioner maximization. In fact, this policy may actually help the Church defeat a serious contender to its membership base. If the military junta eliminates a potential or real threat, fewer pastoral resources need to be expended on combating the challenger directly. Considering the dearth of priests and other pastoral agents, supporting the activities of an anticommunist government provides a low-cost method of eliminating competition, thereby maintaining the Church's ideological monopoly in society. The Argentine and Uruguayan episcopacies both supported efforts by their respective governments to suppress nascent guerrilla movements.

However, if a government is unable to eliminate the communist presence and its actions (e.g., severe repression) serve only to promote further defections to guerrilla organizations, the Church then has an incentive to distance itself from the regime. This was the case in Central America, where military dictatorships in El Salvador and Nicaragua could not effectively subdue leftist guerrillas. As the revolutionary presence intensified in Nicaragua and stalemated in El Salvador, indiscriminate government repression increased, creating sympathy for the rebels. Although the bishops in these countries were suspicious of the guerrilla movements and avoided legitimating them, close identification with barbaric and ineffective regimes damaged the credibility of the Church. Opposition was a better strategy with which to win the hearts and minds of the poor.[31] In effect, the government's capacity to deal with a Marxist threat determined whether the Church would support or oppose a dictatorship.

## Protestantism

Unlike its sister Churches in Europe, the Latin American Catholic Church avoided the Protestant Reformation. A small yet significant number of Protestants did immigrate to Latin America shortly after Independence, especially to the Southern Cone, but these groups were nonproselytizing and, as such, represented no threat to the parishioner base of the Catholic Church. Most Protestant gains among nominal Catholics came after the 1930s. North American missionary efforts turned to Latin America just as the rumblings of war were making Asia and Africa too dangerous. Religious-freedom laws instituted by Liberal governments in the late 1800s and early 1900s made it possible for Protestant missionaries to enter the region. Meanwhile, an indigenous brand of evangelical Protestantism began spreading in the early 1950s—Pentecostalism.

Evangelical Protestants represent a direct challenge to the Church in that they offer different interpretations of the Christian religion. In effect, Protestantism embodies the closest religious alternative to Catholicism. And Pentecostalism, with its emphasis on emotionalism and the importance of the individual, may be a very close substitute for "folk Catholicism," which exhibits similar tendencies. Even under ecumenism, the Catholic Church directly competes with Protestants for the hearts and minds (and wallets) of the population. If the Church seeks to maximize its parishioner base at the lowest possible cost, the most likely method of meeting the Protestant threat would be to appeal to the state to eliminate it or to give the Church a substantial competitive advantage through some positive level of subsidization. This situation is not unlike an uncompetitive business firm seeking protection from competitors. The firm would most prefer the complete elimination of its rivals. Barring that outcome, it would settle for any level of subsidization that would enable it to either reduce its costs or lower its price and thereby compete more effectively. For the Catholic Church, government subsidies could be used to pay for the training and fielding of more pastoral agents (e.g., priests, nuns), giving the Church a greater presence in areas of intense competition. Another important form of assistance is allowing the Church to teach the Catholic religion in public schools, reaching potential adherents at an impressionable age. Absent this, the Church would have to commit its own resources to increasing pastoral activity in areas where competition is most intense. For this reason, the attitude of government officials toward Protestants significantly affects Church policy.

When deciding whether to commit resources to eliminate a threat, military leaders must determine whether the marginal benefits received from such actions outweigh the marginal costs. Rational-acting government leaders will not incur costly expenses to undertake actions that yield no return on their investment. The suppression of communist guerrillas or socialist labor unions typically experienced under right-wing authoritarian rule allowed leaders to pursue the economic and social reforms deemed necessary without opposition. However, while the Catholic Church may reap immense benefits from the elimination of Protestants, state leaders use a different calculus. For the most part, Protestant denominations focus on individual self-improvement and thus pose no collectivist threat to the state from below. In many cases, Protestants even give governments benefits they would have otherwise lacked. For example, Protestant missionaries frequently provide certain social-welfare services to the poor, relieving the government of the cost of having to dispense these same services. This is not to say that the Catholic Church never tended to the needs of the poor. It did. However, Catholic aid (which was scarce given the size of the institution) came more along the lines of charity to alleviate the symptoms of poverty while Protestant assistance was offered in the form of self-help. So long as welfare gains appeared at the individual level, such work was nonthreatening to right-wing military regimes. Historically, most Latin American governments rarely provided welfare services to the most impoverished sectors that evangelical Protestants typically focus on. In this respect, Protestant social activity represented a pure net gain in social welfare at no cost to the government, a situation that all but the most genocidal governments would welcome.

On the other hand, abolishing Protestantism means incurring the costs of identifying Protestant leaders and repressing their proselytizing activities. Given that Pentecostalism (the predominant form of evangelical Protestantism in Latin America), became indigenized quite rapidly, the effort to eradicate its influence would have consisted of more than simply withholding the visas of foreign missionaries. The evangelical population having gained a strong foothold in the region prior to the most recent wave of authoritarianism, efforts to eliminate it would have proved costly indeed. Protests from the United States also would have to be factored into the regime's calculus. In terms of the government's cost-benefit analysis, the marginal costs of eradicating Protestants would far exceed the marginal benefits, which would likely be zero or negative. Having negative marginal benefits means that for every unit of resources spent on eliminating Protestants, there would be a net loss of welfare to the government regardless of costs. Under such circumstances, it would not be rational to devote any resources to this task.

In sum, there is no reason for the state to eliminate Protestant competition. The only possibility that would make such an endeavor worthwhile for the state would be the Church's promise to increase the legitimation benefits it provides to the government. Therefore, the only available option for Church leaders on this front is to engage in pastoral activity that would enable them to retain parishioners where competition was most fierce—among the rural and urban poor. In this manner, Protestant competition among the poor increased the likelihood that a Catholic episcopacy would criticize a bureaucratic-authoritarian regime.

### Spiritism

Spiritism encompasses numerous religious movements that have their origins in Africa or indigenous communities in the Americas. Often these faiths fuse their beliefs with Catholicism. The incentives posed by Spiritism are essentially the same as those of Protestantism. The Catholic Church is strongly opposed to these religions, as they challenge the fundamental message of Catholicism (more so than Protestants since Spiritists are neither Christocentric nor monotheistic). However, the state has little interest in these groups since they pose no security risk and may in fact serve to vent economic and political frustrations in a nonthreatening manner. Lacking state assistance, direct pastoral action among potential Spiritist converts becomes the only available strategy for the Catholic Church. Likewise, the opportunity costs of cooperation with a right-wing military regime increase proportionately.

## Conclusion

The unique nature of religious goods creates a particular set of incentives for church-state relations. Given the partially intangible nature of spirituality and the associated problem of free riding, suppliers of religious goods have a strong incentive to seek state assistance to ensure an adequate level of compensation for their services. Additionally, the susceptibility of religious organizations to competing messages creates an incentive for the clergy to seek monopoly over competition. States may find association with a religion beneficial in that it provides another source of legitimacy for their rule. Subsidizing one religion is generally cheaper than funding all competing religions; thus a state will also prefer religious monopoly to competition, ceteris paribus.

However, the private-consumption component of spirituality provides conditions wherein monopolized religion will tend to underproduce religiosity. Once the state guarantees payment for religious goods, spiritual leaders have little incentive to conform their product to the needs and desires of their parishioners. This is especially true among the people less capable of donating additional resources to the church. In Latin America (as elsewhere) this condition leads to the general neglect of the poor by a monopolistic Catholic Church. But, given the low barriers to entry of the religious market, competitive religions can make substantial (and rapid) gains by providing for the needs of the ignored. Ironically, it was not the establishment of religious freedom that directly resulted in tremendous gains for Protestants; religious liberty existed on a regionwide basis as early as the late nineteenth century. Rather, it was a shift in supply during the 1930s that led to the tremendous growth in Protestantism—from Asia and Africa to Latin America.

Faced with competition, the dominant religion can either rely upon the state to eliminate the competitors, or it can increase its pastoral activities among those most susceptible to alternative religions/ideologies. As the first method is the most cost-effective for the monopoly church, maintaining a close association with the ruling elite remains in its interests. If government officials consider the religious or ideological challenge threatening, they will be willing to cooperate with the church and church-state relations will remain friendly. However, if the religious competition is not inherently threatening, the state will be less willing to assist the church. In this case, religious leaders will be pressed to engage in increased pastoral activity and must evaluate whether such action is worth any potential political repercussions.

Under right-wing authoritarian governments, the ruling elite often views organization among the lower classes with great distrust. For the Catholic Church in Latin America, a pastoral strategy emphasizing a preferential option for the poor would be likely to raise the ire of the regime. Moreover, it would be viewed as a betrayal of the traditional "cross and sword" alliance. If religious competition is intense, bishops are more likely to risk conflictual relations with the state to prevent additional membership loss among the poor. Considering the traditional alliance of the Church and upper classes, a strong antiauthoritarian position (via a more assertive position for the rights of the poor) will be the only credible means of retaining the allegiance of Catholic parishioners.

Finally, church-state cooperation is dependent upon the type of competition being faced by the Catholic Church in Latin America. Under anticommunist regimes, Marxist competitors provide an incentive for Church-state collaboration, unless the state proves incapable of eliminating the threat. Protestantism and Spiritism, on the other hand, are not inherently threatening to the state and thus the ruling elite are less likely to devote resources to combating this threat. In this case, the Church is left to combat these forces on its own through increased pastoral organization among the poor. Thus, Church-state relations will suffer more under intense Protestant or Spiritist competition than they would under a significant communist threat alone.

# FOUR

# Luther's Shadow

## *Protestant Competition and the Catholic Response*

*[A]n attitude of lack of religious toleration can only do great damage to the prestige of the authentic Catholic apostolate, which is to convert and not to persecute.*

William J. Coleman, M.M., *Latin-American Catholicism: A Self-Evaluation*

For nearly five centuries, the Catholic Church had a virtual monopoly over Latin America's religious landscape. For all intents and purposes, it was the only supplier of religious services until the mid-1800s, when a wave of liberal governments opened the doors to non-Catholic religions. Even with this opportunity to expand, Protestantism remained a benign challenge to Catholicism's dominance until the mid-twentieth century when North American missionaries turned their proselytizing energies toward the region. The growth of Protestantism was enhanced by events in Chile and Brazil that led to the creation of an indigenous derivative of North American Pentecostalism. These Pentecostal movements were able to expand more rapidly than foreign missionary movements. By the 1960s, Protestantism had become a significant pastoral challenge for Catholic bishops in a number of countries, including Brazil, Chile, El Salvador, and Nicaragua. Other countries, such as Argentina, Honduras, Paraguay, and Uruguay, avoided this evangelical onslaught until well into the 1980s.[1]

Today, evangelical Protestants pose one of the greatest challenges ever faced by the Catholic Church in the Western Hemisphere. Although the Catholic Church continues to be the region's largest single supplier of religious services, the collective force of evangelical churches rivals Catholic influence in many countries. Phillip Berryman has noted:

Although the vast majority of Latin Americans when polled still identify themselves as Catholics, relatively few attend mass regularly. The upshot is that the number of active Protestant churchgoers is comparable to that of practicing Catholics. The number of practicing Protestants is greater than the number of members of all other kinds of voluntary organizations—in politics, culture and sports—combined. (1994, 7)

As a consequence, the amount of attention paid to this phenomenon by Church organizations, personnel,[2] and scholars[3] has skyrocketed in recent years.

Even prior to the 1980s, evangelical Protestantism was a major concern in several parts of Latin America.[4] The intensity of Protestant growth in some countries provoked a change in episcopal thinking with regards to its evangelizing mission. At a minimum, competitive pressure by Protestants from below persuaded bishops to rethink their traditional neglect of the popular classes. In many cases, Protestant influences actually helped shape the Church's new preferential option for the poor. Given the Church's major presence in the Latin American political arena, this shift in pastoral method had important political ramifications, notably a growing opposition to policies and regimes that hurt the interests of the popular classes.

This chapter examines the empirical basis of the religious-competition hypothesis laid out in the previous chapter. Both comparative-historical and statistical techniques are brought to bear on three critical questions. First, was the Catholic Church threatened by Protestant advances in the hemisphere? Second, did Catholic pastoral activity and hence political strategy actually respond to evangelical competition? And third, does a positive relationship exist between increasing competition and the rise of an antiauthoritarian Catholic episcopacy? Combining the answers to all these questions, it is possible to determine the likelihood of a causal relationship.

We begin by surveying the history of Latin American Protestantism, paying particular attention to the successful missionizing techniques used by evangelicals. Many of these methods later influenced Catholic pastoral action. The Catholic response to Protestantism is examined next, showing that Church leaders were threatened by this form of religious competition and reacted in the manner hypothesized earlier. Statistical evidence then confirms the positive relationship between religious competition and an antiauthoritarian episcopacy. The chapter concludes with a brief overview of the cases contained in the statistical analysis. A detailed comparison of Chile and Argentina is saved for the following two chapters.

## A Brief History of Protestantism in Latin America

Despite being a topic of only recent scholarly attention (at least in the United States) Protestant roots in Latin America can be traced back to the early 1800s. There were sparse traces of Protestantism during colonial times, but none of it had the potential for serious expansion. Prior to Independence, most Protestants were associated with small trading outposts (Mackay 1933, 231-32; Bastian 1992, 314-18). Over time the nature of Protestantism changed dramatically, making it difficult to speak of a single Protestant movement. To simplify matters, three major waves of Protestant expansion can be identified: ethnic Protestantism (mid-1800s–early 1900s); foreign missionary movements (1919–present); and Pentecostalism, a form of Protestantism that rapidly developed indigenous characteristics (1930s–present). The dates presented here are only approximate. Different countries experienced these waves at different times and with varying intensities. For example, ethnic Protestantism was mostly a Southern Cone phenomenon, and Pentecostalism emerged much earlier in Chile and Brazil than anywhere else. In large part, this variation in Protestant growth helps explain the divergent responses of Catholic episcopates to authoritarianism in the 1970s.

### First Wave: Ethnic Protestants

Protestant influence in Latin America began shortly after Independence, when several governments encouraged the immigration of skilled workers from Europe, many of whom came from Protestant countries such as Germany and Britain. Even immigration from predominantly Catholic countries included Protestants. For example, a sizable number of Italian Waldensians and French Reformists migrated to Argentina in the mid-1800s (Martin 1990, 56). Naturally, this trend was more pronounced in labor-poor countries such as Argentina, Chile, and Uruguay. Nonetheless, the desire of Liberal governments throughout the region to integrate themselves into a Protestant-dominated world economy required that a minimal amount of religious freedom be guaranteed to foreign traders (Goodpasture 1989, 148–50). Furthermore, Liberal reformers thought Protestantism would weaken the hold of the Church over society and encouraged non-Catholic immigration (Bastian 1992, 319). Unfortunately for the Liberals holding this view, these Protestants never threatened the Church's cultural hegemony. Ethnic Protestants practiced their respective faiths as a means of preserving cultural identity and avoided proselytizing their views and therefore were not much of a threat to the Catholic status quo.

### Second Wave: Foreign Missionary Movements

Until the first few decades of the twentieth century, Protestant missionaries ignored Latin America because they considered the region already Christianized, albeit by Catholicism. A few missionaries trickled into Latin America during the 1800s, sometimes encouraged by Liberal governments (Mackay 1933, 234–41; Damboriena 1963, 20). These early missionaries (usually from British or United States Bible societies) aimed their efforts at the literate upper classes that were either firmly under the control of the Catholic Church or irreligious. As one would expect, their success remained extremely limited (Millett 1973, 369; Cavalcanti 1995, 297).[5] Because of the perceived limited growth potential, North American evangelical organizations turned attention elsewhere. The 1909 Edinburgh Conference of Protestant mission organizations focused on the non-Christian world (i.e., Asia and Africa) and intentionally excluded Latin American participants, thinking that this region offered little growth prospect (Dehainaut 1972, 5/9; Nuñez and Taylor 1989, 153).

Responding to this intentional oversight, and seeing the potential for Protestantism in the region, Latin American missionaries organized their own meeting seven years later. The Panama Conference, as it was known, proved to be a watershed for evangelical Protestantism (Damboriena 1963, 24-25). Learning from their earlier mistakes, missionaries directed their energies toward the popular classes. Given the neglect of these sectors by the Catholic clergy, there was a great deal of untapped demand for religious services that could be easily filled. To counteract the suspicion of foreigners that plagued earlier evangelizing efforts, these missionaries began using indigenous leaders to propagate their message. Success came quickly.

In the decades following the Panama Conference, several Protestant scholars began actively promoting Latin America as a mission field, arguing that the Catholic Church had failed to connect with the majority of the population (Mackay 1933; Navarro 1933; Rycroft 1942; Howard 1951).[6] This wave of evangelical Protestantism gained momentum in the 1930s, when mission fields in Asia closed due to political turmoil and war.[7] Many young missionaries slated for work in China were redirected toward Latin America (Wallis, interview). By this time, the work performed by previous missionaries had lowered many of the cultural barriers that made earlier growth problematic (e.g., fear of foreigners, problems with indigenous languages). The successful expansion of foreign missions continued over the next several decades but their rate of growth soon was outpaced by the most prodigious of the three major waves—Pentecostalism.

## Third Wave: Pentecostalism

Although Pentecostalism developed from foreign missionary churches that came to Latin America in the second wave, it quickly became a truly indigenous movement. For example, Chilean Pentecostalism originated when several native Chilean pastors split from the Methodist Church to form the country's first Protestant church independent of foreign funding (Gutiérrez, interview; Poblete and Galilea 1984, 16). Elsewhere in Latin America, Pentecostalism branched out from a variety of Protestant denominations and faith missions. While Chilean Pentecostalism is associated with Methodism, Brazilian Pentecostals are closely associated with the Assemblies of God (Willems 1967, 65). In this sense, Pentecostalism does not represent a single denomination as does, say, Presbyterianism. Rather, Pentecostalism is an umbrella term used to describe evangelical Protestants sharing certain theological and organizational features described below. Leadership of the Pentecostal movement is almost exclusively native, and because of its appeal to the poorest groups in society Pentecostalism has been called the "first popular manifestation of Protestantism" in Latin America (Martin 1990, 53).

The Pentecostal movement is distinct from other Protestant missions in a number of ways. Theologically, Pentecostals share three common traits that differentiate them from other evangelicals: faith healing, glossolalia (i.e., speaking in tongues) and prophecy (Stoll 1990, 49). Like other Protestant denominations, Pentecostals emphasize one's direct link to God. However, they stress emotional and spiritual connections over the more intellectual tendencies of the older mainline denominations (e.g., Methodism). Charisma (versus scholarly knowledge of the Bible) figures as the most important leadership quality among Pentecostals.

The unique organizational structure of Pentecostalism facilitates rapid expansion. Due to the prominence of charismatic leadership, the movement is highly schismatic. New Pentecostal churches often arise when the dynamic members of one congregation leave to form their own ministry. Each Pentecostal church is more or less an autonomous entity. Schismatic growth is further enhanced by the low start-up costs of a congregation. Ministers do not have to undergo rigorous theological training beyond what they have received in their parent denomination. And although elaborate church buildings exist, Pentecostals commonly are found worshipping in humble surroundings such as storefronts, garages, or residential houses (Consejo Episcopal Latinoamericano 1984, 35). These factors, combined with the lack of a costly central bureaucracy, has allowed Pentecostal churches to expand at unprecedented rates. A report issued by the Catholic Church went so far as to characterize Pentecostals as "spontaneous religious groups" (Consejo Episcopal Latinoamericano 1984, 141). Today, Pentecostals account for roughly 66 to 75 percent of all Protestant growth in the region (Stoll 1993, 3; Nuñez and Taylor 1989, 44).

## Other Movements

Given the increasingly diverse nature of the Latin American religious landscape, a simplified tripartite categorization falls short of capturing all the non-Catholic religious groups in the region. A few words are in order regarding some of the smaller movements not covered above. Of these, the best known are the politically active, conservative organizations commonly affiliated with the "religious right" in the United States. Stoll 1990 provides the best account of these groups. Among the most prominent groups are Jim Bakker's PTL Club, Pat Robertson's Christian Broadcasting Network, and the Jimmy Swaggart Ministries, which were able to enter the region via the proliferation of radio and television. Unlike previous North American missions that were largely apolitical, these organizations are fervently anticommunist and entered the region (especially Central America) following the 1979 Sandinista revolution in Nicaragua with the intention of reversing the region's apparent radicalization (including liberation theology). Although attracting a great deal of media attention, these groups have been relatively inconsequential in the religious arena. Compared to the indigenous Protestant movement, these groups accounted for only a tiny fraction of evangelical growth. Their stadium-style preaching (reminiscent of traveling religious revivals in the United States) enabled them to whip up tremendous amounts of fervor in the short term, but enthusiasm fizzled soon after they moved on. Despite follow-up efforts to plant local churches, converts (or "witnesses") claimed during large-scale revivals usually returned to their old ways once the momentary fervor of the evangelical crusade passed, a process known as "backsliding" (Holland, interview).

Another set of religions having some influence in Latin America include the religions normally considered to be on the fringes of Protestantism: Seventh Day Adventists, Jehovah's Witnesses, Mormons, etc. Despite their claim to be Christian movements, Catholics and mainline Protestants often view them as illegitimate. These churches appeared on the scene mainly in the 1970s. Although showing some growth potential (especially the Mormons), the foreign nature of these groups prevented them from rivaling the more rapidly expanding Pentecostals. Foreign leadership and small, concentrated numbers made them easy targets for government repression in some countries, notably Argentina and Paraguay (Foreign Broadcast Information Service 1978 and 1979).

Finally, Spiritism has made an impact comparable to Pentecostalism, but only in Brazil and the Caribbean. Spiritism refers to a broad array of African-influenced religions such as Umbanda, Candomblé, and Santería, as well as the more European Kardecist movement (see Hess 1994). These religions have the same popular-class appeal as Pentecostalism, possess a similar schismatic tendency, and operate very cost-effectively. However, they worship, at least partially, non-Christian gods (or spirits). Some groups have been known to synthesize Catholic beliefs and practices into their rituals. Although its influence rivals Pentecostalism in Brazil, Spiritism remains innocuous in continental Spanish America. What is said below about the Catholic reaction to evangelical Protestantism generally holds true for Spiritism as well.[8]

## Winning the Souls of the Poor: Protestant Opportunities and Tactics

The tremendous success of evangelical Protestantism in several Latin American countries provoked many Catholic bishops into reevaluating their own pastoral objectives and methods.[9] In fact, Protestants did more than merely awaken bishops to their historic neglect of the poor; many of the techniques they used to win converts eventually found their way into Catholic grass-roots projects. Drawing attention to these methods reveals that the concurrent growth of Protestantism and the Catholic Church's preferential option for the poor was more than mere coincidence.

Before discussing the specific methods employed by evangelicals, it is worth looking at one exogenous factor that added to their success: the scarcity of Catholic priests. The lack of priests presented Protestants with a tremendous opportunity to expand. As argued earlier, monopoly churches are like monopoly firms in that they do not meet the quality and quantity demands of their customers. Both table 4.1 and figure 4.1 indicate a strong, inverse association ($r = -.75$) between religious monopoly and church strength. Interestingly, Latin America contains the highest concentration of Catholics in the world, but suffers from a chronic dearth of clergy. The number of priests per 10,000 Catholics in the United States and Great Britain—two minority-Catholic countries—is nearly five times as great as in most Latin American countries. Whereas the typical Latin American country has approximately 1.9 priests per 10,000 Catholics, the numbers are 9.8 and

**Table 4.1**  Penetration of Religious Personnel (Latin America and Selected Countries)

| Country | (A) Year | (B) Catholic Clergy* per 10,000 Catholics | (C) Population Catholic % | (D) Indigenous Clergy % |
|---|---|---|---|---|
| Latin America | | | | |
| Argentina | 1971 | 2.0 | 95.8 | 59 |
| Bolivia | 1973 | 1.8 | 93.2 | 30 |
| Brazil | 1970 | 1.5 | 90.2 | 58 |
| Chile | 1971 | 3.0 | 84.3 | 45 |
| Colombia | 1972 | 2.4 | 96.7 | 82 |
| Ecuador | 1972 | 2.7 | 96.7 | 76 |
| El Salvador | 1970 | 1.1 | 96.8 | 61 |
| Guatemala | 1970 | 1.2 | 95.0 | 13 |
| Guyana | 1972 | 6.5 | 16.0 | 15 |
| Honduras | 1972 | 0.9 | 96.3 | 21 |
| Mexico | NA | 1.9 | 96.1 | 13 |
| Nicaragua | 1970 | 1.4 | 95.5 | NA |
| Paraguay | 1972 | 2.2 | 95.6 | 46 |
| Peru | 1970 | 2.1 | 95.5 | 37 |
| Puerto Rico | NA | 2.8 | 92.2 | NA |
| Uruguay | 1970 | 3.8 | 61.0 | 64 |
| Venezuela | 1972 | 2.3 | 94.8 | 25 |
| Selected countries | | | | |
| Australia | 1972 | 10.8 | 28.6 | 90 |
| Austria | 1971 | 9.3 | 89.2 | NA |
| Belgium | 1973 | 8.9 | 91.9 | NA |
| France | 1973 | 2.0 | 80.3 | 94 |
| Great Britain | 1972 | 10.5 | 13.0 | 90 |
| India | 1974 | 11.9 | 1.2 | 88 |
| Netherlands | 1972 | 13.3 | 43.0 | 96 |
| Philippines | 1972 | 1.4 | 85.0 | NA |
| Poland | 1976 | 6.7 | 82.1 | 100 |
| Portugal | 1972 | 6.2 | 96.6 | 98 |
| South Africa | 1972 | 6.5 | 8.7 | 10 |
| Spain | 1972 | 4.4 | 97.6 | 99 |
| Sweden | 1970 | 10.4 | 1.2 | NA |
| Switzerland | 1970 | 8.3 | 49.6 | 90 |
| United States | 1975 | 9.8 | 28.1 | 95 |
| West Germany | 1971 | 45.9 | 48.5 | 96 |

*Source:* Barrett 1982.
Correlation between (B) and (C) = −.75. Statistically significant at the .01 level.
*Aggregation of diocesan and religious order priests. NA = not available

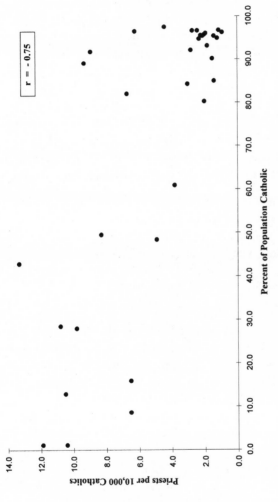

r = − 0.75

**Percent of Population Catholic**

Priests per 10,000 Catholics

Figure 4.1    Penetration of Religious Personnel as Compared to Catholic Density (Selected Countries)

10.5 for the United States and Great Britain respectively. The problem is even more acute when one considers that often a majority of priests in Latin America came from other countries (e.g., United States, Germany) to compensate for the scarcity (see below).

Priests per 10,000 Catholics is used as a measure of Church strength for two reasons. First, it indicates the number of parishioners the Church can adequately service. Obviously, parishioners receive less attention when the ratio of priests to Catholics is lower. Second, a low priest/parishioner ratio reveals an inability to recruit clergy, indicating that the Church is somewhat unpopular. Lodwick observes that "part of the failure of the Roman Catholic Church in Latin American to recruit young men for the priesthood is the immorality and ill-repute of the clergy" (1969, 108; see also Poblete 1970, 47).

Given that the number of parishioners the Catholic Church can reach in Latin America was (and still is) severely limited, evangelicals faced a wellspring of untapped demand. As one Presbyterian minister and scholar observed:

> The very fact of the small number of priests to care for the religious needs of the people is significant, especially when the priests are not of the highest moral quality and in a religion which emphasizes the clerical power to the exclusion of lay leadership. These facts make Latin America a valid field for Protestant missions. (Lodwick 1969, 109)

The lack of clergy was most pronounced in the poorest barrios and in rural areas where parishioners received only periodic visits from priests. Catholic priests traditionally concentrated their time and effort on serving wealthy parishioners who were more apt to contribute financially to the Church's coffers (Illich 1972, 158). Not surprisingly, this created a great deal of resentment toward the Church among the popular classes (Stewart-Gambino 1992, 70-73). Protestant missionaries fed on this disaffection and pent-up demand by providing religious services to persons long neglected by Catholics (Thorp, interview). In essence, Protestants became the first to develop a preferential option for the poor.

The subsequent techniques used by Protestants to acquire converts was conditioned by the fact that their greatest gains could be made among the poor. Providing material goods and other economic incentives to the desperately poor became a way of winning them to the faith (Mackay 1933, 242; Rycroft 1942, 159–75; Klaiber 1970, 102; Turner 1979). Evangelical missionaries dispensed medical care, engaged in agricultural projects, built rural cooperatives and recreational centers, and provided other material goods and services.[10] Missionaries generally distributed assistance unconditionally; converts and nonconverts alike received aid. Popular imagery to the contrary, most foreign missions rarely pressured individuals to join, knowing that coerced conversion rarely led to sustainable membership. Although free riding was an ever-present problem, the trust that Protestants built among the communities they served eventually paid off in increased membership.

Incentives were not strictly limited to handouts. One of the most popular methods of recruitment was to offer parishioners the opportunity for self-improvement. Education figured prominently in Protestant missionizing (Mackay 1933, 243–45). In part, this stemmed from the emphasis on Bible reading. When faced with an illiterate population of potential converts, teaching people to read became a necessity. Although the Catholic Church operated schools, the episcopacy diverted most educational resources to the upper class. Moreover, the Church downplayed the connection between literacy and reading the Bible, fearing it would produce another Protestant Reformation. In fact, the importation of the Bible was banned for most of Latin American history (Montgomery 1979, 89; Wegmueller, interview). As the Jesuit scholar Jeffrey Klaiber noted, this led to some unintended consequences:

> It is not merely a present-day ecumenical joke that today the Catholic missionary in Latin America must carefully explain to his faithful that the Bible was not written by Protestants and that it is not heretical to read it. The Bible came to Latin America as popular literature virtually with the Protestant missionaries. Even today the best and most readable translations of the New Testament in Latin American Spanish are done by Protestants. (1970, 99)[11]

Protestants interested in spreading the Gospel via the written Word of God introduced literacy campaigns in rural areas long before the Brazilian episcopacy introduced the Basic Education Movement, a forerunner of CEBs (see below).

Other forms of self-improvement promoted by Protestants included job training programs, classes on managing personal finances, and treatment groups for alcoholics and abusive husbands. Most of these programs were designed around the philosophy of "redemption and lift," wherein parishioners first found virtue in evangelical teachings and then improved their social conditions (Holland, interview). Considering the way the incentives ran, however, the more appropriate phrase may have been "lift and redemption," as some parishioners were undoubtedly attracted first to Protestantism because of the social mobility these groups provided. Overall, these efforts did improve the lives of many converts (Martin 1990, 230).[12]

The emphasis placed on lay involvement also made conversion more attractive. Protestants generally stress one's personal relationship with God, while the Catholic Church emphasizes priestly mediation. For this reason, evangelical church members participate more actively in services than Catholics do during the Mass.[13] Participation in Protestant church organizations and leadership roles further developed many of the skills that made conversion attractive in the first place. Small groups would also meet in private homes to read the Bible and discuss its relevance to their own lives. This favorite Protestant method of internalizing their religious faith in new converts preceded the same practice in Catholic base communities by several decades. All said, Protestant churches made members feel useful, whereas Catholic services alienated worshippers. Prior to Vatican II (1962–65), the majority of the Mass was said in Latin and parishioner involvement was limited to reciting prayers from memory, often without knowing their meaning. On top of this, the priest would perform his duties with his back to the audience, hardly the best way to make churchgoers feel welcome!

Protestants also mastered the use of technology to attract converts. They pioneered the use of radio and film to reach a wider audience (Finkenbinder, interview; Wegmueller, interview). Although reliance on technological evangelism would appear to benefit conversion of the middle and upper classes, it was actually aimed at the poor and was quite effective. Despite the poverty of rural villages and urban *favelas*, at least some people had access to radios and would invite neighbors to listen. Films, often shown in open fields on bedsheets, attracted large crowds in rural areas, where such entertainment was rare. Exposure to Protestantism in group settings facilitated conversion since it provided the necessary communitarian aspects needed to build a congregation from scratch. One person alone may be reluctant to join a Protestant church out of fear of ostracism from the community. But the psychological costs of conversion are much lower when many members publicly announce their desire to join. In this respect, forming a Protestant church represents a collective action problem that can be solved by lowering information costs (see Lichbach 1995, 111–14). All members of a community may be better off if a new congregation is established, but not knowing the intentions of others, each person will refuse to join; a suboptimal outcome arises since no one establishes the congregation. Only when the intentions and preferences of the entire neighborhood are revealed (and are believed to be credible) is a new church likely to result.

Not all Protestant churches had the resources to offer material incentives or employ fancy technology. This was especially true for indigenous Pentecostal churches in poor barrios. Nor could they realistically offer everyone leadership roles in the church. Moreover, many churchgoers did not want the opportunities for social advancement that these churches offered; they simply desired religious services on a regular basis. Even with these resource limitations and limited consumer desires, Pentecostals still offered parishioners something the Catholic Church did not—religious "entertainment." Pentecostals earned a reputation for boisterous religious services filled with popular music, charismatic preaching, and an almost uncontrollable atmosphere. Church services typically leave one feeling personally "touched" by the Holy Spirit. In many ways, Pentecostalism offered the festive environment of popular Catholic holiday processions,[14] but on a weekly basis. Contrast this with the solemnity of the pre-Vatican II Catholic Mass. For many, the choice between religious services that were fun versus ones that were staid was simple. Protestantism carried the day.

## The Catholic Reaction

How serious was the Protestant threat to the Catholic Church in Latin America, and how did Church officials respond to this challenge? The fact that Church agents responded directly and fervently to Protestant encroachment indicates that they did consider it a serious problem. Nevertheless, to alleviate some initial doubt as to whether Protestantism represented a serious threat, it is best to refer to the thinking of the Church's top official:

> Pope Pius XII, in his second speech at the World Congress of the Secular Apostolate [c. 1955], mentioned four mortal dangers for the Catholic Church in Latin America: Protestantism, laicism,[15] marxism [sic] and spiritism. He said that in order to overcome these necessities and dangers, it is necessary to provide able priests in sufficient numbers. . . . As the lack of native or local clergy cannot be solved in the short term, the pontifical documents asked for the help of clergy from other nations. Even this cannot solve the problem of Latin America in a quick and definitive way; therefore a call is made to the laymen. Further, these documents do not refer only to the persons who may help, but also mention the necessity of

finding new methods which may be adequate for the peculiar conditions
of this time, the best use of technical means, methods, and forms as instruments to help achieve better the virtue and diffusion of truth. (Vitalis
1969, 3/1)

Even before the pontiff's concerns became public, Protestants were on the
mind of Catholic episcopacies throughout Latin America. Consider a joint
pastoral letter issued by the Peruvian bishops on 18 December 1943:

> We are duty bound to raise today a warning voice against a grave and
> widespread danger which seriously threatens the purity and unity of our
> religious faith. . . . [W]e refer to Protestant propaganda. . . . We have
> sketched some remedies whereby . . . we may know how to resist the com-
> mon enemy, holding ourselves firm in the faith; all united in one purpose
> of defending our Christian values with a high sense of Catholicity, deny-
> ing all cooperation to Protestant work, in money, support, attendance at
> its services and schools, reading its literature, membership in its societies,
> even athletic ones such as the YMCA and YWCA. Beware of false
> prophets who come to you in sheep's clothing but inwardly they are
> ravening wolves. (Quoted in Howard 1944, 60–61)

Several other national Churches raised similar concerns during this time
(Turner 1971, 169-70).

A further gauge of whether various episcopates considered Protestantism a significant challenge is to observe how Church officials actually responded. Through the actions and statements of bishops and their agents, it
becomes clear that the growth of Protestantism was taken seriously by
Church officials. At first, bishops tried to solve the problem by physically ex-
cluding Protestants from the region. This strategy had little if any impact. As
Protestants rapidly increased their numbers among the poor in certain countries, many prelates felt obligated to reach out to the popular classes and
make up for four centuries of pastoral neglect. The Church's historical response to Protestant competition reveals how pastoral (and political) strategy shifted as the nature of Latin American Protestantism changed.

### Early Response: Blame the Liberals

Ethnic Protestants never posed a serious threat to the Church's parishioner
base. Nonetheless, the episcopacy regarded the arrival of Protestant immigrants as symptomatic of a more immediate problem—the desire of Liberal
governments to circumscribe the socioeconomic privileges of the institutional

Church. In addition to seeking skilled foreign labor, Liberals promoted religious diversity with the hope of reducing the Church's stranglehold over Latin American culture. Needless to say, the trickle of Anglicans, Lutherans, and other denominations never made a dent in Catholic dominance. Religious liberty represented a Potemkin village for more serious issues such as the *patronato*, church funding, control over education, and clerical reform. If Liberal leaders truly wanted to modernize Latin American society based on Enlightenment philosophy, they would have opted for complete separation of Church and state. Instead, they fought vigorously to preserve the *patronato*, which guaranteed them direct control over many episcopal affairs. The issue was one of control over a hegemonic cultural and political institution, rather than a deep-seated belief that separation of church and state was a prerequisite for modernization. Likewise, episcopal critiques of Protestantism were mostly veiled attacks against Liberal rulers: the great religious/ideological battles of the nineteenth century were actually fights between Catholics and Liberals more than Catholics and Protestants.

## A Defensive Reaction to Early Missions

The arrival of evangelical Protestants beginning around 1900 presented a bigger problem because they stole parishioners directly from the Church (even if those parishioners were Catholic only in a nominal sense). For this reason, Church leaders and activists turned their ire to foreign missionaries. The immediate response was defensive: bishops favored ridding their countries of foreign competitors over strengthening the loyalty of those (nominal) Catholics most vulnerable to the Protestant message. The Church responded with a two-pronged strategy—prelates appealed for government assistance while clergy and lay activists engaged in grassroots intimidation.

Despite professing a philosophy based on human compassion, intimidation and violence were not beyond many in the Church when it came to dealing with evangelicals. One former missionary recounted how a Catholic priest enticed local government officials into chaining shut their meeting hall (Wegmueller, interview). Another faced a hail of mud and stones as he and a fellow minister tried to preach from an outdoor pulpit in rural Brazil. That same person witnessed a number of Bible burnings organized by Catholic priests (McIntire, interview).[16] Slashing tires on missionary vehicles and disrupting evangelical meetings were also tactics commonly employed (Turner 1971, 170). Such activity occasionally ended with missionaries seriously wounded or killed. These countermeasures were common during the first half of the twentieth century, when evangelical Protestants were predominantly foreigners and thus vulnerable targets of intimidation. But far from stopping the advance of Protestant missions, such actions only strengthened their resolve.

At a higher level, bishops tried using their connections with the political elite to impede the entrance of missionaries. Cavalcanti cites a Catholic scholar as saying "Brazil is Catholic and will always be so. . . . To make it Catholic, to liberate it from Masonry, from Protestantism, from Spiritism, and from Positivism, it is necessary that we intervene, organized and cohesive, in political struggles, that we reconquer that place which belongs to us" (1995, 302).[17] Laws were passed, strengthened, or enforced in several nations making it illegal to import the Bible (Wegmueller, interview). At the urging of several bishops, president Getúlio Vargas pressured the United States government to limit the number of evangelical missionaries entering Brazil in the 1940s (Pierson 1974, 177; Lodwick 1969, 103). This issue arose when the United States tried to persuade Brazil to join the Allies in World War II. Vargas, not particularly interested in getting militarily involved, delayed Brazil's entry until the war was assuredly won. The negotiations over Protestant missionaries, while directly beneficial to the Catholic hierarchy, probably served as one of Vargas's many stalling tactics, rather than representing a sincere desire to help the Church. The restrictions were never enacted.

Similarly, Juan Perón enacted antimissionary legislation in Argentina but rescinded it following vitriolic exchanges between himself and the episcopacy in 1955. The Colombian government signed a treaty with the Vatican in 1953 that essentially restricted Protestant activity throughout the majority of the country (Goff 1968, 3/27–36). Overall, though, legal restrictions were hard to come by and rarely enforced. Governments typically had little interest in obstructing the activities of Protestant groups, as they rarely caused trouble. Being "strangers in a strange land," Protestants avoided political activity. Public positions on government policy were normally restricted to issues surrounding religious liberty, in which they had a direct stake. Furthermore, Protestant leaders did not need to take political stands because they were untainted by past church-state alliances. This inaction appeared as support for the status quo and has given Protestant missionaries a conservative image both in the United States and Latin America. This view is incorrect, though. My own interviews with former and current missionaries revealed a wide diversity of political opinions.[18] Survey evidence shows that the political views of Protestants approximate the distribution of views found in the general population (Fontaine and Beyer 1991; also see the various essays in Garrard-Burnett and Stoll 1993).

These governments also benefited from the community services (e.g., medical clinics) that evangelicals provided. Ironically, in the 1940s, it was the United States government that hindered Protestant missionary activity via passport restrictions. It was reported in 1944 that

> Baptists were disturbed by the passport situation, alleging that while on the one hand transportation has been available for outgoing missionaries and Latin American governments have been willing to grant the necessary visas, the [U.S.] State Department has delayed and sometimes refused the issuance of passports. (*Latin American Newsletter*, August 1944, p. 3)

United States bishops, upon requests from their Latin American colleagues, lobbied the U.S. government claiming that Protestant activities were endangering the Good Neighbor Policy.

Despite efforts at controlling their influx, missionaries entered Latin America at an increasing rate, especially after Asia became inaccessible in the mid-1930s. Having only minor success at legally blocking the efforts of foreign evangelicals, the Catholic Church actively sought to bolster its competitive position by regaining a number of socioeconomic privileges it had lost in the late 1800s. This was nowhere more noticeable than in Brazil and Argentina, where the Church negotiated a substantial degree of reestablishment under the populist regimes of Vargas and Perón (Gill 1993). In Central America, the bishops maintained tacit alliances with the various governments that came to power, preserving their privileged social position (Cardenal 1992, 256). Needless to say, the Church pursued these privileges irrespective of Protestant advances, although receiving educational subsidies helped its long-term competitive position by indoctrinating children in the faith early.[19]

### A New Approach: Preferring the Poor

The defensive reaction of the Church ended, by and large, during the 1950s for three reasons. First, reactionary tactics (e.g., intimidation) were ineffective. The flow of missionaries never abated. Governments were reluctant to restrict religious liberty and provide the Catholic Church with the amount of public assistance it needed to remain truly competitive.[20] Second, in 1958, Pope John XXIII called for greater ecumenical relations with non-Catholic religions, thereby making it difficult for Latin American bishops to sustain their previous tactics.[21] Finally, as the Protestant movement became more indigenized, the clergy found it increasingly difficult to stir up nationalistic sentiments against Protestants. Moreover, the success of indigenous Protestantism clearly demonstrated that the Church never paid sufficient attention to its parishioners and that the problem was more complex than merely getting rid of a few missionaries.

All this prompted a more positive approach to dealing with the advance of religious competition, one that emphasized a Catholic renewal among the popular classes. In countries where Protestantism (especially Pentecostalism) grew at exceedingly rapid rates, the bishops and clergy could no longer ignore their pastoral responsibility to the poor. With this realization came the difficult decision about whether to retain close ties with the political elite or shift the Church's attention to the grass roots. Under populist and democratic-reformist regimes (e.g., Brazil 1930–64, pre-1973 Chile), it was possible to pursue both: Where the government maintained a significant degree of legitimacy with the popular classes, associating the Church with the state was a reasonably safe strategy, at least in the short term. Church officials cooperated with reform-minded politicians while simultaneously developing grass-roots programs. However, when right-wing authoritarian regimes came to power, supporting the political elite contradicted episcopal efforts to show a preferential option for the poor. The opportunity costs of supporting an unpopular dictatorship were high and measured in terms of lost credibility for the Church and further parishioner defections to competing denominations. Episcopacies that did not face any significant Protestant growth could maintain beneficial alliances with the state, including abusive dictatorships. Their opportunity costs remained unchanged.

The first sign that the Church recognized it was at a competitive disadvantage to Protestants and took remedial action to counter came relatively early. Influenced by Protestant colporteurs, episcopacies in Argentina and Brazil began distributing the Bible to their parishioners in the 1930s (Rycroft 1942, 57, 115–16). Catholics in other countries began adopting the mass-media technology used so effectively by missionaries. In the 1950s and 1960s, numerous Catholic radio schools (modeled after their Protestant counterparts) appeared throughout the region. Paul Wegmueller, founder of the missionary organization Películas Evangélicas, recounts how Catholic priests would often ask for his advice and services. Catholic priests frequently rented his films for use, despite their Protestant content (Wegmueller, interview)!

The Catholic Church's first major organizational effort to reestablish social influence at the grassroots was Catholic Action. The Vatican originally developed Catholic Action to combat socialism among working-class Europeans, but Pope Pius XI saw benefits in a Latin American version—Acción

Católica (AC). The motivation behind AC stemmed from new challenges to the Church's cultural hegemony, primarily communism and Protestantism. As Levine explains, bishops "attempted to develop explicitly Catholic organizations in many fields, particularly among organized labor and students, in order to combat the potential 'loss' of these elements from the Church. These defensive actions were meant to resolve the immediate problems created by social change" (1981, 31–32). It was believed that social change (e.g., urbanization) was the primary reason so many parishioners were converting to non-Catholic religions and other ideological groups.[22] Nonetheless, it was the successful gains of Protestants and communists that awoke the Church to these changes.

As originally conceived, AC had limited appeal because its emphasis befitted a middle-class Europe more than an impoverished Latin America. Acción Católica was established initially among workers and university students in Latin America during the 1930s, a very small segment of the population at the time. Nonetheless, certain innovative episcopacies (notably those in Chile and Brazil) adapted AC programs to meet their specific circumstances. Vallier sums up this transformation:

> Catholic Action programs have not gained a deep, institutional foothold among the Church's membership, nor have they generated new attachments to the faith among those who stand outside the sacraments [i.e., the popular classes]. Catholic Action also brought home the fact that the average member could not be easily mobilized into a militant apostle. The idea of taking up engagement in society as a spiritual agent of the Church carried little, if any, meaning. . . . The failure of Catholic Action to mobilize an auxiliary labor force indicated to Church leaders that new levels of motivational commitment had to be gained antecedent to the formation of apostolic programs. . . . A noticeable shift occurred in the efforts of progressive Church groups following World War II, and especially in the late 1950s. Instead of promoting the formation of Catholic youth and trying to mobilize militant cadres of spiritual apostles, increased amounts of attention were given to creating social, technical and economic programs that would have a direct appeal to marginal status groups, such as the peasants and urban poor. Catholic Action was not abandoned but incorporated as a kind of organizational base on which new activities could be built. (1970, 65-66)

In countries where the Church faced increasing competitive pressure from below, AC groups influenced a broad array of new pastoral projects, including

the *comunidades eclesiales de base* (CEBs). On the other hand, where significant challenges to Catholicism never developed (e.g., Argentina, Uruguay),
AC remained a narrow and unimaginative movement.

In addition to protecting Latin America from socialism, the leaders of
Acción Católica were equally concerned about the growing influence of
Protestantism. In 1953, AC delegates and episcopal representatives from
twenty-two Latin American countries held a major conference in Chimbote,
Peru. Among the main topics of discussion were the causes and consequences
of Protestant expansion:

> The delegates said that they had to accept the necessity of practicing reli-
> gious toleration. This did not mean a compromise with Protestantism; it
> only indicated that modern changes are such that Catholics must now rec-
> ognize a different set of working conditions if they would convert those
> whom they find outside the fold, be they enrolled in Protestant sects or
> not. . . . [One delegate] affirmed that, beyond all question, there is in
> Latin America a vast, North American Protestant missionary campaign,
> that has ample economic resources, uses very efficient technical methods,
> and is characterized by systematic planning. The real though undeclared
> purpose of this campaign is to divert as many people as possible from their
> traditional adherence to the Catholic Church. . . . The Chimbote people
> spent no time denouncing Protestant penetration, but sought means of
> counteracting its adverse influence on the Catholic apostolate. What was
> of great concern was not merely the arrival of more Protestant missionar-
> ies, then numbering over four thousand, but the success attending their ef-
> forts in establishing local seminaries to train local people in the same type
> of aggressive missionary work. It was pointed out that the Protestant pro-
> paganda in general was directed to the weakest elements of the Catholic
> population—people often isolated and out of touch with full Catholic
> life. This element of the population, sometimes almost abandoned be-
> cause of lack of priests, would naturally be a prey to Protestant prose-
> lytism. . . . Credit was given to the Protestants for the fact that conversion
> to their creed normally involved the convert in a moral commitment. (Vi-
> talis 1969, 8/4–5)

The suggested strategy for combating Protestantism reflected a changing attitude on the part of Catholic activists, away from a defensive posture (e.g.,
intimidation and legal restrictions) toward a more constructive engagement
with nominal Catholics. Conference participants agreed that "it is necessary
to resist Protestantism positively. Long-term programs are needed which

may give to Catholic communities the instruction and vitality which they need at present" (Vitalis 1969, 8/15).

One Maryknoll priest in attendance recognized that Protestantism grew where the Catholic Church was most absent (i.e., the poorest barrios) and that countering Protestant activity meant paying attention to previously neglected Catholics: "[I]t was observed that when an abandoned area has been in the control of Protestants for some time, if the place once again receives the care of a priest, invariably most of the Protestant converts return to their traditional Catholic faith, often at the material sacrifice of being cut off from Protestant economic resources" (Coleman 1958, 49). Although this turned out to be wishful thinking on Coleman's part (Protestant converts frequently stayed Protestant converts), it gave indication that the Church was becoming more sensitive to the needs and desires of their poorest parishioners.

Concurrent with the increasing activity of Protestants, the Latin American Church asked other Catholic Churches in Europe and the United States to send priests to compensate for its clerical shortfall. It was reasoned that many of the Church's problems derived from a lack of personnel (Hurtado [1941] 1992, 99–112). Interestingly, clergy shortages had been a fact of life in Latin America since at least the early 1800s but were not considered a serious problem until the mid-twentieth century. Scholars trace this shortfall to the flight of proroyalist clergy during the struggle for independence, expulsion of various religious orders, and the subsequent episcopal disorganization (Poblete 1965, 18–19). But surely, a century was sufficient time to recognize the problem and take remedial action. Granted, rapid population growth made the problem increasingly visible, but bishops rarely invested Church resources in constructing seminaries in anticipation of the problem. Instead, bishops concerned themselves with promoting their institution's socio-legal status via "high politics."

In many countries, this elite-based strategy was no longer tenable by the late 1950s. Competition for parishioners required the Church to boost its forces, especially among the rural and urban poor. Ironically, Catholic Churches from around the world sent priests and lay missionaries to support the world's most "Catholic" region. During the early 1960s, the Vatican sponsored a program called Papal Volunteers for Latin America. U.S. bishops trained lay activists in association with this effort with the goal of placing "one volunteer in Latin America for every parish" (Vallier 1963, III/17). By the early 1970s, the Latin American Church witnessed an overwhelming influx of foreign personnel. Foreign money also flowed into the region. The shift in strategy reflected the changing nature of Protestantism. Early on, it was easy to claim Protestant growth represented a neocolonial invasion since most missionaries were from the United States and Western Europe. Legal restrictions on missionary activity seemed a justifiable method of defending the region's Catholic heritage from foreign values. However, once Latin Americans themselves began building Protestant churches, legal prohibitions became harder to justify. It became obvious to many Church leaders that Latin America may not have been as Catholic as once thought. This is not to say that Church officials stopped considering Protestantism a foreign entity. Bishops and clergy still refer to Protestant expansion as *la invasión de las sectas*. This is ironic, since the majority of Protestant churches in Latin America are created and run by Latin Americans themselves. The invasion comes more from within than without. Even international missionary movements are increasingly led by Latin Americans, such as Luis Palau, the "Billy Graham of Latin America" (Stoll 1990, 121–24).

In countries where indigenous Protestantism advanced early, bishops took note of the problem and expanded pastoral action beyond the limits of AC. This was particularly true in Brazil and Chile, where Pentecostalism made its debut. While in Rome for Vatican II, Chile's Cardinal Raúl Silva commented specifically on the explosion of evangelical Protestantism in his country. He said:

> We can attribute such increase to several reasons. One is the genuine need of the masses for religious experience, which our own ministry has not been able to satisfy fully because of the scarcity of priests at times; because of the aloofness with which some pastors deal with the laity at other times; and mostly because we have based our pastoral action on the assumption that ours is a secure Christianity, when it is really a mission society calling for vital religious revival. (Quoted in Vitalis 1969, 8/7)[23]

Cardinal Silva was one of the principal architects of CELAM's 1968 Medellín conference, where he vigorously championed CEBs and the preferential option for the poor. In his own country, Silva involved himself in numerous progressive programs including an extensive land reform project. His concern for the poor eventually led him to become General Pinochet's most vocal critic.

A more direct connection between the spread of Protestantism and the Church's new pastoral outlook was evident in Brazil:

> The popular catechesis experiment of Barra do Pirai (Northeastern Brazil), in 1956, provides us with the first known link between popular

Protestantism and what was later to become the CEB movement: "It began when an old woman said to the bishop during a pastoral visitation of her area, 'In Natal the three Protestant churches are lit up and crowded. We hear their hymn-singing . . . and our Catholic church, closed, is in darkness . . . because we don't get a priest.' This challenge prompted some fundamental questions such as: If there aren't any priests, does everything have to stop? Cannot anyone else do anything for the life of the church community?"[24] A conservative bishop, Dom Agnelo Rossi, was stung into initiating a lay missionary movement. He mobilized 372 coordinators (lay catechists) who gathered groups of Catholics to pray and listen to the reading of scripture, to hold "Mass without a priest," and in other ways to maintain a sense of community. Instead of the traditional chapels, they built community meeting halls to be used for catechetical instruction, public schooling, and trade schooling. (Cook 1985, 64)

Many of the techniques used in Catholic grassroots projects clearly owe their existence to the pioneering work of Protestant missions (Cook 1985, 64ff.).

Further evidence that Protestant evangelizing methods informed the Church's new pastoral strategy comes from the Maryknoll Fathers, a Catholic missionary order based in the United States and heavily involved in Latin America. Maryknollers are famous for their progressive political positions. In 1954, this group sponsored a conference in Lima, Peru, to map out their pastoral strategy. Laced through the official proceedings are references to Protestantism and communism. For example, referring to Catholic Action and other lay associations, participants declared, "What a bulwark they would be against the inroads of Protestantism and communism" (Maryknoll Fathers 1954, 60).

But more than taking on a defensive posture, the Maryknollers believed they could learn from their competition. The following exchange recorded in the Lima conference proceedings demonstrates the positive influence Protestantism had on progressive Catholic thought:

**Father Comber:** I would remark the ability of the Protestants to conduct schools and hospitals, with a very small amount of foreign personnel by using a great many national workers in their schools and hospitals and other works. We don't seem to have developed that technique very well.

**Father Consodine:** I have three points here. The first would be lay participation in worship. Catholics who have been won to Protestantism in South America remark that their share now is more that of participants than witnesses. Catholics are not supposed to be mere "witnesses" at Mass but this is how these fallen-away Catholics report. The second is lay co-operation in works of religion and social action. Protestants generally make great use of local laity in direct works of religion and social action as Father Comber points out. The third point is their very strong program of social welfare. We sometimes express disdain for their seeming overemphasis on social welfare. Bishop Kiwanuka in Uganda told me how he was harried by the Protestants in Uganda. He threw up his hands and said: "It's almost as if we had divided the two Great Commandments between us. We Catholics practice the first Great Commandment and the Protestants the second. We put great emphasis on the intense life of worship: 'Thou shalt love the Lord, thy God' and I can't help but feel that the Protestants have stolen the lead in regard to the second, 'Thou shalt love thy neighbor as thyself.' Here in this neighborhood the Protestant seems to be the one who is creating neighborliness, going around prompting people to get together, to be kind to one another. These are natural virtues, it is true, but nevertheless they provide a strong foundation for the supernatural and we should make use of them." (Maryknoll Fathers 1954, 287).

Similar references were made to the proselytizing techniques of communism (Maryknoll Fathers 1954, 60–63). Much of the remaining conference report discusses the use of various pastoral techniques that appear remarkably Protestant in nature, including combining evangelization with community projects and medical assistance, literacy training, youth recreation groups, and encouraging heavy involvement of the laity (Maryknoll Fathers 1954). Many of these techniques—lay involvement, small Bible discussion groups, and personal and community development—eventually found their way into the *comunidades eclesiales de base* movement. Interestingly enough, CEBs have been most active in countries with the highest concentration of Pentecostals, namely Brazil, Chile, El Salvador, and Nicaragua.

Several scholars have also noted the relationship between Protestantism and Catholic renewal. Paul Turner's study of religious innovation in Oxchuc, Mexico, makes a forceful case that the resemblance between Protestant churches and CEBs is more than coincidental:

In reaction to the success of Protestantism, some priests started a counter-action using similar methods to those employed by the missionaries. This was an anti-Protestant movement led by ambitious young men seeking converts to Orthodox Catholicism, characterized in part by ascetic living. . . . [T]he Orthodox Catholics living there [in Oxchuc and Yochib]

compare favorably with the Protestants in progressiveness and afflu-
ence. . . . The reason why the Orthodox Catholics are making comparable gains is because they have been influenced by Protestantism. In a
limited but important sense, Orthodox Catholics in [Yochib] *are* protestants [*sic*]. (Turner 1979, 259)

Mexico has not been a major mission field for evangelicals; Protestant growth
there is concentrated in the southernmost provinces. Both Oxchuc and
Yochib are located in the state of Chiapas, which borders Guatemala and is
one of the poorest regions in Mexico. Chiapas has the highest evangelical
growth rate in the country, once again providing anecdotal evidence of how
Protestant gains served to alert the Church of its pastoral responsibilities to
the poor. The lesson of Pentecostal success was not lost on Chiapas' Bishop
Samuel Ruíz, one of Latin America's most outspoken defenders of the poor,
who began his career as a conservative. In response to the advance of evangelical Protestantism in his diocese, Ruíz questioned whether Latin America was
truly Catholic, as many had supposed in the past (Klaiber 1970, 100), and apparently made appropriate pastoral adjustments to rectify the situation.

Other scholars have observed similar connections between religious/
ideological competition and Church change. For example, when discussing
the development of grassroots Catholicism, Vallier notes that "the growing
visibility and influence of Protestant churches and their flexible procedures
for establishing new congregations, organizing worship, involving laymen,
and encouraging voluntarism" had a "positive effect" on many Church leaders (1970, 115). Speaking primarily about the spread of communist groups
in Brazil during the 1950s, Bruneau notes that "while the bishops in the
Northeast had been threatened by all sorts of enemies, had become aware of
social problems and had committed themselves to act, the bishops in the relatively peaceful South noted that some problems existed but interpreted the
Church's role in exclusively religious terms" (1974, 71). Among the "enemies" that Bruneau refers to are communists and Protestants.

Clearly, the growth of evangelical Protestantism in some regions
prompted bishops and their agents into a greater concern for the poor, where
competition was most concentrated. Lacking the legal means to eliminate the
threat at its source, Catholic leaders facing the greatest challenge to their
parishioner base felt obliged to strengthen the "Catholicness" of the popular
classes. However, many of these same prelates realized that four centuries of
pastoral neglect and "high politics" would severely handicap their efforts at
winning the hearts and souls of the masses. The Church had been too closely

associated with unpopular regimes in the past. A full-blown and credible commitment to the poor was required. This implied opposing governments that harmed the popular classes. Nowhere was this more true than under the wave of right-wing military governments that swept across the region in the late 1960s and lasted for roughly two decades. The Church could have received substantial financial benefits had it legitimated these regimes. In several countries (e.g., Argentina) bishops chose this route and were treated well. But where Protestantism was eating away at the Church's membership, cooperation with dictatorship would have only validated the view that the bishops truly did not have the interests of the poor in mind and hastened the exodus to the evangelical camp. In this vein we should expect to see a positive correlation between Protestant growth and episcopal opposition to authoritarianism.

## Religious Competition and Church Opposition to Authoritarianism: A Statistical Examination

The preceding section provided an overview of the Catholic Church's reaction to Protestantism along with anecdotal evidence showing an association between Protestant growth and Catholic concern for the poor, which translated itself into opposition to dictatorial rule. But how strong is this relationship? A statistical analysis of available data demonstrates that religious competition is the best predictor of episcopal opposition to authoritarian rule compared to a variety of other potential explanations.

In addition to the religious-competition hypothesis, three other explanations are statistically analyzed: poverty, repression, and internal Church reform. Briefly, it has been proposed that a growing awareness of poverty and repression, combined with the liberal reforms of Vatican Council II and CELAM's 1968 Medellín conference, contributed to a new "progressive" mindset within the Latin American Catholic Church. This mindset translated itself into "prophetic criticism" of governments that contributed to the worsening social conditions of the popular classes. If this is true, there should be a correlation between these variables—poverty, repression, and internal Church reform—and an episcopacy's decision to denounce right-wing military regimes, which often enacted policies that hurt the popular classes.[25]

To test the predictive strength of these various hypotheses, cases were dichotomously categorized as to each episcopacy's stance toward dictatorship (support = 0; oppose = 1). Categorization of these national episcopates as either proauthoritarian or antiauthoritarian was derived from general remarks throughout the literature on the Catholic Church, especially Mainwaring and Wilde 1989. Not all bishops in a given country hold the same view, of course. Keeping this in mind, we want to identify whether the episcopal "center of gravity" (Mainwaring and Wilde 1989, 5) leans toward support for or opposition to the military. The antiauthoritarian cases of Brazil, Chile, El Salvador, and Nicaragua have been well publicized and are easily identifiable. Even though bishops in Ecuador and Panama were less adamant in their opposition, these two countries also fall into this category.

Since less has been written about proauthoritarian (or neutral) episcopacies, they are more difficult to identify. Although bishops in all Latin American countries have been critical of flagrant human rights abuses at various times, Mainwaring and Wilde note that

> Argentina is only the most dramatic example among many countries where, in the face of dictatorship and violence, the Church did not assume such a political role; the Churches of Guatemala, Paraguay, and Uruguay also supported, more than they denounced, military rule. In these countries, progressive Church sectors criticized authoritarian rule, but they failed to move the ecclesiastical institution as a whole. (1989, 14)

The Bolivian and Honduran Churches were also comparatively silent during the 1970s. Confirming evidence was found in Smith 1979, Barrett 1982, Levine 1984, Cardenal 1990 and 1992, Martin 1990, and the U.S. Army *Area Handbook Series* (for various years and countries). Measurement of competition consisted of the percentage increase of non-Catholic proselytizing faiths (e.g., evangelicals, marginal Christian sects, Spiritists) from 1900 to 1970 (Barrett 1982).[26] Only proselytizing denominations were considered; ethnic Protestants were excluded since they do not actively seek to convert Catholics. A physical quality of life index (PQLI) for the mid-1970s, the height of Latin American authoritarianism, measured relative poverty (Wilkie and Reich 1980).[27] The Freedom House index of civil rights served as a proxy for repression (REP), calculating the average score (1 = most free, 7 = most unfree) for each country's authoritarian period during the 1970s.

Internal Church reform is the most difficult variable to measure because it encompasses a rather vague phenomenon—the qualitative change in official Church thinking with regards to both society and institutional Church structure. As all Church officials knew about the changes proposed at Vatican II and Medellín, an index was created to measure an episcopacy's potential *receptivity* to these reforms. I reasoned that bishops appointed during the tenures of the Church's two most progressive popes—John XXIII (1958–63) and Paul VI (1963–78)—would be more open to implementing these reforms than bishops appointed under more traditional pontiffs. This assumption is based on the observation that popes generally select bishops who concur with their own ideas and objectives (Della Cava 1993a). Furthermore, because the ideas of Vatican II were expanded upon during the 1960s and 1970s, contributing to an increasingly progressive atmosphere, bishops appointed several years after Vatican II are assumed to be more receptive to these reforms than ones appointed before 1962. To measure general episcopal receptivity, a score was calculated for each episcopacy based on the average number of years a bishop was appointed after 1958, the year John XXIII became pope. A higher score assumes an episcopacy is more open to progressive ideas (i.e., a younger episcopacy). Negative numbers indicate the average bishop was elected $x$ years *before* 1958.[28]

Based on the above operationalization of variables, the following relationships with the episcopacy's antiauthoritarian position are anticipated:

| | |
|---|---|
| Competition: | Positive |
| Poverty: | Negative |
| Repression: | Positive |
| Church reform: | Positive |

Remember, the measurement used for poverty measures quality of life, with lower numbers representing greater poverty.

As the raw data show (see table 4.2),[29] ten of the twelve cases appear to support the religious-competition hypothesis. Within-groups averages of the level of competition show a moderately strong, positive relationship between religious competition and an antiauthoritarian episcopacy. On closer examination, in five of the six antiauthoritarian cases—Brazil, Chile, El Salvador, Nicaragua, and Panama—relatively high religious competition (i.e., above the median level of 4.5 percent) preceded the episcopacy's decision to oppose the military. Likewise, five of the neutral or proauthoritarian Churches—Argentina, Bolivia, Honduras, Paraguay, and Uruguay—faced comparatively little competition and did not implement progressive pastoral strategies on an extensive basis. Although small progressive sectors were attacked in these countries, pastoral agents received little support from the hierarchy (Mainwaring and Wilde 1989, 14).

There also appears to be a positive relationship between competition and reform, indicating that the episcopacy's "youthfulness" may have played a role in determining the bishops' political strategy. Four of the six antiauthoritarian cases—Chile, Ecuador, Nicaragua, and Panama—lie above the median (0.8) for the reform index, while four of the proauthoritarian

Table 4.2    Raw Data for Explanatory Variables

|  | Competition | Poverty | Repression | Reform |
|---|---|---|---|---|
| Proauthoritarian |  |  |  |  |
| Argentina | 2.7% | 85 | 5.3 | 2.7 |
| Bolivia | 4.1 | 39 | 4.3 | −2.1 |
| Guatemala | 6.3 | 54 | 3.5 | 0.5 |
| Honduras | 3.1 | 53 | 3.0 | 2.8 |
| Paraguay | 2.1 | 75 | 5.2 | −1.8 |
| Uruguay | 1.2 | 86 | 4.7 | −0.4 |
| Average | 3.3% | 65 | 4.3 | 0.3 |
| Antiauthoritarian |  |  |  |  |
| Brazil | 12.0% | 66 | 4.8 | 0.4 |
| Chile | 15.5 | 79 | 5.0 | 5.0 |
| Ecuador | 2.9 | 69 | 3.7 | 1.1 |
| El Salvador | 5.5 | 64 | 4.4 | −6.0 |
| Nicaragua | 5.6 | 55 | 4.3 | 7.4 |
| Panama | 4.8 | 79 | 5.7 | 5.3 |
| Average | 7.7% | 69 | 4.7 | 2.2 |

Competition: Percentage increase in "competitive religious groups" 1900–70 (Barrett 1982).

Poverty: Physical quality of life index, mid-1970s (Wilkie and Reich 1980, 4). High = higher living standards.

Repression: Average civil rights score for authoritarian period until 1979 (Gastil, various years). High = most repressive.

Reform: Number of years after 1958 average bishop was appointed (Vatican City 1975).

cases—Bolivia, Guatemala, Paraguay, and Uruguay—fall below this boundary. The distribution and within-group averages for poverty and repression provide little evidence of a systematic relationship between these variables and a national episcopacy's position toward authoritarianism.

Multivariate analysis was employed to test the strength of the relationship between the dependent and independent variables. Given the dichotomous nature of the dependent variable (opposition or support), probit was chosen as the appropriate technique.[30] Results of this analysis support the religious-competition hypothesis (see table 4.3). The relationship between religious competition and opposition was statistically significant at the 10 percent level in all models containing that variable. Since significance tests are highly dependent on sample size and the sample used here is small ($n = 12$), this level of statistical significance seems adequate. None of the other three variables was statistically significant. Furthermore, poverty and repression frequently did not have the anticipated signs. From this evidence, religious competition appears to be the best predictor of an episcopacy's position toward military rule. Although measures of fit are somewhat ambigu-

**Table 4.3**   Results of Probit Analysis

|                       | I       | II      | III     | IV      | V       | VI      |
|-----------------------|---------|---------|---------|---------|---------|---------|
| Constant              | −5.67   | −1.42   | −5.80*  | −5.70   | −3.53   | −1.59   |
|                       | (4.37)  | (2.35)  | (4.24)  | (4.24)  | (3.06)  | (2.33)  |
| Competition           | 0.63*   |         | 0.64*   | 0.61*   | 0.43*   |         |
|                       | (0.40)  |         | (0.39)  | (0.37)  | (0.29)  |         |
| Poverty               | 0.05    | −0.01   | 0.05    | 0.05    |         | 0       |
|                       | (0.07)  | (0.03)  | (0.07)  | (0.05)  |         | (0.03)  |
| Repression            | −0.15   | 0.40    | −0.11   |         | 0.35    | 0.40    |
|                       | (0.91)  | (0.66)  | (0.86)  |         | (0.59)  | (0.66)  |
| Reform                | 0.05    | 0.09    |         | 0.05    | 0.06    |         |
|                       | (0.13)  | (0.11)  |         | (0.13)  | (0.12)  |         |
| % Predicted correctly | 83.3    | 75.0    | 83.3    | 83.3    | 75.0    | 41.7    |

Dependent variable = opposition. See table 4.2 for definition of variables.
Standard errors are in parentheses.
*Significant at the .1 level.

ous for probit models, results indicate that 10 of the 12 cases (83 percent) examined were predicted correctly when religious competition was included in the analysis. Looking back at the raw data (table 4.2), we notice that Guatemala and Ecuador do not fit the predicted pattern. Possible explanations for these two anomalies will be discussed below.

It appears that reform contributed to the predictive power of the model. When poverty and repression alone are included in the analysis (model VI), only 41.7 percent of the cases are predicted correctly. Adding reform (model II) boosts the percentage of cases predicted correctly to 75 percent. This confirms eyeball estimates of the raw data showing antiauthoritarian episcopacies tend to be younger on average. However, the coefficients generated for reform are far from statistical significance, indicating the observed results could have occurred simply by chance.

It is likely that the general philosophy of both Vatican II and Medellín played a role in shaping the thought of many bishops in Latin America and that younger bishops were more open to these ideas. Moreover, newly appointed officials are more apt to take reformist positions because they have less invested in the old system. Keep in mind, though, that bishops must work their way through the ranks to obtain their positions, thereby giving them a stake in the system. On the other hand, we have seen examples of conservative bishops changing their pastoral strategy in response to external stimuli (see Cook 1985, 64). Several famous bishops, such as Oscar Romero (El Salvador), Raúl Silva (Chile), Hélder Câmara (Brazil), Paulo Evaristo Arns (Brazil), and Samuel Ruíz (Mexico) were known as traditionalists when they started their careers. Thus, the presence of an old clergy does not necessarily imply a resistance to change. Nor does a young episcopacy necessarily indicate progressiveness; John Paul II has found ample numbers of young, conservative prelates to appoint in Latin America. Admittedly, the index used to measure receptivity to internal Church reform is an inexact proxy. At best, the influence of age is ambiguous: age undoubtedly plays a role in some instances, but is affected by so many other factors that the direction and magnitude of the effect are difficult to determine.

One way of assessing the importance of probit coefficients is to calculate the relative probability of obtaining a result on the dependent variable for various values of the independent variables. So as to include all the other relevant variables, model I was used as the basis for calculation. Assuming median values for poverty (68), repression (4.6), and reform (0.8), a cumulative probability function is calculated for the range of values associated with religious competition, 1 percent to 16 percent (see figure 4.2). From this distribution, we can estimate that the probability a Church hierarchy will oppose a dictatorship when faced with only a 1 percent level of competition will be roughly 0.1. There is an even chance an episcopacy will be antiauthoritarian at a competition level of 4.6 percent, ceteris paribus. At levels of competition above 7 percent, the probability of an antiauthoritarian stance rises to about 0.9. Substantively, these results suggest that a relatively modest increase in religious competition (from 5 percent to 6 percent) can be expected to push the Church into a preferential option for the poor, and the antiauthoritarian stance associated with the exercise of that option.

Overall, the statistical tests indicate there is good reason to believe a relationship exists between Protestant growth and an episcopacy's decision to oppose authoritarian rule. Granted, statistical analysis cannot conclusively prove causality, especially in studies with small sample sizes. But the data do provoke suspicion that a systematic relationship is at work, and when combined with the historical evidence presented above the case for a causal linkage between religious competition and an episcopacy's opposition to authoritarianism appears strong. Examination of the historical contexts of the various countries bolsters support for the primary hypothesis of religious competition.

## Discussion of the Cases

The following survey provides a brief overview of the countries contained in the above analysis. Unfortunately, the number of cases ($n = 12$) does not fa-

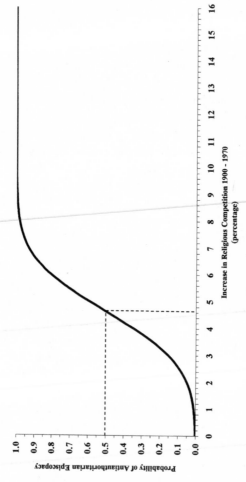

**Figure 4.2** Cumulative Probability Function for Various Levels of Religious Competition (Assuming Median Poverty [68], Repression [4.6], and Reform [0.8])

cilitate the use of a detailed case-study approach for each country. However, a few cursory observations are helpful in demonstrating the linkage between religious competition (primarily evangelical Protestants) and the bishops' denunciation of authoritarianism. I present detailed examinations of Argentina and Chile, which represent the extremes in both Protestant growth rates and support/opposition to dictatorial regimes, in the following chapters.

## The Antiauthoritarian Episcopacies

Six of the twelve cases were of antiauthoritarian episcopacies during the 1970s, some more so than others. The most interesting observation about these cases is that the two countries with the highest levels of religious competition—Brazil and Chile—witnessed the emergence of the region's most progressive episcopacies comparatively early, before Vatican II. This immediately raises the question of how Vatican II could have shaped progressive pastoral reforms in these countries when it had not occurred yet. It is important that both Brazil and Chile experienced rapid growth of non-Catholic religions during the 1930s and 1940s, when Protestant growth was still relatively slow elsewhere. Consequently, bishops in both these nations implemented progressive reforms in the 1940s and '50s in an effort to improve their credibility among the popular classes and slow the exodus from the Catholic faith. As for political alliances, each episcopacy sought state assistance from the democratic regimes preceding military rule, but there was a noticeable drift toward reformist parties that were more in tune with the masses. The case of Chile will be discussed extensively in chapter 5.

The Brazilian bishops first sought to stave off the Protestant advance in the 1930s and 1940s by seeking prohibitions on the entry of missionaries into their country (Pierson 1974). A renewed and strengthened alliance with the state under Getúlio Vargas enhanced their ability to take such defensive actions, although the state's cooperation on this issue was lukewarm at best.[31] Following World War II, Protestantism became more indigenized and various Spiritist and Afro-Brazilian religions gained popular appeal. Many Church leaders realized that a new pastoral commitment was needed if Brazil was to remain a predominantly Catholic nation (Mainwaring 1986, 34–35; Doimo 1989, 213).[32] Learning from the success of Protestant missionaries, the Catholic hierarchy promoted numerous social projects and organizations aimed at improving the lives of the working class and poor beginning in the late 1940s. Many of the techniques employed by the Brazilian Church mirrored the efforts being made by the Protestants, including grassroots literacy campaigns centered around reading and discussing the Bible, health clinics, and rural cooperatives.[33] Eventually, the Brazilian Church gave birth to the base community movement.

The Brazilian episcopacy remained on good terms with populist governments, as they generally offered the Church assistance in aiding the popular classes. The Goulart government (1961–64) offered critical financing for the Church's Basic Education Movement (Movimento de Educação na Base), which provided literacy training for both children and adults living in impoverished conditions (Mainwaring 1986, 66–70). Radio schools were instrumental to this program. As noted before, this method was a favorite of early Protestant missions that did not have the personnel to cover wide areas.

However, in 1964 the Brazilian military came to power with the goal of demobilizing the popular sectors. After it became clear to the episcopacy that the regime intended to stay in power indefinitely, relations deteriorated. Having made a substantial commitment to the needs of the poor, it would have been difficult for the Church to maintain credibility had it supported a dictatorship that opposed their interests.

The three Central American episcopacies included in the antiauthoritarian camp—El Salvador,[34] Nicaragua, and Panama—started experiencing significant growth in Protestantism in the mid-1950s, especially after the Latin American Mission (LAM) intensified its efforts in the region. Incipient Pentecostal movements evolved throughout the 1930s and 1940s, but it was the LAM (based in Costa Rica) and other North American faith missions that provided the organizational visibility indigenous Pentecostals needed to win converts (Rosales 1968; Martin 1990, 89-92).[35] In general, Pentecostalism emerged roughly twenty years later than in Chile or Brazil.

Indicative of the fervor of faith missions invading Central America at mid-century, LAM's 1960 Evangelism-In-Depth campaign in Nicaragua included a parade of approximately seven thousand evangelicals marching past the Catholic Church's national cathedral. They were later addressed by President Luis Somoza Debayle, drawing even greater attention to their movement. All told, the campaign claimed the following accomplishments: "500 prayer cells organized; 65,000 homes visited; 195,000 Bible portions and tracts distributed; 126,000 people who attended the campaign (aggregate attendance)" (Rosales 1968, 3/17). Even if these figures are exaggerated, the undertaking was truly impressive. Similar efforts were carried out in El Salvador and Panama. Needless to say, the Catholic Church took note.[36]

For the better part of the twentieth century, Nicaragua lived under the shadow of the Somoza family dictatorship. Bishops came to expect this as the natural state of affairs and were not very critical of the government's rule until the late 1960s. The turning point in Church-state relations actually came in the mid-1960s, when members of the clergy established several grassroots programs. Though not officially sponsored by the episcopacy, they were allowed to continue their work. Implicit support for these grassroots groups indicated a new pastoral direction for the bishops; there was a growing concern for both the spiritual and material welfare of their most vulnerable parishioners. This new pastoral strategy eventually manifested itself in political conflict with Somoza, whose concern for the poor was nonexistent at best. Small signs of tension between the episcopacy and Somoza government appeared in 1967 when the bishop of Matagalpa, Octavio José Calderón y Padilla, refused a meeting with the president, citing the unjust treatment of political prisoners (Williams 1989, 23). Shortly thereafter, Bishop Miguel Obando y Bravo sold a car given to him by president Anastasio Somoza and turned the proceeds over to charity (Dodson and O'Shaughnessy 1990, 120). Relations deteriorated rapidly following the 1972 earthquake, when Somoza channeled relief funds into his own pockets. Obando y Bravo declined to participate in Somoza's reinauguration in 1974. This represented a serious breach in Church-state relations, one that jeopardized governmental support for the Church. Subsequently, the bishops continually pressured Somoza to step down and allow for a transition to democracy. Episcopal criticism of Somoza typically was couched in terms of his regime's maltreatment of the lower classes. It was this social segment that the Church had to demonstrate a credible commitment to, lest they abandon their Catholicism for alternative faiths.

In El Salvador, the archbishop of San Salvador, Luis Chávez y González (1939–77), introduced a series of pastoral reforms, including rural cooperatives, in order to bring the Church closer to the common folk (Cardenal 1992, 263; Cáceres Prendes 1989, 104–6). Again, the time frame corresponded to an increase in Protestant activity among the popular classes. At first, the archbishop's efforts met with resistance, but throughout the 1960s and 1970s his efforts bore fruit as other bishops began implementing these reforms in their dioceses. Consistent with the idea that the age of bishops may determine their receptivity to reform, it was the younger prelates that vigorously embraced these reforms and challenged the status quo in their country, although they followed the lead of an archbishop who was appointed in 1939. The various social programs sponsored by the episcopacy during this time brought them closer to the popular sectors. As social tensions increased during the 1970s and the military stepped up its clandestine (and not so clandestine) repression of leftists and suspected subversives, the Church, rather than defending the oligarchy as it had in the past, spoke on behalf of the persecuted. If the Church was to maintain credibility in its new pastoral strategy of caring for the poor, it needed to demonstrate it in the political arena as well.

The Salvadoran and Nicaraguan bishops also faced growing competition for the allegiance of the masses from leftist guerrilla organizations. In El Salvador, guerrilla activity began in the early 1970s. Several small bands created an atmosphere of anarchy and attracted increasing numbers of students and peasants, although no single group was able to topple the government. By 1980, these groups joined forces in the Farabundo Martí National Liberation Front (FMLN). Their joint strength forced the government into a stalemated civil war. The Nicaraguan Sandinistas originated in the early 1960s, but did not become a significant force until a decade later, when corruption and elite dissatisfaction with Somoza weakened the government. As these groups demonstrated a growing attraction among poor campesinos, and as the ability of the government to control the spread of revolutionary ideas waned, it became apparent to the bishops that they, like the Sandinistas, needed to embrace a preferential option for the poor lest their credibility as moral leaders fall and more peasants defect to these movements. While many progressive bishops showed sympathy with the goals of social justice professed by the revolutionary armies, they were wary of their Marxist leanings, especially after considering the experience of the Church in Castro's Cuba.

In many ways, the bishops were caught choosing between two unattractive extremes—legitimating a right-wing government or validating a potentially dangerous revolutionary movement. While several priests, nuns, and lay workers in these two countries actively participated in the guerrilla movements, the bishops remained wary of these groups. The bishops publicly championed social justice, but they also urged caution when it came to cooperation with Marxists. Their warnings fell on deaf ears as many guerrilla leaders picked up on the legitimating power of liberation theology and played down the more atheistic characteristics of their Marxist heritage. Although some bishops were open to the sociological methods used by Marxist theorists, they carefully separated theory from the practice of communist regimes, all of which had a history of repressing religious organizations.

In terms of scholarship, the Panamanian Church remains the neglected child of Central America. But like El Salvador and Nicaragua, grassroots

Church development was encouraged throughout the 1960s under the leadership of Bishop Marcos Gregorio McGrath. Again, as in El Salvador and Nicaragua, these changes followed the substantial growth of Protestantism in the late 1950s and 1960s. The 1968 military coup led by General Omar Torrijos resulted in tensions between Church and state almost immediately. To cite Barrett,

> Although the bishops have publicly supported the claims of the new government concerning Panama's sovereignty over the Canal Zone, at the same time they have criticized (as for example in their joint declaration of 2 August 1973) the general lack of freedom in the country and the marginal economic life of the masses living in poverty. The episcopate has also protested against the obstacles placed by the government in the way of efforts by the church to promote social justice. (1982, 549)

These denunciations were sustained throughout the 1970s.

With regard to the religious-competition hypothesis, Ecuador is the outlier in the antiauthoritarian camp. Some in the Ecuadoran episcopacy have become known for their progressive policies regarding land reform, CEBs, and opposition to military rule. Nevertheless, Protestants have been reluctant to target it as a mission field until very recently. Likewise, no indigenous Pentecostal movement developed on a large scale, even as late as the mid-1970s. Interestingly, the few Protestant missionaries who entered Ecuador have been highly concentrated in one area, Chimborazo. By 1976, roughly 10 percent of Chimborazo's Quechua population was Protestant (Stoll 1990, 273), despite a national figure of 3 percent. As the religious-competition hypothesis would predict, this region also happened to be home to the country's most progressive bishop, Leonidas Proaño.[37]

Facing intense local competition, Proaño organized a pastoral conference in 1976 in his Riobamba diocese to discuss efforts at Catholic renewal and pastoral reform. In attendance were several progressive Chilean and U.S. religious officials. The military detained all those present, fearing they were "communist subversives" (Arzube, interview).[38] With international attention focused on the military's actions at Riobamba, such a blatant attack upon the institutional Church could not be ignored by the Ecuadoran bishops who were not in attendance. These other bishops had faced little competitive pressure and were relatively conservative and supportive of the dictatorship until this defining moment. The Riobamba incident galvanized Church opposition to militarism, though such opposition never manifested itself as strongly as in the other cases discussed. The Ecuadoran episcopacy (except Bishop Proaño) represents the most ambivalent of the antiauthoritarian Churches discussed here.

## Proauthoritarian/Neutral Cases

Most of the episcopacies characterized as proauthoritarian or neutral continued to operate throughout the 1970s as they had since the time of Independence—favoring high politics to preserve institutional perquisites instead of revitalizing the institution through a renewed commitment to the majority of parishioners. In a world free of constraints on time and resources, these bishops probably would have devoted greater attention to both the popular sectors and the elite. But in reality, the episcopacy had to choose how to split human and financial resources between the elite and the masses. So long as Protestant gains did not become too large, bishops could afford to pursue an alliance with unpopular dictators without risking the loss of parishioners. Protestantism was a concern, especially as it related to *other* countries and the region in general, but not to the degree that it provoked changes in pastoral strategy. Each of these countries experienced periods of limited pastoral reform, spurred mostly by the example of other countries or at the behest of the pope.[39] However, these programs were not pushed to the point where they caused tensions with government officials. Disputes between the Church and state occasionally erupted in these countries, but they typically were resolved at the elite level.

The Paraguayan Church typified the proauthoritarian response. As did Churches throughout the region, the Paraguayan episcopate promoted Acción Católica in the 1940s and 1950s as a bulwark against communism. A few decades later, some parishes experimented with CEBs. Because of Paraguay's comparatively low level of urbanization, CEBs were primarily found in the countryside and known as Ligas Agrarias Cristianas (Christian Agrarian Leagues). The *ligas* were generally organized by low-level clergy and had little hierarchical support. Overall, their impact was quite limited. Politically, the bishops resigned themselves to living under a ruthless dictator. In a 1968 interview with the archbishop of Asunción, Frederick Turner captured the episcopacy's attitude toward the government:

> In discussing Paraguayan politics . . . [Archbishop Mena] commented—
> in the candid, open manner that he maintained throughout—"They say it
> is a dictatorship here, but you can work and study. You just can't make a
> revolution against the government." The archbishop clearly appreciated
> government financing for Catholic schools, and the fact that, as he said,

his signature alone would allow the Church to import automobiles, motorcycles, refrigerators, and typewriters free of all duty. (1971, 120)

Turner also noted that the archbishop was genuinely concerned about the country's underdevelopment and high level of poverty (1971, 119–20). Saying that a bishop supports a dictatorial government does not necessarily imply that he lacks concern for the poor (as some analysts insinuate). Instead, the prelate may find himself in a situation where protecting the short-term institutional interests of the Church takes precedence over more noble long-term causes such as restructuring the economy. Without any major threat to the Church's cultural hegemony, it was expedient to accommodate the military dictator in exchange for state-guaranteed privileges.

Paraguay was not without its Church-state tensions, though. Conflict erupted between the episcopacy and General Alfredo Stroessner's government in 1969, after the military shut down a Catholic publishing office and harassed several progressive priests (Carter 1990, 77–79). Citing unwarranted intrusion into Church affairs, these actions essentially allowed the episcopacy to break free from the restrictive *patronato*, still in effect after nearly five centuries. The conflict did not engender any critique of authoritarianism per se. Rather, it was a battle over Church autonomy, a struggle that had existed since colonial times. Once the Church gained greater freedom from government control, it reentered a period of détente with the state (Carter 1990, 79-80; O'Brien 1990, 346). Throughout the 1970s, "the Church was in retreat from social concerns in favor of housekeeping matters and issues of conventional morality—their reigning priorities of a Church seeking a way to live in a stagnant, repressed social climate" (Carter 1990, 81). The episcopacy eventually played an oppositional role beginning in 1986. But by this time, the dictator was becoming increasingly unpopular among powerful sectors in society.

Several other episcopal conferences had similar experiences. Bishops in Bolivia, Honduras, and Uruguay implemented, but did not vigorously promote, grassroots reforms in the 1960s and 1970s. Scholarship about these three Churches is almost nonexistent, receiving only brief mentions for scattered "progressive" acts in works such as Lernoux 1980. Mainwaring and Wilde 1989 categorizes the Uruguayan episcopacy as proauthoritarian. Evidence for Honduras can be found in Cardenal 1990 and Rudolph 1984. Both Barrett 1982 and Hudson and Hanratty 1991 contain evidence for classifying Bolivia's episcopacy as neutral. Of the three countries mentioned here, Bolivia comes closest to being outspoken and perhaps could best be considered a fence sitter.

With minor exceptions, the episcopates in each of these countries remained silent during recent periods of military rule. They verbally protested attacks on progressive clergy but never called into question the status of the regimes. None of these countries witnessed significant increases in Protestantism. Honduras remained cut off from the intensive efforts of the Latin American Mission, and Uruguay has been noteworthy for its irreligious population. Interestingly enough, approximately 31 percent of Uruguay's population consider themselves nonbelievers (atheists or agnostics) (Barrett 1982), yet this has not provoked a major evangelization effort on the part of the Catholic Church. It would appear that Church leaders are more sensitive to active threats that actually steal members (e.g., evangelical Protestants) than passive ones like religious apathy. Bolivia only recently came to know evangelical Protestantism on a large scale (Damen 1988). Evidently, in the absence of any competitive pressure the urgency of defending the poor was rated lower than maintaining good relations with the political elite.

At first glance, the Guatemalan case is inconsistent with the religious-competition hypothesis. Throughout the 1970s, both Protestants and communist guerrillas successfully recruited the indigenous population living in Guatemala's highlands (Stoll 1990, 202–3). Despite the mass slaughter of Indians, the archbishop of Guatemala City, Cardinal Mario Casariego, looked the other way and accommodated the various military governments that came to power. In part, this reluctance to criticize the military may have resulted from the Church's active participation in the 1954 coup that ousted the democratically elected president, Jacobo Arbenz Guzmán (Schlesinger and Kinzer 1982, 154). Arbenz encouraged the growth of Protestantism to undermine conservative opposition to his presidency. In response, certain Church officials placed their faith in the military and conservative politicians to ensure that anticlerical politicians would not return to power. In essence, the Guatemalan Church was still fighting its battle with liberalism, whereas most other countries had resolved this dispute in the first decades of the twentieth century.

It is also important to note that not all Guatemalan bishops expressed promilitary sympathies in the 1970s. Church officials working in rural areas were highly critical of the country's brutal dictatorships. One progressive bishop, Juan Gerardi, fled the country in 1980 after being targeted for assassination (Berryman 1984, 204–6). Cardinal Casariego offered little objection to the government actions leading up to this bishop's exile. Following Casariego's death in 1985, the Guatemalan hierarchy began taking a more critical view of military rule and its associated abuses. In this case, it appears as if one well-positioned prelate controlled the Church's agenda and effectively blocked a growing progressive movement within the Church's leadership. The probabilistic nature of the religious-competition model predicts that such an outcome is unlikely, though not impossible. Understanding the uniqueness of the Guatemalan case requires an examination of internal Church decision making. Unfortunately, space limitations forbid such an inquiry here. The fact that internal Church politics remains quite cloistered does not help matters either.

An interesting comparison with the study's other outlier—Ecuador—should be drawn here. Given the geographic concentrations of religious competitors in both Guatemala and Ecuador and the observation that progressive bishops were located in the areas of greatest competition, it becomes apparent that an examination of the Church in Latin America could be improved by employing the diocese as the primary unit of analysis. Unfortunately, Protestant data do not conform to Catholic definitions of parish organization. Given current data restrictions, analysis of the episcopacy as a national unit is the best available test of the competition hypothesis.

One final qualitative consideration should be noted here. The Catholic Church is an international institution and cross-national transfers of information are relatively easy. Problems and solutions to competition in one country can teach other national episcopacies to take preventive measures before their problem grows too large. Thus, countries that do not appear to have much to worry about may nonetheless engage in pastoral reforms after observing other countries confront "alien sects." In other words, the competitive threshold for significant pastoral reform should decrease as time progresses. Chile and Brazil, arguably two of the most progressive Churches in Latin America, were the first to face intense competitive pressures and were also the first to initiate progressive reforms. Today, as part of the Church's call for a "New Evangelization" (Hennelly 1993), almost all episcopacies support some degree of pastoral reform among the popular sectors.

## Summary

For most of its Latin American existence, the Catholic Church enjoyed the comfort of being the sole provider of religious goods and services. This changed during the twentieth century. Although the doors for Protestantism opened as early as the mid-1800s, significant expansion waited until after 1930. Not only did Protestant missionaries challenge the hegemonic position of Catholicism, but an indigenous derivative of North American Protestantism—Pentecostalism—awoke many bishops and clergy to the fact that the region may not have been as Catholic as previously thought. If the Church was to remain a spiritual and moral force in Latin American society, it needed to match the pastoral efforts put forth by Protestant churches. Having been associated with the political and economic elite for so long, a credible commitment to the poor meant publicly distancing itself from abusive governments.

It would be myopic to say that the need to compete with Protestantism was the only factor affecting the bishops' decision to oppose military rule. Growing poverty and repression, reforms promoted at Vatican II and Medellín, courageous decisions on the part of individuals, and martyrdom catalyzed the new attitude toward military rule. However, religious competition was a key component in explaining the variation in responses throughout the region. Competition furnished the wake-up call the Church needed to realize that poverty and repression were serious problems that demanded more than temporary acts of charity. More than just a wake-up call, however, Protestant advances also provided the motivation to do something about these problems.

All this should not imply that bishops in the proauthoritarian cases were unconcerned about poverty and repression (no matter how callous their behavior appeared). Surely, the heavy-handed tactics of dictatorships in Argentina, Paraguay, and Bolivia unsettled many bishops in those countries. But the costs of opposing the government (e.g., loss of funding for Church programs or physical repression) outweighed the benefits (measured in membership retention). Thus, the episcopacy had an incentive to maintain friendly relations with an unpopular government in the short term while hoping for better social conditions in the future. Moreover, without an exit option, parishioners could not effectively express their discontent with Church policy. True, there were some who pleaded with the episcopacy to rethink its association with the ruling elite, but most parishioners just remained quiet, as they always had. In other words, there was no mechanism (or alarm) to inform the bishops they were not acting in accordance with popular desires. With this in mind, we now turn to a detailed comparison of Chile and Argentina.

# FIVE

# Chile

## A Preferential Option for the Poor

*Even in those days Protestants were everywhere, distributing their Bibles, preaching against the Vatican, and hauling their pianos through heat and rain so their converts could celebrate salvation in public song. Such competition demanded the total dedication of the Catholic priests.*

Isabel Allende, *Eva Luna*

Of all the countries examined in the previous chapter, Chile and Argentina offer the two cases in Latin America that best approximate a controlled scientific experiment. Both share a number of characteristics that make it possible to hold constant (within reasonable limits) a number of cultural and economic factors that many scholars have considered important in explaining the rise of progressive Catholicism. First, Argentina and Chile are similar in that they are among the most "European" cultures in Latin American. Although Argentina, by virtue of its wider immigration, is more heterogeneous than Chile, neither country confronted the divisive problems associated with large indigenous populations. Second, by the standards of Latin America, both countries are relatively prosperous. Finally, each country experienced a period of severe military repression that certainly challenged the humanitarian doctrine of the Catholic Church, spelled out at Vatican II and Medellín. To borrow Penny Lernoux's phrase, the "cry of the people" in both countries was sufficiently loud to be heard by the bishops.

However, when confronted with military rule, the two episcopacies chose different political strategies. The Chilean episcopacy became an outspoken critic of the Pinochet regime, even at the expense of severe persecution of its clergy (Escobar 1986). The Argentine bishops, on the other hand, gained notoriety for not only ignoring the abuses of military rule, but for actively participating in the government (Mignone 1988). The following two chapters trace the differences between these two episcopacies to the presence (or absence) of competitive pressure among the lower classes.

Chile was one of the first Latin American countries to develop both a strong socialist movement and a substantial evangelical Protestant population. To compete with these challenges, the Chilean hierarchy developed extensive pastoral projects aimed at serving the working class and poor. As the success of these projects rested on the Church's credible commitment to the lower classes, the episcopacy found it necessary to *publicly* denounce the abuses of the Pinochet regime. In contrast, the Argentine Church faced little serious competition from either Marxists or evangelical Protestants. With no exit option available to parishioners, the Argentine Church found it comparatively easy to ignore the concerns of its members and support various military regimes in return for special treatment.

Obviously, no social phenomenon has a single cause. The deeper one digs into the historical specifics of a single case, the more evident the multiplicity of causes becomes. Church support for, or opposition to, authoritarianism is no exception. The previous chapter isolated the cause that best accounted for the variation in Church political strategy across countries: religious competition. This variable remains the primary focus of the comparison between Chile and Argentina. Nonetheless, other conditioning factors will be mentioned when appropriate. Specifically, the long-standing tradition of multiparty government in Chile constrained the elite political options available to the episcopacy, whereas in Argentina the political instability of the past four decades facilitated the Church's decision to accommodate military rule. However, as seen in El Salvador, Nicaragua, and Brazil, neither democracy nor political stability is a necessary condition for Church opposition to authoritarianism. Finally, to better understand the relevancy of choosing the Argentine and Chilean cases for study, greater attention will be paid to the historical context of each country since Independence. This detailed history is necessary to convey the strong similarities between the two cases until the 1930s, when their paths diverged dramatically. We begin with an examination of the better-known case—Chile.

## *From Independence to Separation*

The development of Church-state relations in Chile during the first century of independence approximated the situation elsewhere in Latin America but without the violence experienced by the Catholic Churches in Mexico, Colombia, and Ecuador. During the struggle for independence, both the royalists and patriots swore allegiance to the Church, recognizing its ideological clout with key segments of the population. For their part, Church officials[1] remained loyal to Spain, while the creole clergy generally favored separation (Barrios 1987, 58–59).

Although the republican government established in 1818 desired friendly relations with the bishops, its officials still sought to control Church authority. After Chile's two bishoprics became vacant in 1825, a battle ensued between the Vatican and the government over who had the right to nominate replacements. President Bernardo O'Higgins, Chile's first president (1818–30), pursued the matter with great tact, sending a propatriot clergyman to negotiate a reasonable settlement. Still, a series of miscommunications and political wrangling left the two Chilean sees unoccupied until 1832, when the pope reluctantly agreed to the Chilean claim of *patronato nacional* (Mecham 1966, 72–75, 203–5).

In return for control of the selection of bishops, the state guaranteed the Church a privileged place in society. The Constitution of 1818 declared Catholicism the state religion with all the dispensations this entailed (Aliaga 1989, 125). What this meant in practice remained unclear. For the most part, the Church continued to operate in society as it did during the colonial period, receiving most of its funding through state-collected tithes. In 1853, the tithe per se was eliminated, although the government continued its role of funding the Church. The rapid series of new constitutions during the 1820s and 1830s preserved the provisions of the 1818 Constitution with regards to Church and state. For all intents and purposes, the state regulated the Church during the immediate post-Independence period, largely due to the absence of Church leadership. Prior to 1825, the bishop of Santiago, José Rodríguez Zorrilla, was largely impotent. Because of his proroyalist sentiments, Rodríguez was exiled from 1817 to 1821. Upon returning, he exercised little power until his death in 1825 (Barrios 1987, 63-64; Salinas 1987, 136). With the exception of a few minor confiscations of Church property (Dussel 1981, 93), the Church did not suffer any serious anticlerical attacks.

In contrast to Argentina, the various Chilean governments curtailed religious liberty as a matter of *official* policy. Until the middle of the nineteenth century, laws prohibited the organized exercise of non-Catholic religions. Quite paradoxically, the 1828 Constitution declared that people could not be persecuted based on religious belief even though the law forbade Protestants from practicing their faith. In reality, the government never enforced restrictions on Protestant worship. De facto religious freedom developed due to the economic importance of Protestant foreigners. Under President

O'Higgins, Protestants were encouraged to worship freely in the country (Sepúlveda 1987, 248). The situation mirrored that of Argentina, where politicians realized that increasing economic ties with North America and Protestant Europe meant cultivating toleration for non-Catholic beliefs (Ramírez, interview). It appears that prohibitions on non-Catholic religions merely served to placate Catholic bishops and were never meant to be seriously enforced.[2]

As the nineteenth century wore on, hostility between Church and state increased, paralleling an increase in liberal political strength. Philosophically, liberals viewed both the separation of Church and state and freedom of conscience as essential to modernization. The liberal pursuit of integrating Chile into a world economy dominated by the heavily Protestant North Atlantic countries led to the realization that a zealous defense of Catholicism created unwanted problems. For example, during the middle of the nineteenth century, problems erupted between the United States and Chile when the U.S. ambassador, Seth Barton, married a Chilean. The Catholic archbishop of Santiago became infuriated when it was revealed that Barton was not only a Protestant, but divorced as well. In retaliation for the verbal abuse he received from Church officials, the ambassador condemned the bishop *and* the Chilean government, creating a diplomatic furor in both countries (Mecham 1966, 209). In 1865, President José Joaquín Pérez solved this problem by introducing the Ley Interpretiva, which permitted Protestants to worship in private and to create schools (Sepúlveda 1987, 248). The Church responded by creating *La Revista Católica*, an intellectual weapon against liberal thought. The episcopacy also forged a political alliance with the rural-based Conservative party, which in turn used the "religious question" against its Liberal political enemies (Aliaga 1989, 157–58).

Even with Church support, the Conservatives failed to halt the advance of the middle-class Liberal and Radical parties. Liberal President Federico Errázuriz (1871–76) proposed several changes to Church-state relations, including the elimination of the *fuero eclesiástico*—an ecclesiastical court system established for clergy and other Church officials accused of violating civil or canon law—secularization of cemeteries (allowing Protestants equal access to burial rights), civil marriage, and the legal separation of Church and state. Only the elimination of the *fuero* passed Congress.[3] A compromise settled the cemetery issue by designating portions of Catholic cemeteries for Protestants. Civil marriage and full disestablishment proved too controversial and failed passage (Mecham 1966, 211).

Throughout this period, the episcopacy struggled against further encroachment on its power. Once again, the *patronato* ignited hostilities. When the archbishop of Santiago died in 1878, tensions arose between the Liberal government and the Holy See over the next appointment. The Vatican refused to recognize the government's choice. This conflict lingered into the next administration and President Domingo Santa María broke relations with Rome. Relations were restored after a compromise candidate was named in 1886 (Aliaga 1989, 155–61). The Liberal political elite sought greater restrictions on episcopal power in retaliation for the Church's intransigence on the *patronato* issue. In the early 1880s, José Balmaceda (while minister of the interior under Santa María) introduced a series of laws known collectively as the Leyes Reformas Teológicas. These laws secularized cemeteries, the registry, and marriage, which were important sources of Church income and power (Aliaga 1989, 159–160). Balmaceda contemplated the complete separation of Church and state (a move that implied eliminating the *patronato* and state financial support), but thought it impolitic at the time. Not only would absolute separation arm his Conservative opposition with a volatile issue, but it also would mean complete loss of control over an institution with (supposed) vast social influence.[4] Philosophical arguments aside, disestablishment was an issue of political power. As it stood, the Leyes Reformas made the Church more dependent on the state, both financially and legally, than at any time since Independence.

The Church reacted to these attacks by drawing closer to the Conservative party, an alliance that persisted into the middle of the next century.[5] To this point, the principal threats to the Catholic Church came from above (i.e., the political elite). The episcopal response, in turn, was elite based. Rather than strengthening links with parishioners as a means of bolstering the Church's social status, the bishops preferred allying with other elite who opposed their Liberal and Radical foes (Mecham 1966, 216). Between 1891 and 1920, the Conservatives gained a weak hold on the Chilean legislature. When the Radical party proposed separating Church and state in 1906, Conservative legislators thwarted their efforts. The political fragmentation and instability of this period guaranteed that no changes to the legal status of the Church were made.

The electoral victory of Liberal president Arturo Alessandri in 1920 ensured that separation became reality. The final break (contained in the 1925 Constitution) was peaceful. A negotiated arrangement provided the Church with transitional funding and control over its own educational system. The bargain also permitted the Church to retain its landholdings. For the Catholic prelates, separation meant the end of the *patronato* and a restoration of institutional autonomy. Considering the damage done to the Church's administrative capacity when sees went vacant for an extended period of time, this gain was substantial. In comparison to other Church-state battles in the region, the Chilean Church fared well with this agreement (Smith 1982, 70–74).

The last important change in the 1925 Constitution related to religious tolerance. Article 10 officially granted freedom of conscience to non-Catholics, a situation that had existed in practice since Independence. With little growth in the Protestant population up to this time (and most of the expansion accounted for by nonproselytizing immigrants), the Church did not feel threatened by this addition. Because religious liberty existed in Argentina throughout most of the nineteenth century with no deleterious impact on the Church's religious hegemony, the Chilean bishops probably thought much the same would happen in their country. But significant changes in the nature of Protestantism would transform the religious landscape in short order.

## The Disestablished Church

The 1925 disestablishment in no way implied that the Catholic Church had abandoned the political arena or its preference for elite-based solutions to its problems. Only two days after legal separation, Archbishop Errázuriz declared that "the State is separated from the Church; but the Church is not separated from the State, and will always be ready to serve it" (Mecham 1966, 22).[6] Ironically, this was the same bishop who previously cautioned priests about becoming too politically involved. The Catholic Church's elite persistently sought to influence government policy, specifically through cooperation with the Conservative party, but also by maintaining good relations with all governments in power. Elite accommodation was essential since the episcopacy continually requested public funding (Vallier 1972, 178).

New threats to the Church's parishioner base began arising in the early 1900s. Communism came first.[7] The episcopacy feared that socialist unions would indoctrinate Catholic workers with atheistic beliefs. Chilean bishops preferred to rely on political allies at the elite level. Thus, despite earlier statements purporting noninvolvement in politics, the bishops "combined an official policy of political neutrality with a tacit alliance with the Conservative party" (Stewart-Gambino 1992, 31-32). This led the Vatican to chastise the Chilean episcopate for its direct partisan activity (Barrios 1987, 120–21).

The Vatican's preference for neutrality could be understood as a reaction to the Latin American Church's being used as a political volleyball during the late 1800s and early 1900s, especially in Ecuador (Bialek 1963). By tying itself to one political party, the Church potentially could reap big rewards if that party won office, but also could incur serious losses should its ally fall from power. An appeal to nonpartisanship meant the Church's spoils would not be as great, but neither would its losses. With Liberal parties gaining ground in the 1800s, it was a wise strategy to minimize losses rather than maximize gains. Hence political neutrality became the optimal strategy. However, individual episcopacies still sought short-term gains in an environment of scarce resources and would typically lean in favor of Conservative candidates without being overtly hostile to Liberals. In this manner, a slight difference between the Vatican's overall strategy of neutrality and the Chilean Church's more partisan stance emerged.[8] Papal warnings did little to affect the relationship between the hierarchy and the Conservatives, except perhaps to force prelates to become more oblique in their political dealings and endorsements.

The growing influence of Chilean socialism presented the bishops with a serious political dilemma. Because recent Church doctrine—*Rerum Novarum* (1891) and *Quadregesimo Anno* (1931)—emphasized the need to circumvent communism by defending workers against the abuses of capitalism, Church officials felt obliged to increase pastoral activity among this social sector.[9] Such activity, though, was costly in terms of Church resources. Given the priest-centered nature of Catholicism, clergy were needed in the battle against foreign ideologies. Unfortunately, the Chilean Church lacked a sufficient number of priests to carry out even moderate outreach programs among its parishioners (Hurtado [1941] 1992, 99-112; Poblete 1965). A less costly method of containing communism was to rely on the Conservatives to manage the situation. However, this solution ran the risk of alienating the working class, who had a vested interest in unionization. Stewart-Gambino aptly summarizes the bishops' dilemma:

> Would the church implement progressive policies that might inadvertently lead to an increase in Marxist strength, or would the church continue its tacit alliance with the Conservative party against the spread of Marxism, in spite of the party's often open disregard for the social doctrine of the church? . . . [P]rogressives within the church believed that the church's identification with the Conservatives only hastened the defection of significant portions of the working class to the Marxist or anticlerical parties . . . [but] [p]rogressive policies in the countryside, it was

reasoned, would present a double risk: the possibility of creating a division between peasants and owners that could be manipulated to the advantage of the Marxist left, and the possibility of a subsequent erosion of the Conservative party's base of electoral strength that would undermine its ability to protect the national interests of the Church. (1992, 83–84)

Caught between the horns of a dilemma, the Church tried steering a middle course: The episcopacy initiated new pastoral efforts to bolster its image among the lower classes while simultaneously supporting elite-based measures against communism when available.

Although designed as a counterweight to communist activism, Catholic pastoral action often created conflict with the traditional elite. A famous case involved the rural unionization efforts of Acción Católica Chilena (ACC). Two wealthy *hacendados*, Rosendo Vidal and Carlos Aldunate, claimed that some local priests were inciting "class struggle" in their "defense of the poor" (Larson and Valenzuela 1940, 13). The priests responded by claiming that it was better them organizing the poor than the communists.

[Vidal and Aldunate] ignore that S.N.E.S. [Secretariado Nacional Económico-Social, a division of ACC] exists in Chile . . . to manage the social action of Catholics, just as Marxist organizations exist that manage the social action of their followers. And the absence—felt for a long time—of a Catholic social organization is precisely the cause of the loss of thousands of Catholic workers, gone to the Marxist ranks. (Larson and Valenzuela 1940, 63)

Consistent with other Latin American Churches at the time (notably Argentina), ACC became the Church's principal counterweight against communism (Acción Católica Chilena 1946, 391). Officially created in 1931, ACC had earlier forerunners including Acción Católica Feminina (1921) and Federación Chilena del Trabajo (1922). The former differed substantially from ACC in that it was a charitable organization of women from wealthy families. ACC, when created, stressed self-help over charity.[10] The Federación Chilena del Trabajo more closely approximated ACC in spirit if not actual organization. ACC leaders placed their greatest emphasis on organizing youth and workers (Acción Católica Chilena 1946, 428–29). However, success was limited, as other organizations offered better alternatives for workers and students (Smith 1982, 95–96; Sanders 1984, 239). In addition, the Church had an image problem to overcome: Its association with the Conservatives left many people suspicious of its motives, and the situation was not helped when the bishops supported measures curtailing workers' organizations during the 1940s and 1950s.

Faced with ambiguities and difficulties in organizing workers to resist communism directly, the Church continued relying on elite-based solutions to meet new social challenges. This traditional strategy paid some dividends. Following modest electoral gains for the Communist Party in 1947, Conservative and Liberal legislators passed the Permanent Law in Defense of Democracy (1948), which outlawed the party. This action came only one year after the Law of Peasant Unionization prohibited labor organization in rural areas. The episcopacy, after some internal debate, provided muted support for these policies (*La Revista Católica* 1948a and 1948b; Stewart-Gambino 1992, 55).

Reliance on elite measures did not rule out pastoral activity. The Church continuously nurtured grassroots organizations, largely in response to a new pastoral threat—evangelical Protestants (see below). New groups such as Joventud Obrera Católica (JOC), Joventud Agrícola Católica (JAC), and Acción Sindical Chilena (ASICH) demonstrated a growing concern for the interests of the Church's less wealthy parishioners, targets of both communist and Protestant recruitment. During the 1940s, the bishops also began urging greater social action to alleviate the plight of the poor (e.g., *La Revista Católica* 1946). Although mild by today's standards of progressivism, the Chilean episcopacy became the first in Latin America to shift substantial attention to the lower classes.

The increasing concern shown by the Chilean episcopacy toward the poor and workers can be understood as a response to escalating competition for the loyalty of its parishioners and, in part, to the political environment. Elite-based solutions aimed at eliminating competition (e.g., communists) became untenable for several reasons. First, it was morally difficult to justify legal proscriptions on workers' rights in a democracy, especially in light of Church social doctrine and the episcopacy's own efforts at unionizing labor. Supporting such restrictions only weakened Church credibility and made the lower classes more susceptible to enemy ideologies. For this reason, the implementation of the Law in Defense of Democracy and Law of Peasant Unionization provoked severe debates within the Church and among its allies.[11] Even with these laws, grassroots communist and socialist activity continued. It soon became apparent that these laws would not be able to stand the test of time. They were repealed in 1958.

Second, a split within the Conservative ranks reduced the coherency of the episcopacy's primary ally. In 1938, several Conservative Party members broke with the party to form the Falange Nacional party (Fleet 1985, 47–58). The bishops opposed this new faction, fearing it would destroy the unity of their chief political ally. Such a position was difficult to maintain publicly given Vatican warnings about political activity. Moreover, many of the Falangists were prominent members of ACC who argued that the Conservatives were not true to the spirit of papal social encyclicals. In essence, the Church's own activity was indirectly responsible for dividing its allies. When another group split from the Conservatives in 1956 and joined with the Falange to form the Christian Democratic Party, the Church realized that it could no longer rely upon the Conservatives. Rather than disassociating from elite alliances completely, however, the episcopacy shifted support to the Christian Democrats. As this party's platform resembled the Church's new emphasis on social action, the association was natural and alienated fewer lower-class parishioners.[12]

The Church's new position most certainly alienated some wealthy parishioners. However, Protestantism never made significant inroads among the upper class and the rich remained faithful Catholics. They may have decreased financial contributions (their primary exit option), but outside resources compensated for this loss. Moreover, the wealthy vented their frustrations by joining conservative Catholic organizations (e.g., Opus Dei, the Society for the Defense of Tradition, Family and Property) in the 1960s (Smith 1982, 136–40). Such action by some members of the upper class was consistent with the Church's goal of minimizing parishioner loss and thus was not of grave concern to the episcopacy.

Finally, the Church faced an additional new challenge to its hegemony among the lower classes, one that their elite political allies did not feel compelled to restrict legally: evangelical Protestantism. Lacking any legal recourse to eliminate these new challengers, greater pastoral activity was the only method of dealing with this threat. To regain the credibility the Church had lost after years of neglecting the lower classes, the episcopacy began defending publicly the rights of the poor where religious competition was the most fierce.[13] This position, designed to win the confidence of their poor parishioners, eventually led the bishops into conflict with a military regime that pursued policies antithetical to the interests of the poor.

## Chilean Protestantism and the Catholic Reaction

Legal prohibitions notwithstanding, most Protestants had practiced freely in Chile since 1818. However, for the first hundred years following Independence, Protestantism remained largely an ethnic (i.e., immigrant) phenomenon and showed no expansive tendencies. North American missionary efforts developed slowly because of the population's suspicion of foreigners (Willems 1964, 94). Although the episcopacy, fearing that Protestant activities might expand, fought to maintain legal restrictions on them, Protestants were not really a competitive force in Chile until the 1930s.

The turning point for Protestant growth actually came in 1910, when a rift occurred among members of the Methodist Church in Chile.[14] The conflict pitted those emphasizing a rationalistic approach to worship against others calling for spiritualistic and emotional methods. This latter group was composed almost entirely of native Chileans who subsequently founded Chile's first genuinely indigenous Protestant church: La Iglesia Metodista Nacional (Sepúlveda 1987, 254–56). Another split followed in 1932, when this new church further divided into the Iglesia Metodista Pentecostal and the Iglesia Evangélica Pentecostal (Gutiérrez, interview). The restructuring of Chilean Methodism into a highly decentralized Pentecostal movement fueled the rapid growth of evangelical Protestantism in the 1930s and beyond.

Given the emotional and indigenous appeal of these new churches, they rapidly attracted converts among the poor, where their efforts were concentrated. The Pentecostal strategy was to go where religious demand was high and supply was low; Catholic priests had long neglected the poor because they failed to contribute to the Church's coffers. By providing material incentives, social networks, and an enjoyable religious alternative to the highly ritualistic Latin Mass, Pentecostals attracted numerous converts. The original Methodist Church remained characteristically middle-class and intellectual and did not experience the phenomenal growth rates of the Pentecostal churches (Chacón, interview). Spurred by the success of the indigenous Protestant movements, missionaries flooded Chile. These groups adopted the methods of the Chilean Pentecostals and rapidly indigenized their movement. Nonetheless, the greatest success belonged to the Methodist-inspired Pentecostals. The schismatic nature of Pentecostalism allowed this branch of evangelical Protestantism to multiply rapidly (Willems 1967, 103–18).

This phenomenon, occurring only in Chile and Brazil at the time, provoked alarm among Church officials. As evidence of the Church's alarm, consider a report prepared by Ignacio Vergara, a Catholic priest. Vergara estimated that 11.36 percent of Chile's entire population was evangelical Protestant in 1955 and then compared this to a report published by the Catholic bishops in 1936 that estimated that only 10 percent of the Catholic population attended Mass regularly (Vergara 1955, 261). As Protestantism grew, doubling its adherents every ten years, so did the episcopacy's concern. Throughout the 1940s and 1950s, one could page through *La Revista Católica* or *Mensaje* and discover numerous articles concerning the subject.[15] Unlike in Argentina, where Protestantism was considered a problem related only to foreign missionaries, the problem was more threatening in Chile, not only because of its size and rate of expansion, but because it was uniquely Chilean. The fact that Chileans themselves led the call to conversion shocked many bishops and priests who considered their country to be unquestionably Catholic.

For the bishops, the immediate question became how to deal with this new challenge. They could have either appealed to the political elite to eliminate the threat through legal roadblocks or altered the Church's pastoral emphasis to address the concerns of those most likely to convert to Protestantism.[16] The former option was unavailable for two reasons. First, Chile's long-standing tradition of de facto religious liberty prevented politicians from banning Protestant activities. Prohibitions were especially difficult to enact since Protestant growth was indigenous. A democracy cannot easily ban its own citizens from doing what the law stipulates (although the practice has not been uncommon in Latin America). Second, and more significant, the political elite (even the Conservatives) had no incentive to undertake the effort necessary to rid Chile of Protestantism. Pentecostals, because of their apolitical nature, were simply no danger to politicians (Stoll 1990, 111; Chacón, interview). Thus, although the Church could rely on some help in its battle with communism, it was on its own in facing Protestantism. Since both communist and Pentecostal expansion occurred largely among the same sectors of society (the popular classes),[17] the best defense for Church leaders was to develop a social policy that would regain the allegiance of these sectors. The connection between the threat of Protestantism and the need for Catholic social action was explicit almost from the beginning.

In 1941, Padre Alberto Hurtado, a Jesuit priest active in numerous Catholic social projects, published a book entitled *¿Es Chile un país católico?* (Is Chile a Catholic country?). This work deserves extensive examination, as it was widely read and influenced the episcopacy's social thinking. Alberto Hurtado was perhaps Chile's most influential Catholic. So great was his influence that there is currently a movement to have him beatified, the first step toward sainthood.[18] Of his book's six chapters, one was exclusively devoted to the Protestant campaign in Chile.[19] Although communism was mentioned occasionally, Protestants were by far Hurtado's greater preoccupation.

When examining the cause of the rapid growth of Protestantism in Chile, Hurtado placed the blame squarely on the shoulders of the Catholic Church itself.

> One of the causes of the success of this [Protestant] campaign in Chile is the lack of religious cultivation of our popular masses. They are sheep without pastors, but with a profoundly religious nature. . . . The responsibility for the success of the Protestant campaign in Chile belongs to the Catholics who have not knowingly cultivated their church and of all those who have not heard the divine voice. . . . Protestantism in Chile lives on our errors: it grows where Catholic life has been uncared for and nourishes the Christian nature of our people. (Hurtado [1941] 1992, 83, 91)[20]

Indirectly, Hurtado revealed the link between religious monopoly and clerical apathy toward parishioners that Adam Smith saw 165 years earlier. Protestants delivered the wake-up call the Catholic Church needed to realize the failure of past evangelization efforts.

Hurtado further emphasized the fact that the Chilean Church was to blame by noting that the growth of Chilean Pentecostalism was not the result of cultural imperialism but an indigenous movement.

> [I]t has not been the case that the Protestant movement was above all a campaign of foreign money. The majority of the money that they earn in Chile is from Chileans. The Pentecostals or *canutos,* the national sect, do not rely solely on foreign pastors and they cover all their expenses with tithes and offerings gathered among their faithful. (Hurtado [1941] 1992, 84)

This is an important distinction because in Argentina evangelical Protestantism was considered exclusively a foreign problem and never challenged the episcopacy's belief that the majority of Argentine citizens were truly Catholic.[21] Indigenous Pentecostal expansion proved to many Church leaders that Chile was Catholic only in name. This induced the episcopacy to undertake concrete action to improve the spiritual and material lives of its parishioners, rather than blame Yankee imperialism.

In seeking to further explain Protestantism's popularity, Hurtado admired and took note of methods employed by evangelical pastors. What he observed is worth repeating, since Catholic pastoral efforts would later mimic these very same techniques.

> The first principle of their propaganda is to multiply their locations and meet in small groups to educate them [converts] thoroughly. Even when they [Protestants] meet many people in the same site, they divide them into groups of ten or fifteen brothers in the charge of a class guide or catechist. People are grouped in such a way as to obtain the best homogeneity of religious culture: and, if possible, they are concerned that they live in the same barrio, to make it easy for the class guide to visit his catechized. . . . Another great pedagogical principle applied by Protestantism is that one knows each individual, [and] each group has its own individual manner of seeing and feeling and one-on-one nature. . . . The religious instruction given by the evangelicals is based on the Bible. Study is done book by book, at times in the form of "Biblical themes," or an exposition of a dogmatic or moral point grouped around all the pertinent Biblical passages. . . . I hope our Catholic Action will employ [these methods] since they serve to make knowledge of the Sacred Scriptures intuitive. (Hurtado [1941] 1992, 86–87)

Indeed, Protestant techniques influenced Catholic Action and many other pastoral organizations (Ossa, interview). Reading this passage today without reference to when it was written or knowing that it focused on Protestants, one might think that it described a CEB.

Hurtado entitled the closing section of his chapter on Protestantism "Lessons of the Protestant Campaign" and ends with the following passage:

> It makes us see that if we had more apostles evangelizing our people, they would be profoundly Catholic, as is demonstrated by all the progress the Church makes in the *popular* barrios where new parishes and religious communities are founded that cultivate souls. . . . More than campaigns against Protestantism, what we need is a positive campaign for Christianity; to go to the people, give them a knowledge of our sacred religion. (Hurtado [1941] 1992, 94–94; emphasis added)

Rather than taking a defensive posture toward a perceived threat, Padre Hurtado called for the Church to positively engage itself more directly in the lives of the poor. Improving the spiritual lives of the poor meant improving their material conditions (Hurtado [1941] 1992, 55–57). Hurtado backed up his words with action, founding a Catholic labor organization (Acción Sindical Chilena) and the Hogar de Cristo, organizations devoted to helping workers and the destitute. His words and deeds eventually became hall-marks of progressive Catholicism as represented at the 1968 Medellín conference. The connection is hardly coincidental. Bishop Manuel Larraín of Talca, one of the principal architects of the Medellín conference, was personally close to Hurtado and delivered the eulogy at Hurtado's funeral in 1952, wherein he referred to Hurtado's now-famous book.

Observations similar to Padre Hurtado's were made by fellow Jesuit Ignacio Vergara. He concurred with Hurtado's observation that the growth of Chilean Pentecostalism resulted from the Church's pastoral apathy. "[T]he first cause of Protestant success in Chile," he wrote, "is the *thirst for God.* . . . The soul of a Chilean is essentially religious, but has been cultivated poorly. It is as if fertile land is waiting for a seed. . . . [Catholic] evangelization has been disgracefully insufficient" (Vergara 1962, 226-27). Noting that evangelical Protestantism is a popular (i.e., lower-class) movement, he described how evangelicals often provided economic assistance to their converts in the countryside (1962, 233–34). Curiously, in a manner that indirectly championed Catholic pastoral activity, Vergara then accused Pentecostals of not paying adequate attention to "social promotion" (1962, 238). By this he probably was criticizing Protestantism's tendency to emphasize the individual over the community. Catholic efforts supposedly favored the latter.

Acting upon the wisdom of Padre Hurtado (and later Vergara),[22] the bishops responded with concern of their own. In 1947, Bishop Jorge Larraín of Chillán reacted to the expansion of evangelicals in his diocese with the same observation made by Padre Hurtado—that the lack of Church resources encouraged Protestant growth:

> The Protestant pastors have understood, with skill one cannot deny, the necessity souls have to practice Religion [*sic*], and therefore, profiting from the lack of Catholic temples or priests, respond, with speed, especially to those towns . . . where no one preaches the true and only doctrine of Christ, the teaching of the [Catholic] Church. (Larraín 1947, 1116-17)

The bishop concluded that "we should pray for the conversion of the heretics" and suggested "that Catholic Action undertakes a serious campaign . . . so that the faithful do not fall into Protestant errors, and so that the souls led astray return to the unique and true traditional Christian faith, taught by the Catholic Church" (Larraín 1947, 1118–19).

Four years later, the entire episcopacy issued a pastoral letter concerning various threats to the Church. First on the list was Protestantism. Like

Bishop Jorge Larraín's earlier comments, the tone of the document was defensive. "[W]e should indicate the danger of the propaganda of those who are vulgarly called 'evangelicals,' that, although divided into numerous sects, unite themselves in a common campaign attacking the Catholic Church and its teachings" (*La Revista Católica* 1951, 119). But in addition to Jorge Larraín's earlier solution to these problems (i.e., promote Catholic Action), the entire episcopacy recognized the importance of actively involving the laity in Church life, including the Mass (*La Revista Católica* 1951, 120), much as Protestants did. This recommendation preceded Vatican II by a full decade and indicated that Church thinking was moving, albeit slowly, in the direction of Christian base communities (CEBs). Admittedly, the gap between lay involvement in the Mass and CEBs is a fairly large one, but remember that CEBs rely heavily on lay involvement. For bishops to publicly express support for greater lay involvement in holy rituals a full decade before Vatican II was quite extraordinary, especially in the highly ritualistic Latin American Church.

The other threats (*las amenazas*)[23] mentioned in the episcopal text were Freemasonry and Marxism. Thus, despite the debate over the Law in Defense of Democracy, which divided Catholics, the hierarchy remained wary of communism. Without adequate means from the government of eradicating their competitors, the bishops gradually moved toward a position of active involvement with their neglected flock. This position, if it was to have any degree of credibility, eventually led the bishops to disassociate themselves from the political policies that hurt the parishioners they most needed to win back. Under the dictatorial rule of General Pinochet, this meant outright conflict.

In a survey of the Chilean episcopate conducted in late 1968, Thomas Sanders noted a continuing concern over Protestantism well into the 1960s despite a lack of public statements regarding it. He concluded:

> Critics now generally assume that most Catholics lack significant understanding of their faith, strong convictions, and that they do not effectively relate their beliefs to their actions. They look with interest and admiration on the rapidly growing Protestant sects, which combine fervent piety with community spirit, extensive lay activity, and changed lives. The bishops of the new line would presumably continue parochial functions, but would like to dedicate chief attention to the stimulation of small cells or communities, whose members would have greater sophistication and conviction in the faith. . . . This group of bishops also believes that the

Church should concentrate more attention on the lower class, for several reasons: its traditional neglect by the Church, its importance for the future, its greater freedom from the economic and social interests that inhibit fulfillment of the social teaching of the Church. . . . They do not think that previous social activism was a mistake, because the Church had to disengage itself from the image of collusion with the groups in power. (Sanders 1969, 1/45)

Although Sanders never stated precisely who the "critics" were, the passages preceding this citation indicate that he was referring to a number of younger pastors and bishops who were critical of previous pastoral efforts.

By 1957, the Protestant problem had become so acute that the bishops called for help from the United States' Catholic Church "to counterattack the evangelical penetration" (*La Revista Católica* 1957, 1873). The U.S. Catholic Church complied with this request and sent numerous religious personnel and funds to their brethren in need. On the home front, the calls by Chilean prelates for increased social responsibility grew in frequency and intensity. More attention was being paid to the plight of the urban and rural worker, as well as the poorest of the poor.

Although already on a trajectory toward increased social activism, several events catalyzed the Church's drift toward progressivism. The first change dealt strictly with Church policy toward Protestants. In 1958 Pope John XXIII called for greater ecumenism with non-Catholics. No longer could the Church's reaction to Protestantism be defensive; the challenge posed by Protestant growth had to be met with a positive engagement with Catholic parishioners. Episcopal condemnation of Pentecostal activities dropped off noticeably following John XXIII's declaration. In contrast to earlier accusatory works (*Mensaje* 1952; Espíndola 1954; Vergara 1955), *Mensaje* reflected this new cooperative attitude by publishing articles more ecumenical in tone (Villegas 1963; Blomjous 1964; Ossa 1964; Pape 1967).[24]

Nonetheless, concern among Church officials continued. Ecumenical relations between Protestants and Catholics were never very strong, and the episcopacy remained worried about the rapid growth in Pentecostalism. Ecumenical relations were best with the more traditional, mainline Protestant churches (e.g., Lutherans, Presbyterians, and the "old" Methodists). However, these churches represented a minority of Protestants. Relations were difficult to establish with Pentecostals because the Church considered them too aggressive, and their highly decentralized nature made cooperation difficult.[25] In 1959, several Jesuit scholars created a religious think tank—Centro Bellarmino—to investigate social problems in Chile. From its inception, this organization was closely associated with *Mensaje* and was interested in the study of Protestantism in Chile. Perhaps not so coincidentally, the center's namesake, Robert Bellarmine, was a Jesuit renowned for his struggle against Protestants in Europe during the 1700s.[26]

The second change affecting Church policy was the repeal of the Law in Defense of Democracy in 1958. With Marxists now legally competing for the allegiance of the urban and rural proletariat, the Church hierarchy had no option but to increase pastoral action among the lower classes. Finally, the rise of the Christian Democratic Party and subsequent election of Eduardo Frei in 1964 convinced Church leaders that its traditional alliance with the Conservatives was no longer sustainable. The Christian Democrats represented a reformist option to the revolutionary fervor sweeping Latin America (Frei 1964). With public opinion rapidly shifting away from the Conservative position, the bishops decided it was better to join the reformist bandwagon than lose influence over their flock (Sanders 1984, 230). Catholic pastoral activity, now with a strong progressive tone, expanded rapidly in the 1960s.

## Social Justice and the Expansion of Pastoral Action

By the bishops' own admission, "evangelization is the great task of the Church" (Conferencia Episcopal de Chile 1960a, 86). Said differently, bishops want to maximize the number of Catholic believers. In chapter 3 I predicted that when competition increases in the religious/ideological marketplace, the episcopacy will respond by altering its sociopolitical strategy to accommodate the new situation. If competition occurs among the lower classes, the bishops would be expected to show an increasing concern for the poor. As challenges to the Chilean Church's social influence intensified throughout the 1960s, noticeable changes occurred in official Church policy. Due to the success communist organizations and Pentecostal churches had in attracting the working class and poor by improving their material conditions, many prelates realized that preaching the Gospel per se was not enough to retain members. To demonstrate a true commitment to the poor, the Church needed to care for the more earthly needs of its parishioners as well.

Official Church documents in the early 1960s began connecting the need for evangelization with social justice (Conferencia Episcopal de Chile 1960a, 1960b). A lengthy and highly controversial document entitled *La*

*Iglesia y el problema del campesinado chileno* (The Church and the problem of the Chilean peasantry) made this connection explicit. Using the mission of the first Apostles as an allegory for the pastors of the Church, the document states:

> [T]ogether with spiritual problems, [the Apostles] attended to human problems: the distribution of bread and food, the care of widows and orphans. Even knowing their primary mission consisted of the interpretation and preaching of the Gospel, they did not renounce their duty of caring; they called upon their converts, charging them with material concerns. So were born the deacons [i.e., the Catholic Church]. (Conferencia Episcopal de Chile 1962, 131)

Although perhaps sounding like traditional Catholic charity, this document went on to advocate land reform (156–57), a radical position considering both that the Church's long-standing allies came from the landed elite and that the Church itself was a major landholder. This position, consistent with the Christian Democrats' platform, naturally shocked Conservatives. Many in the upper class considered such a position a betrayal (Sanders 1969, 1/24). Another pastoral letter released that year—"*El deber social y político en la hora presente*" (Social and political responsibility in the present hour)—also declared support for social reform (Aliaga 1989, 225–26).

However, words were just that—words. If the episcopacy was to be credible in its commitment to the poor, action was needed. After all, nearly five centuries of neglect and recent support for the Conservative Party undoubtedly sowed cynicism among many poor parishioners. Fortunately for Church officials, the increase in pastoral support from abroad (both financial and personnel) made such action possible. An influx of foreign resources shifted the opportunity costs of the various strategies available to the episcopacy. With outside funding, soliciting state assistance became less critical and the Church could afford to promote policies that would win poor parishioners at the expense of potentially alienating the rich. Again, though, the rich remained firmly within the Catholic faith despite their dissatisfaction with the Church's new social policies.[27]

Shortly after the spate of concern expressed by the episcopacy about Protestantism in the 1950s, the episcopacy created the Oficina del Sociología Religiosa (OSORE) "to conduct empirical studies of religious attitudes, practices, and needs throughout the country and to evaluate existing pastoral programs" (Smith 1982, 113). A large number of other social projects and think tanks were funded by various Church organizations that sought to improve the lives of the lower classes (Sanders 1969, 2/12–21). Such activity included educational assistance to the poor, land reform programs, the creation of cooperatives, and expansion of the role of the Church in labor unions. CEBs officially appeared in Chile in 1968 (González and Goic 1989, 4). With all this activity, the Chilean episcopacy became famous for its preferential option for the poor. Not surprisingly, evangelical Protestants were also active in similar activities throughout the 1960s (Sepúlveda 1987, 268). In fact, Catholics borrowed many of the Protestant techniques of blending social action (e.g., providing material incentives to potential converts) with religious evangelization (Ossa, interview; Ramírez, interview; Rosales, interview).

The 1970 presidential victory of Salvador Allende, a member of the Socialist Party who led a coalition of left-wing parties, presented an unique problem for the Catholic hierarchy. Church leadership was still adamantly anti-Marxist, but Allende received his greatest support from the popular sectors the Church most needed to "re-Catholicize." A public confrontation with Allende's Popular Unity coalition would not have served Church interests, as it would only have spread distrust of the bishops' motives among the poor: If the bishops spoke against the candidate of the poor, could they truly have had a preferential option for the poor? On the other hand, the bishops did not want to endorse the general ideological program promoted by the Popular Unity, which included hard-line Marxists.

The episcopacy distanced itself from the regime while seeking peaceful coexistence. Relations during Allende's abbreviated term remained "mutually respectful" (Mella 1987, 34). The bishops even went so far as to issue a pastoral letter saying that socialism (the non-Marxist variant) could be consistent with Catholic doctrine.[28] Nevertheless, tensions existed. When the president introduced a proposal in 1973 to teach "socialist humanism" in the schools, the Church reacted with swift and firm disapproval (Silva and Oviedo 1973; Tagle 1973a; Vicuña 1973). The controversy between the Church and Allende over education had its roots as far back as 1971, when the government sought to increase its regulation of Catholic schools since they received public funds. Naturally, the episcopacy resisted (Santos and Oviedo 1971). Given the myriad of troubles the president was facing at the time, Allende let the education issue drop without a struggle.

As noted above, the call for ecumenical relations muted Catholic-Protestant conflict, and the episcopacy turned its attention to presenting the Church in a new light in order to regain members. But the growing presence of evangelical Protestants continued to be an important issue. This recognition came from an unexpected source—Salvador Allende, who was not a practicing Christian. Given his narrow electoral base of support, he recognized the growing importance of the Pentecostal vote, roughly 14 percent of the electorate in 1970 (Barrett 1982, 226).[29] Contrary to the widely held stereotype, Latin American evangelicals were (and still are) an ideologically diverse lot (Garrard-Burnett and Stoll 1993). Finding a left-leaning Pentecostal in Santiago is not particularly difficult, especially since many Pentecostal ministers do their work among the poor. Furthermore, given their relative cultural isolation, evangelicals represent a potential single-issue (religious equality) voting group that transcends political ideology. Reaching out to Pentecostals, who were historically neglected by Conservatives and Christian Democrats, would have provided a net gain of votes for Allende's coalition. At the behest of the president, Chile held Latin America's first ecumenical Te Deum on 12 September 1971 (*La Revista Católica* 1971). A Te Deum is a Christian blessing frequently associated with official government functions in Latin America. The Chilean Te Deum traditionally occurs on the country's Independence Day, 12 September. (Note that thirteen years passed between Pope John XXIII's call for ecumenism and the inclusion of Protestants in this important function.) The inclusion of Protestants in a traditionally Catholic-only event indicated that the social influence of the Catholic Church was wearing down, no matter how hard the bishops tried to reverse it. Nonetheless, the Catholic hierarchy said nothing, either because the bishops were truly filled with the ecumenical spirit or because statements of opposition would have contradicted their public support for ecumenism.

## Church-State Conflict under Pinochet

Despite cordial relations between the episcopacy and Allende, most bishops initially welcomed the 1973 military coup (Yañez 1989, 51–52; B. Smith 1986, 273–74; Tagle 1973b). There are two major reasons for this. First, although progressive, the bishops were nonetheless anti-Marxist. Actions taken by Allende (e.g., his education policy) did not alleviate their misgivings about his version of socialism. On top of this, Chilean society was becoming more and more divided along class lines, which created unwanted tensions for an organization said to speak for all humankind (*La Revista Católica* 1973).[30] Second, given Chile's experience with stable democracy, no one, most of all the prelates, thought the military would remain in power. This outlook was apparent in a pastoral letter issued two days after the coup. It asked citizens to cooperate with the armed forces so that "Chile can return to institutional normality, as the participants of the military junta have promised" (Oviedo 1974, 174).

Relations soured between the episcopacy and Pinochet after about one year. The episcopacy wanted to continue its social policy, which ran into conflict with the government's demobilization of the lower classes. Pinochet's economic policies (e.g., drastically cutting social services to control inflation) severely hurt the working class and poor. Additionally, the military's crackdown on dissidents hit the middle and lower classes particularly hard and affected many priests and lay activists within the Church itself (Escobar 1986). Because of the their previous commitment to the poor, the bishops could not easily ignore the cry of the people if they wished to remain credible. Allying with the military would blacken the name of the Church at a time when it was seriously worried about maintaining parishioners. Faced with a choice between supporting or opposing the regime, a credible pastoral commitment to the poor demanded the latter. The decision was facilitated by an increase in foreign financial aid for the Chilean Church, mostly from organizations supporting its human rights programs. Funds from abroad lessened the episcopacy's reliance on state funds, thereby making the decision to oppose the regime less costly.

Immediately after the coup, Church officials in ecumenical cooperation with several mainline Protestant churches established the National Committee to Aid Refugees (CONAR) and the Committee of Cooperation for Peace (COPACHI). In both organizations, though, the Catholic Church took the lead. CONAR and COPACHI provided emergency relief services and counseling for individuals affected by the military's crackdown. Legal services were provided to citizens unjustly accused by the government of subversive activity (Lowden 1996, 34–43). The mere fact of monitoring human rights abuses and offering assistance to the victims of such abuse represented a serious challenge to the regime. That many dissidents used these organizations to shelter their activities from the regime also provoked tension between Church and state. The military government viewed both CONAR and COPACHI as subversive and closed them in late 1975 (Smith 1990, 329–30).

The Protestants who participated in these ecumenical programs were predominantly from the mainline churches—Lutherans, Anglicans, and (non-Pentecostal) Methodists. These Protestants did not actively proselytize and were more apt to be on ecumenical terms with the Catholic Church than their rapidly expanding Pentecostal brethren (Galilea, interview). The Pentecostal response to authoritarian rule reflected the diverse nature of their denomination. A small minority of Pentecostal pastors assisted in humanitarian efforts that were considered subversive. Another group, discussed below, actually took advantage of the tensions between the Catholic Church and the military and supported the regime, even to the point of raising money for the military's program of reconstruction. The majority of Pentecostal ministers, however, remained publicly neutral, preferring to focus exclusively on religious activity (Lagos, interview).

With the growing rift between the Pinochet regime and the Catholic Church, several Pentecostal ministers saw an opportunity to boost their political standing. Like most other social groups, the more conservative Pentecostal ministers initially supported the coup. Unlike other religious groups, though, these ministers were more adamant and persistent in their backing. As the authoritarian regime actively sought religious legitimation for its rule,[31] and the Catholic Church became less willing to provide it, Pinochet welcomed the advances of the Pentecostals. The resulting cooperation between the two stirred a great deal of controversy, especially within the Catholic Church.

Beginning in 1974, a group of right-wing Pentecostal ministers, known as the Consejo de Pastores, began accusing the Catholic Church of being infiltrated by Marxists. On 13 December of that year, the Consejo organized a meeting of twenty-four hundred evangelical Protestants in Diego Portales (the military government's headquarters) to show their support for General Pinochet. Then in 1975, they sponsored the first in a series of evangelical Te Deums celebrating and legitimating the actions of the dictatorship.[32] Pinochet used the proclamations and actions of these Pentecostals to demonstrate his commitment to religious freedom and continue his repressive campaign against "Marxist subversion." In return for their support, the government built the Pentecostals a large church in downtown Santiago (Smith 1982, 313) and provided funding for various religious activities.[33]

Showing its sensitivity to the criticisms launched against it by the Consejo and its disapproval of the Pentecostal influence in the government, the Catholic Church responded with an extensive study detailing the collaboration of the Consejo with the military. The resulting report was approximately three hundred pages long and painstakingly documented (Vicaría de la Solidaridad y UNELAM 1978). The report—*La libertad religiosa en Chile, los evangélicos y el gobierno militar* (Religious liberty in Chile, the evangelicals, and the military government)—was produced in three volumes and circulation limited to two hundred copies. (The cosponsoring organization, UNELAM, was a mainline Protestant body that had previously cooperated with the Church in COPACHI.) Obviously, the episcopacy considered evangelical Protestantism a serious enough challenge to undertake such a massive effort. Predictably, the influence of the Consejo in the government increased as tensions between the Catholic bishops and military leaders grew. Not only did Pinochet embrace the Pentecostals for religious legitimation, but he used his close relation with them to punish an uncooperative Catholic episcopacy. The mere existence of the Church's three hundred–page response on the subject indicated that the dictator succeeded in irritating his critics.

After disbanding CONAR and COPACHI on orders of the government in 1975, the Catholic episcopacy created the Vicaría de la Solidaridad, an umbrella organization that coordinated the Church's various social projects. Unlike earlier ecumenical associations though, this organization was a strictly Catholic affair. The World Council of Churches supplied money to the Vicaría, but Protestant churches were not direct participants. Making the Vicaría a strictly Catholic affair was a brilliant strategy on the part of the bishops and one that showed the bishops were growing bolder in their opposition to Pinochet. As Pamela Lowden notes, "[N]ow to attack the Vicaría would mean direct confrontation with the institutional prerogatives of the Catholic Church" (1996, 53). Moreover, the Vicaría's offices were located in Santiago's main plaza, a stone's throw away from where President Salvador Allende died defending himself against the 1973 coup. Such a central location constantly reminded the government of the Church's watchful eye (Lowden 1996, 53). The wide range of services provided by the Vicaría included legal assistance to those arrested by the government, documentation of human rights abuses, housing assistance to the poor, and organizing rural cooperatives. Christian base communities and other Catholic programs continued to function during this time. With political dissidents joining in these organizations because their own organizations had been shut down, the tone of the work they did took on greater political significance. Helping the poor was an act of opposition to a government that implemented policies that further impoverished the lower classes. Despite being at odds with the bishops, the military was hesitant to completely shut down the activities of the Church.

Thanks to financial contributions from abroad, the Church's efforts had a substantial impact on the population (Sanders 1984, 235–39; Smith 1979,

158–62). Church programs also benefited from an influx of personnel who had previously worked in secular organizations now outlawed. Additionally, the episcopacy maintained public pressure on the dictatorship by denouncing its economic policies and human rights abuses.[34] Cardinal Silva preached antigovernment homilies at the Masses he presided over. Many other bishops and clergy followed his lead. Several prelates even went so far as to excommunicate a member of the government's intelligence forces (DINA) for his role in antagonizing Church officials upon their return from the 1976 Riobamba Conference, the same conference wherein the Ecuadoran government detained an international cadre of Catholic leaders (Lowden 1996, 59). Such a move was daring considering the DINA was responsible for most of the "disappearances" in Chile during the 1970s and '80s. In another instance of opposition, the episcopacy declared the pastoral motto for 1978 to be "Every Man has the Right to be a Person," which "underlined the Church's concern that the regime had denied many Chileans just that right: it was designed to be a startlingly simple and hence eminently didactic message" (Lowden 1996, 65). Throughout their statements, it became obvious that the bishops viewed authoritarian rule as inimical to the interests of the poor. To close out the rather tumultuous 1970s, the bishops advocated a "no" vote in the 1980 plebiscite determining if Pinochet would stay in power (Sigmund 1986, 33).

Eventually, the Church brokered negotiations between the Pinochet government and the political coalition that wanted a return to civilian rule (Precht 1992; Fleet 1995). During the 1980s, the episcopacy, headed by Cardinal Silva's replacement Juan Francisco Fresno, kept an open dialogue with secular opposition groups. Direct confrontation with Pinochet's government subsided so as to provide space for compromise. Although not publicly confrontational, this strategy nonetheless represented a form of opposition to the regime, one that had the realistic goal of gradually transitioning back to democracy. Despite a severe economic crisis in the early 1980s, the Chilean military was still unified and strong enough to maintain power in the face of growing public opposition, unlike its neighboring junta in Argentina. Cardinal Fresno realized that Pinochet held the greater bargaining position and that low-intensity compromise was the only means of bringing civilian rule back to Chile. Ironically, the Church's tenacity at keeping dialogue alive between Pinochet and his opponents created a situation where "Church-state relations deteriorated to an all time low" (Fleet 1995, 70). Repression against the Church increased. Nonetheless, Monsignor Fresno held his course and proved to be an important protagonist in the eventual return to democracy in 1989.

Overall, the image of the Church among the general population improved immensely. For the first time in several decades, the Church experienced a significant increase in seminarians (Precht, interview) and involvement in Church-sponsored programs swelled. Although the latter phenomenon can be explained by the participation of social activists who had nowhere else to go, it remains likely that many in society felt that the Church was genuinely on their side. Unfortunately, it is empirically impossible with current data to determine whether the Church's efforts impacted its parishioner base by slowing conversions to Pentecostalism. Evangelicals consistently won converts throughout the 1970s and 1980s. Arturo Chacón (interview) estimated that between 20 and 25 percent of the population was Protestant as of 1990.[35] Even with resources flowing into the Church, the bishops still could not field enough priests, nuns, and lay activists to compensate for the years of pastoral neglect. For purposes of this study, though, the consequences of episcopal actions on parishioner retention are not as important as the motives behind those actions: The bishops sincerely believed that their efforts on behalf of the poor would bolster the credibility of the Church as a true evangelizing body.

## Summary

From Independence to the 1930s, the history of the Chilean Church resembled that of Churches throughout the region. Beginning in the 1940s, however, the needs and concerns of the poor began playing a larger role in episcopal thinking, and bishops promoted numerous reforms that foreshadowed Vatican II. By the 1960s, the Chilean Church was a trendsetter in progressive Catholicism and many of its leaders set the agenda for CELAM's 1968 Medellín conference. The dramatic shift in pastoral emphasis was provoked, in large part, by the realization that efforts to evangelize the lower classes had been insufficient. Without Catholic pastors caring for their needs, workers and the poor quickly strayed to other ideological and religious organizations that did. The substantial success of communist organizers and Pentecostal churches prodded many in the Catholic Church to redouble their pastoral efforts among these social groups.

Due to these challenges to their religious hegemony, Church officials faced a political dilemma. To deal with their competitors, the bishops could either increase pastoral activity in the areas of fiercest competition or rely upon the state to eliminate the challengers. Pastoral action was hindered by a general lack of resources. An alliance with state officials was a more cost-effective solution. However, the elite proved unsuccessful at eliminating the competition. Chile's democratic tradition made it difficult to completely prohibit the activities of communists and Protestants, although efforts were made to block the former. Furthermore, politicians had no incentive to eliminate evangelical Protestants since they did not threaten national security and they were becoming a significant constituency unto themselves.

Throughout the 1940s through 1960s, the episcopacy wanted to have it both ways and supported elite measures to prohibit certain types of competition (e.g., the Law in Defense of Democracy), while increasing Church social activity through Acción Católica and other organizations. Herein lay a subtle dilemma. Association with certain elite groups (i.e., the Conservatives) in the presence of unabated competition hastened the defection of parishioners who distrusted the motives of the Church: Did the bishops truly want to help the poor, or did they merely want to prevent them from joining socialist unions and evangelical churches? For a time, this dilemma was resolved by a change in the political environment. The emergence of the Christian Democrats as a political force in the 1960s allowed the Church to shift its alliance from the Conservatives to a more reformist party while preserving credibility for its commitment to social action. The fact that Christian Democratic policy (e.g., agrarian reform) paralleled Church objectives made for harmonious relations between Church and state, and enhanced the image of the Church as a "voice for the voiceless." Episcopal political strategy under the Allende administration was similar, although the bishops were less willing to give full endorsement to the government's more radical measures, especially considering the presence of Marxists in the governing coalition.

The Church's political dilemma surfaced again after 1973, this time in a way that presented the episcopacy with a stark choice between supporting the dictatorship or the poor. Unlike the Christian Democrats, General Pinochet's policies were diametrically opposed to the interests of the lower classes. Association with this regime would have meant destroying the credibility the Church had built slowly over the past few decades. Given that reevangelizing society had become one of the Church's most immediate concerns, lost credibility was too high a price for whatever benefits accommodation with the dictatorship would have bestowed. Moreover, increased financial support from abroad lessened the Church's reliance on the government, making the decision to oppose Pinochet a bit less costly. Faced with a growing Pentecostal population among the popular classes, any support for a right-wing authoritarian regime meant betraying the interests of those the Church most needed to win. In the final analysis, the episcopacy opted for the poor.

# SIX

# Argentina

## Complicity with the Devil

*The antiguerrilla struggle is a struggle for the Argentine Republic, for its integrity, but for its altars as well. . . . This struggle is a struggle to defend morality, human dignity, and ultimately to defend God. . . . Therefore, I pray for divine protection over this "dirty war" in which we are engaged.*

Argentine Bishop Victor Bonamín

Unlike its counterpart west of the Andes, the Argentine episcopacy has no history of political progressivism. Except for a much-publicized conflict with Juan Perón in 1954–55, the episcopacy's political strategy has been consistently one of accommodation with the political elite.[1] Argentine bishops, with very few exceptions, failed to defend publicly the interests of their parishioners against government abuses during recent periods of military rule. Concomitantly, pastoral efforts aimed at improving the lives of the poor were minimal. Rather than Catholicizing society from the bottom up, Church leaders chose to impose Catholicism from the top down by preserving cordial relations with whatever government was in power, concentrating their efforts on guaranteeing control over Argentine culture by legal decree. This policy led the vast majority of Church officials to endorse a series of military regimes and interventions, including the most recent authoritarian government (1976–83), arguably the most abusive in Argentine, if not South American, history.

In further contrast with Chile, the Argentine Church did not face any serious challenge to its parishioner base from below, at least prior to 1983. Pentecostals and other evangelical Protestants were virtually nonexistent there until the mid-1980s. Communism presented a threat, but state officials were more than willing to deal with this problem. The episcopate, lacking any competition, did not concern itself with poor parishioners. Bishops freely pursued political strategies that improved the socio-legal status of the Church but were often unpopular with the majority of Catholics. Occasionally, various governments sought to reduce the Church's privileged legal and financial position in society. In terms of Church political strategy, elite-based threats demanded elite-based responses. The episcopacy fought off attacks from above by allying with the pro-Church landed elite or certain segments of the military that were willing to do its bidding. All told, the bishops had little incentive to adopt a preferential option for the poor and several reasons (morally reprehensible as they may have been) to opt for dictatorship. This strategic preference becomes clearer with a historical examination of Church-state relations in Argentina.

## From Independence to the Constitution of 1853

The history of the Argentine Church during the struggle for independence resembled the situation elsewhere in the region. All three bishops in the colonial territory that would eventually become Argentina were fervently proroyalist, including the creole bishop of Salta, Nicolás Videla del Pino (Farrell 1992, 48–49). The appointment of a creole bishop was an oddity in colonial America. One might have thought that del Pino would sympathize with his creole compatriots, but concern for his institutional position under a liberal, independent government probably weighed heavily in his decision to back the royalist cause. In keeping with the general situation in Spanish America, most creole clergy in Argentina favored the patriots (Casiello 1948, 68–70).

The liberators recognized the importance of religion as a way to legitimate their cause and actually courted the bishops despite their opposition to independence (Farrell 1992, 44). It has been asserted that the liberator of La Plata, José de San Martín, was "privately anti-Catholic" (Villalpando 1970, 12). Nevertheless, he was politically astute enough to suppress his sentiment so as not to alienate the clergy. The power of religion to legitimate (or delegitimate) political movements was never lost upon Argentina's secular leaders, with the exception of Perón in 1955 (see below). Given this realization, the history of Church-state relations throughout the nineteenth century becomes the story of secular rulers attempting to control and coopt this source of legitimacy. For their part, Church officials tried to maintain autonomy while still gathering the benefits offered by the state.

As in other Latin American nations, the central issue concerning Church-state relations in the immediate aftermath of Independence was the control of the *patronato* (see Ivereigh 1995, 39–62). In Argentina, this question was settled in favor of the state largely by default. While King Ferdinand VII was imprisoned by Napoleon (1810–14), several Catholic offices fell vacant. The ruling junta at the time consulted two Catholic scholars as to whether the right of *patronato* belonged to the Spanish king per se, or to the territorial sovereign. Not surprisingly, the government-appointed scholars responded that it belonged to the sovereign, setting a precedent for the exercise of *patronato nacional* (Gustafson 1992, 21–22). Confusion followed. The pope refused to recognize the state's episcopal nominations for the empty sees. By 1819, all Argentine bishoprics fell vacant and remained so for several years (Gandolfo 1969, 68-69).

With the Church lacking leadership to promote its interests, the state easily dictated the terms of Church-state relations. Politicians crafted laws that gave the Church a privileged status yet kept it firmly under control of the government. Article 1 of Argentina's first constitution (1819) declared Catholicism to be the state religion and mandated the government to provide the Catholic Church with "effective and powerful protection" (Lopresti 1993, 26). Unlike Chile, though, this protection coexisted with a de jure tolerance for all religious denominations. Many of the liberal residents of the port city of Buenos Aires saw their economic future tied to Protestant Europe. They correctly argued that British merchants were less likely to establish trading relations in countries persecuting their faith.[2] Furthermore, a shortage of skilled labor persuaded the government to encourage immigration regardless of religious belief. Irrespective of official support for the Catholic Church, Article 1 contained Latin America's first guarantee of religious liberty (Lopresti 1993, 26). This same constitution also codified the *patronato nacional*, giving the president power to nominate bishops for papal approval (Mecham 1966, 228).

The state's attempt to limit and control the power of the Catholic Church did not end with the 1819 Constitution. In 1822, liberal reformer Bernardino Rivadavia brought the Church more tightly under the control of the state by abolishing the tithe and the *fuero*, confiscating Church properties, and regulating religious orders (Gandolfo 1969, 75–81). Although Rivadavia claimed to implement these laws in order to reform a corrupt clergy, it was undoubtedly an attempt to usurp the moral authority and material resources of the Church when episcopal leadership was at its weakest. The state was also in desperate need of revenue and ideological support. The Church did not lose out entirely. In exchange for these measures, the government agreed to pay episcopal salaries and fund other Church activities. Dussel has even argued that Rivadavia's reforms represented an attempt to "create a national Church" (1981, 81). Despite losing substantial autonomy over their institution, the clergy fared well financially under this new situation (Gandolfo 1969, 79).[3]

In spite of the 1822 reform measures, the actual status of the Church was far from determined. Being financially tied to (and regulated by) the state did not guarantee a completely servile Church. Summing up the era between 1826 and 1853, Gustafson notes that "the church, for its part, looked for opportunities not to be separated from politics, but to be more independent of and influential over the state" (1992, 26). Throughout the mid-1800s, the Catholic hierarchy demonstrated a tenacious ability to defend its interests against unwanted government intrusion and even recaptured a substantial degree of autonomy.[4] For example, when the see of Buenos Aires became vacant in 1829, Rome designated a bishop independent of the desire of the government, which agreed to the appointment only ex post facto (Sweeney 1970, 6). The aggressiveness of the papacy at this time, combined with the desire of new governments to obtain the blessing of the Church, provided the episcopacy with a greater degree of autonomy than legal proscriptions implied. Moreover, since the state had successfully expropriated the various sources of revenue available to the bishops, thereby reducing their power, there was little harm in allowing the Church a degree of self-governance provided that the clergy remained loyal to the state.

## The Triumph of Liberalism and the Catholic Reaction: 1853–1943

The year 1853 marked the beginning of a new period in Church-state relations that would last roughly ninety years. This period was characterized by the triumph of liberalism and the waning legal influence of the Catholic Church. Despite the challenge liberalism posed to Church privilege, this period also saw a renewed (albeit limited) interest on the part of the episcopacy in seeking social influence of its own accord. Greater pastoral action replaced the strategy of, though not the preference for, government-mandated Catholicism.

This period began with the drafting of the 1853 constitution. Although this constitution did not proclaim Catholicism as the official state religion, Article 2 stipulated that "the federal government will sustain the Roman Catholic religion" (Lopresti 1993, 92).[5] Given Argentina's continued need for immigrant labor and an economic relationship with Protestant Europe, freedom of conscience (Article 14) remained intact. Still, it was recognized that Argentina was at its heart a Roman Catholic nation and its rulers should have the interests of Catholicism always in mind. To guarantee this, Article 76 required the president to be Roman Catholic, as the Church did not trust a non-Catholic making decisions pertaining to the funding of the Church per Article 2 (Centeno, interview).[6] All said, the 1853 constitution balanced the liberal reforms of the 1820s with a respect for the special status of the Church in society. Church-state relations proceeded without overt conflict over the next three decades, but the growing liberal rhetoric in politics kept the episcopacy on the defensive. Though official relations did not reflect it, the political status of the Church was declining.

The conflict between the Church and the liberal state reached its apogee during the first presidency of Julio Roca (1880–86), with the latter claiming victory. A major setback came in 1884 with the passage of Law 1420 which secularized education throughout the country (Farrell 1992, 102). The Church no longer had access to public schools to teach religious belief, a serious blow considering this was (and remains) one of the most efficient means of propagating the faith.[7] Education reform was followed by civil control of the registry (1884), the banning of public religious processions (1886), and a civil-marriage law (1886).

Like other episcopacies in Latin America, the Argentine bishops begrudgingly accepted these legal challenges. The Church lacked the institutional strength required to win important political battles. As long as its monopoly position in society remained intact, the hierarchy could lay low and wait for a more favorable time to improve its legal status. (Officials of a two thousand-year-old institution tend to have long time-horizons.) With neither cross nor sword seeing any benefit in further antagonisms, the next half century witnessed generally good relations between the two entities. Mecham summarizes the political situation as follows:

> After the passage of lay education and civil marriage laws in the 1880's religion ceased to be a political issue. The two principal parties, the Conservatives (National Democrats) and the Liberals or "Radicals" (Radical Civic Union) were not disposed to disturb the placid waters, but not so the Socialists who advocated separation of Church and State. The Socialists, however, never threatened to become a majority party. The Conservative party, that of the landowning aristocracy, was consistently backed by the Church. (1966, 247)

All political forces, conservative and liberal alike, agreed to maintain the Church-state status quo.

Throughout this period, the Church sought every possible opportunity to improve its legal status, but such attempts were generally rebuffed. State financial support continued but other legal perquisites were not reestablished. Without access to public schools and other guaranteed channels of social influence, the Church needed to rely more upon its own resources to maintain a social presence than it had in the past (Auza 1962, 122–23). Like a subsidized firm cut off from governmental assistance, the Church was in a situation of having to restructure itself or face gradual obsolescence. Instrumental in this process was Acción Católica Argentina, created in 1928. ACA represented the episcopacy's only major organizational effort to actively engage parishioners in the faith during the twentieth century.

Acción Católica Argentina, inspired by Pius IX's efforts to rebuild Catholic influence in Europe, resembled Catholic Action groups throughout Latin America. Nonetheless, ACA did have its indigenous forerunners. During the final decade of the nineteenth century, the specter of socialism and the influx of European immigrants prompted some clergymen to begin organizing the growing urban working class. Many bishops and priests feared that foreigners would bring with them a European fondness for socialism. This was the closest that the Church would get to a threat from below for at least another century. Inspired by *Rerum Novarum* (1891), Padre Federico Grote formed the Círculos Católicos de Obreros in 1893 and the Liga Democrática Cristiana shortly thereafter (Siwak 1992, 70). Like the Chilean formation of Catholic labor organizations, these actions were predominantly defensive in nature (Donini 1985, 43). Although Grote could be characterized as Argentina's Padre Hurtado,[8] his impact on the course of social Catholicism was negligible in comparison, due in large part to the episcopacy's lethargic attitude toward his ideas and organizations. Without the intensity of threats from below, the Argentine hierarchy lacked the passion to encourage these programs further (Siwak 1992, 110–11).

The episcopacy met as a cohesive body for the first time in 1905 to discuss ways to rally support for Catholic political causes. Changes were slow in coming, though. The hierarchy remained wary of Grote's social work and sought to control it wherever possible (Ivereigh 1995, 69).[9] However, with the electoral success of the liberal Unión Cívica Radical (UCR)[10] in 1916, the Catholic hierarchy seriously reconsidered its lethargic attitude. Again, although communist activity among workers worried the clergy, the primary threat motivating episcopal action originated from the political elite, not from below (as was the case in Chile during the same time period).

Above all, ACA must be understood as the episcopacy's bulwark against liberalism. The lackluster performance of socialism in Argentina presented only a minor nuisance (Ivereigh 1995, 63–64). Church officials were more concerned about the attitude of the elite. Juan Casiello, whose reading of Church history approximates the episcopacy's,[11] summarizes the threat succinctly:

> The liberal doctrine that has infiltrated the public arena, following foreign models, spoke against all institutions with the intent of changing the Christian orientation these institutions had inspired. Laicism, in all its forms, tried to affect the Christian bases that constitute our national essence. And, unfortunately, it began having repeated successes in various aspects of public life. Attacks against Christian marriage and religious schooling have had their desired results. On the other hand, Catholic elements that occupied visible positions suffered, without provocation, arbitrary persecutions. (1948, 269)

Although exaggerating the real threat that liberalism posed,[12] this passage reveals the defensive posture of the prelates at the time.

From its inception, ACA was almost explicitly political and conservative. Although Article 5 of ACA's charter officially proclaimed political neutrality (Casiello 1948, 280), episcopal directives urged ACA members not to vote for politicians who advocated separation of church and state, secular education, and legalized divorce. From this observation, Kennedy concluded that ACA "provide[d] the hierarchy with a block of votes which [could] be swung one way or another as the bishops may decide, and hence the organization [was] a means of episcopal interference in the electoral process" (1958, 183–84). In hindsight, it is quite clear that Acción Católica was designed as a counterweight to the Radical Party.

Acción Católica Argentina eventually grew to 66,099 members in 1945 (Frías 1960, 527). Constructed primarily to spur middle-class involvement in Church organization, ACA groups were found mostly among university students and urban professionals, those most attracted to the middle class—based Radical Party. The organization's leaders "provided religious instruction and social formation, but they did not emphasize direct action" (Sweeney 1970, 10). Contrast this with Chile, where Acción Católica targeted the blue-collar working class and stressed direct action. The difference between the focus and style of AC movements in Argentina and Chile resulted from the type of threat to which each episcopacy responded. The Chilean Church confronted Protestant and communist competitors active among the popular classes, thus ACC targeted the poor. Argentine bishops, faced with a political threat only from above, directed their initiatives at the elite.

Over time, it became apparent that the hierarchy's renewed pastoral vigor was only a second-best strategy for dealing with the Church's waning political influence. Rather than competing with the Radicals for the hearts of the Argentine population, the bishops opted to support a military solution. When the armed forces overthrew Yrigoyen in 1930, the editor of *Criterio*[13] "praised the military coup of [General José Félix] Uriburu, whom he defined as a 'fervent Catholic,' and would shower him with sympathy during his entire term as provisional president" (Donini 1985, 44). Donini further states that this position should not have been surprising considering that "at the root of the conflict between liberalism, personified by the government of Roca, and the Catholic Church, many Catholics came to look upon democratic institutions with distrust" (44). Pike echoes this perspective:

> Increasingly concerned over how long they could keep a majority party out of power through electoral manipulations and fraud, many traditional elements responded approvingly to the right-wing nationalism that prominent Catholic leaders, both clerical and lay, had begun to preach. . . . [These leaders believed that] if Argentina was to be redirected toward worthwhile and exalted national goals, the higher values of life would have to be protected through a system of authoritarianism that was to be the political manifestation of a hierarchical social structure. (1970, 55)

The 1930 coup became the first in a string of military interventions in politics that would plague twentieth-century Argentina. It also provided the Catholic hierarchy with a new political option. Rather than relying upon their own resources to fight governments that opposed their interests, bishops could now rely on generals to intercede on their behalf. The relationship was mutually beneficial: The Church provided military dictators with the ideological justification needed to intervene in politics in exchange for a restoration of Church privilege. From this date on, the Church became an implicit, and often explicit, coconspirator in military rule, irrespective of what such support meant for the majority of Catholic parishioners. As one observer of the Argentine Church in the 1970s wrote,

> [B]ishops are terrified that they might have to face a situation in which they would not have at their disposal the resources to which they have become accustomed for their own personal expenses, office expenses,

and maintaining the seminaries that provide continuity to their mission. This fear of losing a source of income . . . turns them into courtiers during dictatorial regimes and coup supporters during democratic regimes. (Mignone 1988, 87)

## Church Complicity with Dictatorship from Perón to Videla

On 4 June 1943, the Argentine military toppled the elected government of Ramón Castillo. Having fought a century-long battle against liberalism (which tended to triumph in electoral contests) the episcopacy embraced military rule (Donini, interview; Pérez del Viso, interview). The episcopacy even ended up defending the military's intervention against critics in Chile and Uruguay (see *Criterio* 1944b; Franceschi 1944). Given the tenuous nature of the Ramírez administration and the contentious rise of Juan Perón (Crassweller 1987, 99–114), it was natural for the military to reach out to a major cultural institution for moral support during the regime's period of consolidation. Though not a devout Catholic, Perón realized that a continued embrace of the Church yielded substantial political benefits. In a speech on 28 June 1944, Perón emphasized the critical alliance between "*el Evangelio y la Espada* [Gospel and Sword]" (Lubertino 1987, 35).

Church support for Perón was reinforced during the national campaign of 1945. The bishops, as in the past, firmly prohibited Catholics from voting for candidates who advocated legalizing divorce, preserving secular education, and separating Church and state any further than it had been already (Donini, interview; Pérez del Viso, interview). Though the bishops evaded any outright endorsement of Perón, the message was clear to voters. Perón's only viable opposition—the Unión Democrática—endorsed these principles in its published platform (Lubertino 1987, 36). In a country where roughly 94 percent of the population was nominally Catholic, episcopal endorsement provided a significant moral advantage in political competition.

In return for its support of Perón, the Argentine Church was amply rewarded with numerous pro-Catholic policies, including the reinstatement of religious (i.e., Catholic) instruction in public schools (Tessi 1944).[14] It has been reported that several, if not all, bishops also received luxury automobiles from the government (Sweeney 1970, 11). Furthermore, "the Church saw in *peronismo* a means to warn the working class of the dangers of socialism and communism" (Lubertino 1987, 35), a major concern of the international Church. As the most extensive English discussion of Church-state events during this period says:

The decree [of 1943] is alleged to have been the coin in which the Roman Catholic hierarchy was paid for its support of—or at least its lack of opposition to—the revolutionary government, over which in the immediately succeeding months Perón was to establish his domination. Perón's government was notoriously undemocratic and quasi-totalitarian. Hence, it has been alleged, the decree demonstrates conclusively that the bishops were ready to cooperate with an anti-democratic program and to use the revolutionary conditions of 1943 to gain an advantage for their creed, an advantage which sixty years earlier had been denied through constitutional procedures. (Kennedy 1958, 196)

That Argentine bishops preferred state-mandated Catholicism over greater pastoral action became apparent in the episcopacy's reduced devotion to Acción Católica. As table 6.1 indicates, episcopal commitment to this organization suffered when the Church renewed its alliance with the state. Peaking just prior to the 1943 military coup (Donini 1985, 59), membership in ACA dropped 11 percent over the next fifteen years, with the critical youth branches registering a decrease of 29 percent.

The honeymoon between the Church and Perón was short-lived, at least from the latter's perspective. Immediately, the president began implementing methods of consolidating his rule and building popular support that lessened his need for Church legitimation. Key among these methods was *justicialismo*, a secular ideology emphasizing the need for state action to ameliorate conflict in society. Although purportedly based on papal encyclicals, Perón's philosophy sought state supremacy in both secular and spiritual matters, a perspective not shared by Church officials (Crassweller 1987, 227). One must wonder how committed Perón was to promoting Christian principles, since he himself was never a practicing Christian and occasionally dabbled in the occult (Pérez del Viso, interview). Nonetheless, use of Catholic writings

Table 6.1    Membership in Acción Católica Argentina, 1945–59

| Branch | 1945 | 1959 | Percentage Change |
|---|---|---|---|
| Men (adult) | 9,352 | 8,305 | −11.2% |
| Women (adult) | 17,700 | 20,900 | +18.1 |
| Men (youth) | 13,647 | 9,888 | −27.5 |
| Women (youth) | 25,400 | 17,800 | −29.9 |
| Students* | NA | 2,000 | NA |

*Source:* Frías 1960, 527. Percentage change calculated by present author.
*Student branch did not exist in 1945.

to build a personal ideology would be considered a safe move in a country that was overwhelmingly Catholic (in name at least).

While government officials claimed to be sympathetic to Christian principles, the Catholic Church remained suspicious of Perón's new philosophy (Bustos 1969, 185). Many prelates saw *justicialismo* as the means by which the secular government usurped the Church's traditional role of charity (Lubertino 1987, 81). Perón's organization of labor unions and other societal organizations—based on the principles of *justicialismo*—further alarmed these bishops. Fearing a loss of adherents to an "alien" ideology, the Church tried countering belatedly with Acción Católica. Naturally, Perón took offense at these rival organizations. Intimidation followed. The earliest attack upon Acción Católica came in May 1952. Following a screening of an erotic film, several ACA youths took to the streets protesting the lurid material. Riots broke out and several youths were arrested. In reaction to the disturbances, Perón's minister of the interior, Angel Borlenghi, publicly declared that "Latin America was being overrun by Catholic missionaries from the U.S., and that Catholic Action societies in Paraguay and elsewhere were engaging in anti-Peronista propaganda" (*Hispanic American Report,* June 1952, 30). Though not directed at the Argentine Church per se, it clearly embodied a warning.

As the Argentine economy deteriorated in the early 1950s, Perón intensified his program to instill *justicialismo* among the working classes and military—his two primary bases of power. Catholic bishops continued to voice opposition to this political strategy. The fears the bishops had of Perón's intentions were only aggravated further with the death and "deification" of "Saint" Evita, the president's second wife. When Perón suspended the observance of several Catholic holidays in favor of a celebration of his late wife, the episcopacy became vocally infuriated (*Hispanic American Report,* December 1954, 33).

Perón did not accept criticism lightly. Alluding to ACA in 1954, he proclaimed that "if organizations are legal and legitimate, and consequently enjoy the right of carrying on a given activity, they should limit themselves to this activity. If they interfere in the legal activities of other associations, they should immediately be abolished and prosecuted" (Perón [1954] 1964, 186–87). Revealing the regime's myopic preoccupation with its secular ideology, the official *peronista* newspaper declared "that the Church should defend its interests . . . but it seems to us absolutely intolerable that it should pretend to teach norms of conduct to the civil power" (*Hechos e Ideas,* [1955] 1964, 191). In 1955, Perón went so far as to legalize divorce and prostitution and proposed the definitive separation of Church and state, cutting off the Church's flow of public funds and denying religious educators access to state-run schools.[15]

On another front, the holistic philosophy of *justicialismo* did not prevent Perón from playing social actors against one another. Believing power lay in the urban population, the president developed policies favoring the proletariat. To raise the living standards of urban workers, the regime depressed food prices through the monopsonistic purchase of agricultural goods at artificially low prices. This policy angered the agricultural elite, a traditional stronghold of the Catholic Church. Not surprisingly, both the agricultural sector and the Catholic Church, with the aid of sympathetic elements in the military, allied to bring Perón's regime to an end. The Catholic Church was by no means the direct cause of Perón's demise, but the open conflict between Church and state provided one more reason for disgruntled sectors to take power (*Hispanic American Report*, 1955, various issues).

From 1955 through 1983, civil and military officials avoided direct confrontation with the Church hierarchy. They feared providing potential rivals with ideological fodder. In a political environment as shaky as Argentina's, the fate of Perón reminded leaders that the Church could potentially tip the balance against them. Apparently, even Perón himself learned this lesson before his return in 1973. Over the next three decades, political leaders treated the Church with kid gloves and the Church benefited (Galán, interview). In fact, the episcopacy actually made further gains with respect to its institutional autonomy.[16] Under Radical president Arturo Frondizi, the subsecretary of religion, Angel Centeno, initiated negotiations with the Holy See to end the *patronato nacional*.[17] The move was primarily a symbolic gesture of goodwill toward the Church, as the *patronato* had not functioned as originally intended for decades (Centeno, interview).[18] Whereas the government was legally required to draw up and present a list of three names to the Holy See when a diocesan post was vacated, Church administrators actually provided the list to the supreme court, which then rubber-stamped the pope's decision.

Negotiations were conducted directly with the Vatican on the issue of filling diocesan posts. The Argentine bishops themselves gave little input, although they were generally pleased with the course of events (Centeno, interview; Galán, interview). Although an agreement between Rome and the Argentine government would seem to be an easy matter, negotiations dragged on through three administrations until the document was finally signed by the military dictator, General Onganía. The agreement was originally slated to be signed by President Arturo Illía on 29 June 1966, the day he was ousted by a military coup d'etat.[19] The reasons for the delay were mostly outside the control of both parties and did not indicate hostility on either side. The preoccupation of Rome with Vatican II, the death of Pope John XXIII, and political instability in Argentina all contributed to delaying the inevitable agreement.[20]

As far as the Argentine episcopacy's concerns went, no major changes were made in the status of the Church during this period. Relations with the various governments remained good (Galán, interview). There was some concern among Church officials regarding Frondizi's handling of the *peronista* party during his term in office. From the beginning, the Church questioned the willingness of the government to rid Argentina of *peronismo* (*Criterio* 1958, 1959a). Bishops even called for military action (*Criterio* 1959b). All told, however, the hierarchy was not important in the president's expulsion even though the Church supported military intervention in 1962. So long as the Church's institutional interests remained unharmed, the hierarchy took little interest in public affairs.

Considering the growing political unrest in the country under President Illía, the bishops welcomed the June 1966 coup. The conservative nature of the bishops toward social unrest manifested itself in attempts to quell political dissension among clergy and laity. On 21 January 1966 the Conferencia Episcopal Argentina (CEA) issued a declaration to certain (unmentioned) clergy to cease their propaganda activities ("Declaración de la comisión permanente de la Conferencia Episcopal Argentina sobre ciertas publicaciones de algunos sacerdotes," in Conferencia Episcopal Argentina 1982, 16–17). Several months later, several Catholic university students occupied a church in Córdoba to protest the military coup. Instead of offering asylum to the protesters or offering to negotiate a settlement, the archbishop of Córdoba ordered the students to simply leave (*Criterio* 1966a). When pressed to take a position on the coup d'etat, the secretary of the CEA, Bishop Antonio Quarracino, declared, "The political community and the Church are independent and autonomous, each with its proper territory. The Church does not pretend to interfere in any manner in the temporal government" (*Criterio* 1966b). Considering the episcopacy's history of political maneuvering, this public neutrality towards the Onganía government was widely interpreted as support (Turner 1971, 89).

As the 1960s progressed, Argentina saw an increase in student protests, labor strikes, and the appearance of a number of small guerrilla organizations. On the religious front, the Catholic Church witnessed the creation of

Movimiento de Sacerdotes para el Tercer Mundo (Movement of Priests for the Third World), heavily influenced by Vatican II, *peronismo,* and progressive Catholic thinkers throughout Latin America (Donini 1985, 69–73).[21] Needless to say, the episcopacy did not endorse this group.[22]

The bishops also expressed growing displeasure with the country's increasing chaos. Beginning in 1969 and lasting until 1973, most issues of *Agencia Informativea Católica Argentina (AICA),* which reports on Catholic news including statements by the hierarchy, contain references to episcopal condemnations of violence and pleas for peace. However, blame is never placed on the military for the level of violence the country was experiencing. With the military seemingly incapable of stopping the violence, the solution promoted by virtually all sectors of society was returning Juan Perón to Argentina. It was hoped that his presence, and elections in 1973, would placate the most militant groups in society and ease the unrest the country was experiencing (Crassweller 1987, 339). Among the coalition agreeing to Perón's return from exile was, surprisingly, the Church (Gustafson 1992, 37). For the Catholic hierarchy, Perón's return appeared to be the only remaining way to quell civil unrest (Galán, interview). Episcopal support for ending its former enemy's exile was cautious. Reacting to a speech by Perón, the apostolic administrator of Mendoza revealed a certain wariness on the part of the hierarchy: "I listened *with true anxiety* to the message of the ex-president and leader of *justicialismo* and found it calming, clear, positive, and actually constructive" (*AICA,* 28 April 1973, 18; emphasis added). Knowing that they would have to work side by side with Perón, the episcopacy avoided alienating the leader. For his part, Perón had either learned his lesson or was too busy with other matters to bother with the Church. Relations remained cordial throughout his brief term in office.

The hope that Perón's presence would ease social tensions was short-lived. Not only did *peronista*-influenced organizations break ranks with their leader when his rule did not meet their expectations, but his death in July 1974 left the country essentially leaderless. Perón's third wife and hand-picked successor, Isabela, proved incapable of leading the country. Argentina once again spiraled toward anarchy. With the *peronista* option of guaranteeing social order exhausted, the Church reverted to supporting the military as the country's savior. Although the later years of Onganía's administration (and those of his successors Levingston and Lanusse) disappointed the episcopacy, the Church fared much better under military dictators than under democratic regimes.

From the outset, Argentine bishops played an active and supportive role in the military government. Just prior to the coup, two leaders of the junta (General Jorge Videla and Admiral Emilio Massera) met with influential members of the Church hierarchy to notify them of their intentions and obtain their blessing. This meeting was followed by a lengthy visit with the president of CEA, Monsignor Adolfo Tortolo, on the day of the coup (Mignone 1988, 2). Considering that dictators typically have busy schedules on their first day in office, these meetings indicate the importance the military placed on a close alliance with the Church. Furthermore, several bishops may have known of plans for a coup long before March 1976.

> On 23 September 1975, in a homily given in the presence of General Roberto Viola, Monsignor Victorio Bonamín, Vicar of the Army, wondered "will Christ not wish someday for the armed forces to go beyond their normal function." And on 29 December of the same year . . . Monsignor Adolfo Tortolo prophesied that a "process of purification" was approaching. (Mignone 1990, 356)

In 1966, the bishops' silence signified cautious approval of the military regime. Having experienced a decade of political turmoil since that time, the episcopacy was prepared to speak out in favor of the regime. When asked by reporters to comment on the similarity between a pastoral letter issued in August 1975 condemning civil unrest and statements made by General Videla, Archbishop Adolfo Servando Tortolo (president of CEA) responded that Videla's ideas "are the same as mine, the principles sown by the conduct of General Videla are those of a moral Christian" (*AICA*, 22 April 1976, 19). This also suggests that there may have been significant communication between the episcopacy and the eventual junta leaders well before the actual coup. Tortolo later appeared at various military installations stressing the importance of the relationship between "la Patria y la cruz" (the Fatherland and the cross) (*AICA*, 1 July 1976, 7).

Not only was the leadership of CEA in concordance with the military junta, but the vast majority of the bishops approved of the government as well. Of the "more than eighty active prelates" in Argentina at the time, "[o]nly four of them took a stand of open denunciation of the human rights violations committed by the . . . regime" (Mignone 1988, 19).[23] In a collective pastoral issued shortly after the coup, the bishops, cognizant of the repressive tactics being used by the military, condemned the tactics of left-wing terrorists (kidnappings and assassinations) as a sin, while at the same time dismissing the excessive repression of the military as only errors in defense of the common good. The pastoral letter, dated 15 May 1976, also stated that "[w]e [Argentines] must keep in mind that it would be easy to err with good intentions against the common good, if one were to insist that the armed forces must act with the precision [*pureza química*] of peacetime while blood runs each day" (Conferencia Episcopal Argentina 1982, 287).

Not all within the Church supported the military, and those who did not suffered the consequences. The most notorious example of repression against Catholic clergy occurred on 4 July 1976, when three Pallottine priests and two seminarians were assassinated, undoubtedly by government forces (Mignone 1988, 146–47). Given the grisly nature of the crime (Andersen 1993, 187) and the publicity surrounding it, the bishops could not ignore the matter. Although they sent a letter to the government expressing their concern over the matter, no accusations were made as to who the perpetrators were. In fact, the bishops went out of their way not to accuse the government by stating that "we know . . . the military high command, like the government and armed forces, share our pain" (Conferencia Episcopal Argentina 1982, 290).[24] Numerous other incidents occurred (see Lernoux 1982, 3–9; *AICA*, 29 July 1976, 3, 5–6; *AICA*, 12 August 1976, 15–16), including the intimidation and suspicious death of Monsignor Enrique Angelelli[25] (Mignone 1988, 138–45), but the episcopacy generally ignored such abuses. When these incidents are placed beside the Pallottine murders, it appears that the episcopacy reacted only to well-publicized atrocities; the hierarchy never brought such matters to the public's attention.

Over the entire course of the dictatorship, Church officials dismissed allegations of abuse against the government and in many cases were part and parcel of the process of repression. In fact, the Comisión Nacional sobre la Desaparición de Personas (CONADEP) published eyewitness accounts of clergy and high Church officials asking detainees to cooperate with their military captors (1992, 259–63). Mignone further accused several well-placed bishops with covering up human-rights abuses (1988).[26]

Given the intensity of government repression and pleas by parishioners to take action, the bishops found it hard to ignore completely problems such as the fate of the *desaparecidos*—i.e., those people kidnapped, tortured, and often killed by the military (see Comisión Nacional sobre la Desaparición de Personas 1992; Andersen 1993). However, the statements they made in reference to the subject were crafted to avoid blaming the regime. For instance, what appeared as a condemnation of military repression by the hierarchy also blamed left-wing terrorists as equally culpable for the current situation:

The disturbance [of social order], as well as a mistaken concept of personal and collective security, has led many consciences to tolerate and even accept the violation of basic human rights created in the image of God and redeemed by Christ; it has led also to admitting the legality of enemy assassination, psychological[27] and physical torture, the illegitimate loss of liberty, or the elimination of all those who are assumed to be adversaries of personal and collective security. . . . Although it is true that the national government has clarified and published the situation of many . . . still there exists the problem of disappeared persons, *be it by subversion or by repression or also by free will.* . . . Although subversion has been restrained in large part, nonetheless this harmful action has ultimately resurfaced in isolated instances . . . [W]e must condemn it as inhumane. (Conferencia Episcopal Argentina 1982, 359; emphasis added)[28]

Terrorist acts were of course committed by left-wing insurgents, but the disproportionate amount of abuse emanated from the military. The hierarchy's declaration could be interpreted as an effort to appease public opinion without directly implicating the regime. The bishops further asked for "national reconciliation," a position tantamount to the military remaining in power. They never demanded punishment for those officers responsible for human-rights violations.

The institutional Church was rewarded well during the dictatorship. Given the Church's legal status at the time, the episcopacy obtained a "defence of 'Western and Christian civilization', and the consolidation of the Church's privileges" (Mignone 1990, 360). As part of this defense, and in response to Church complaints about proselytizing sects (*AICA,* 23 September 1976, 36–37), the military banned the Jehovah's Witnesses (*AICA,* 23 September 1976, 38–39).[29] Laws regulating non-Catholic denominations were also altered with little prior notice, making it difficult for many religious organizations to properly register and obtain legal status (Ligget, interview).[30]

State funding for Catholic education and other projects continued. Church personnel were also well cared for.

At the height of the military dictatorship . . . the episcopate had the . . . idea of negotiating and obtaining, among other privileges, a state salary for each diocesan and auxiliary bishop, equivalent to 70 per cent of the income of a state judge, also special retirement terms for them, a salary proportionate to that of a civil servant for seminarians and even a grant towards a new house for the archbishop of Buenos Aires. (Mignone 1990, 366)

It was no doubt difficult for bishops to bite the hand that fed them. Note that the Catholic prelates initiated negotiations, demonstrating that they were willing participants in the military government and not simply innocent puppets.

For the duration of the military government, the Church remained reasonably supportive. Only in 1981, in the midst of a severe economic crisis, did the episcopacy echo the growing concern of many in society about the military's competence to rule. In May of that year, the bishops issued a document entitled *Iglesia y Comunidad Nacional*, wherein they called for restoration of citizens' rights (Conferencia Episcopal Argentina 1981, 16) and very tepidly endorsed democratic values. Obviously concerned about Argentina's volatile experience with democracy and *peronismo*, the hierarchy warned against the perils of democratic demagoguery (Conferencia Episcopal Argentina 1981, 46). This document preferred reconciliation to condemnation and never approached the strong denunciations of militarism being issued from the Churches in Chile, Brazil, or El Salvador.

When the governing junta released its "final document" with the intention of dismissing charges of human rights abuses against the military, the "only group [in society] that attempted to defend the communiqué was the executive commission of the Bishops' Conference of Argentina" which summarily published a document of support (Mignone 1988, 39). With the return to democracy assured, several bishops who had remained silent throughout the military's rule expressed discontent with the official Church position (Mignone 1988, 39–40). By this time, the damage had been done; the Argentine Church had earned a reputation as a coconspirator with one of hemisphere's most brutal dictatorships. Even today, more than ten years after the return to civilian rule, the Church suffers from a lack of credibility among parishioners. The hierarchy's image has been so bad that in 1995 the bishops publicly asked the Argentine citizenry to forgive them for their sinful participation in the regime (López 1995; Rouillon 1995).

## Protestantism and Church Political Strategy in Argentina

I save for last an examination of the effect that evangelical Protestantism had on Catholic political strategy from 1930 to 1983 for the simple reason that it was extremely limited. Prior to the early 1980s, the Argentine Church never faced a serious grassroots threat to its parishioner base from Protestants (Donini, interview; Galán, interview; Pérez del Viso, interview). The interests of the majority of Catholic parishioners remained a secondary concern to an episcopacy that was more interested in bolstering its legal status in society.

This is not to say that Protestantism did not exist in Argentina. Numerically, Argentina contained one of the largest *absolute* populations of Protestants in Latin America, although proportionately it was quite small.[31] More important than sheer numbers, however, was the type of Protestants found in Argentina. As mentioned above, Argentina's trading relationship with Northern Europe, shortage of skilled labor, and consequent need to attract immigrants led to the early establishment of religious liberty. Protestant workers were encouraged to migrate to the country in the nineteenth and early twentieth centuries. For the most part, these "transplanted" churches served as a means of preserving ethnic identity (Villalpando 1970, 13–15).[32] Read, Monterroso, and Johnson note, "Many contingents of European immigrants brought their churches with them, resulting in a number of ethnic churches, some of which do not conduct services in Spanish, and *most of which do not try to evangelize the Spanish-speaking people who surround them*" (1969, 82; emphasis added). Lacking missionary zeal, Protestantism never represented a significant threat to the parishioner base of the Catholic Church.

Until the early 1900s, Chile and Argentina closely resemble one another. Protestantism initially established itself in these Southern Cone countries as enclave communities. After 1930, the Protestant paths of these two countries diverged dramatically. As David Martin points out, "[T]he main increase in Argentinian Protestantism was by migration prior to 1930, and the main increase in Chilean Protestantism was by conversion after 1930" (1990, 74). To my knowledge, a systematic investigation of why this divergence occurred has never been undertaken.[33] For immediate purposes, it is only important that evangelical Protestantism took hold in one country and not another. The varying rates of Protestant growth are considered exogenous in this study. The experiences of Argentina and Chile support the assumption of exogeneity. Both introduced religious liberty relatively early (be it official or de facto), and the persecution of non-Catholic missionaries was not as intense as in other Latin American countries such as Colombia (Goff 1968). In essence, there was an equal opportunity for Protestantism to develop in both countries.

Protestant missionary activity was not entirely absent from Argentina. But in contrast to Chile and Brazil, Argentine Protestantism failed to indigenize itself and remained limited in its appeal. Sweeney attributes this failure to higher literacy rates and the lack of a strong Pentecostal presence (1970,

183–84), although given the expansionary nature of Pentecostalism the latter causal factor is a truism. The critical question for Sweeney becomes why Pentecostalism never took hold, a question outside the purview of this study. Whereas in both Chile and Brazil the Pentecostal movement became indigenous almost immediately, Protestant evangelism remained a foreign matter in Argentina and after 1961 missionary efforts dropped off significantly.

The Catholic reaction to Protestant evangelism was primarily elite based and influenced by anti-imperialism. Articles on the subject of Protestantism by leading Catholic thinkers (e.g., Franceschi 1944; Criterio 1944a, 1944c, 1945) appealed to missionaries to stop their activities rather than focusing on rethinking the way Catholicism presented itself to the majority of the population. Given the massive influx of North American missionaries following the closure of mission fields in Asia and Africa, this approach was in vogue throughout much of Latin America at the time. For the Argentine episcopacy, the problem with Protestant encroachment was less an internal pastoral challenge than a regionwide phenomenon to be dealt with through legal proscriptions on the activities of foreigners (Criterio 1944a). Church leaders focused their attention on enacting laws that would restrict the flow of foreigners. They met with moderate success under Perón. Interestingly, the few articles pertaining to Protestantism in Criterio show greater concern with Protestants in other Latin American countries than in Argentina (Criterio 1944b, 1956a, 1956b, 1956c; Centeno 1957).

In addition to preaching religious anti-imperialism, the episcopacy sought legal means to block Protestantism. In addition to privileging Catholic access to public schools (an advantage Protestant teachers did not enjoy), Perón prohibited Protestants from evangelizing by radio and implemented a registry (el fichero) for all non-Catholic denominations (Sweeney 1992a, 225–26). Many Protestants considered this the first step toward state regulation and an outright ban, but in reality these actions were not severe impediments to Protestant growth. Radio transmissions, albeit a powerful tool, were used by only a few missionary organizations, and the registry did not lead to a suppression of church activities. Not surprisingly, these laws were revoked in 1954 when Perón and the Catholic Church were at odds.

During the most recent military regime, the Church was able to persuade the military to outlaw several "marginal Protestant" groups (e.g., Divine Light Mission, Jehovah's Witnesses) operating in the country. These groups were mostly new to the religious scene and were quite visible in their proselytizing activities. As such, they made easy targets for a military ban. Groups that were slightly more established (e.g., Mormons) were not affected by the political situation, except for having to register with the government. Such obstacles were easily overcome by the better-organized churches.

Given the weak impact of evangelical Protestantism in Argentina, the episcopacy was never pressured to reevaluate its pastoral role at the base of society. Protestantism remained a foreign threat, and was dealt with at the elite level through legal proscriptions. The greater threat to Church interests came from the elite in the form of liberalism and *peronismo*. Although *peronismo* was a working-class movement, it was organized from the top down. In this sense, the threat to the Church came from above. Despite Acción Católica and other small movements that were primarily middle- and upper-middle-class in nature, pastoral commitment to the poor remained weak. No major works of pastoral introspection, comparable to Padre Hurtado's works or *Mensaje*, were produced by Church personnel.

The lack of any serious introspection on the part of the Argentine bishops was reflected in their traditionalist stance toward both the Medellín (1968) and Puebla (1979) conferences. The sociopolitical problems raised at these conferences were not considered to be Argentine problems by the episcopacy; the bishops viewed their situation more akin to Europe than the Third World (Donini, interview). Along with the Colombian episcopacy, the Argentine bishops provided the primary front against the progressive tone of these conferences. Reacting to demands by progressives at Medellín to activate the Church in the temporal liberation of the poor, Bishop Quarracino responded, "It is negative . . . to think of a temporal Church, considering it as a factor of power, or as a promoter or in charge of creating the idea of an 'earthly paradise,' or to think of the faith as nothing other than mere 'social responsibility'" (AICA, 12 March 1969, 32). Although the episcopacy made speeches about caring for the poor, its commitment to pastoral innovations (e.g., CEBs) promoted at Medellín amounted to little more than traditional charity. A decade later, the episcopal contingent attending the Puebla meeting "unsuccessfully tried to bar the use of the word *liberation* from the documents" (Gustafson 1992, 40). To them, the ideological doctrine of "national security" (condemned at Puebla) was not at odds with Church teachings (Mignone 1988, 81).

For all practical purposes, the Argentine Church maintained a religious monopoly over its parishioners until the mid-1980s, when evangelical Protestantism began making substantial headway. Consistent with the prediction that religious monopolies provide less care for their parishioners than do competitive churches, the needs and desires of Argentina's Catholic laity were ignored during the past several dictatorships. While those harmed by the policies of the military looked to the Church for moral support, the bishops looked the other way and reaped the benefits that cooperation with the state brought.

## Summary

For the first century following independence, Church-state relations in Argentina and Chile proceeded along similar paths. Bishops in both countries sought to preserve their institutions' privileged status against the onslaught of liberal political forces that simultaneously tried reducing and controlling the Church's grip on society. Furthermore, each episcopacy fought for greater autonomy in the realm of internal Church decision making (i.e., eliminating the *patronato nacional*). To accomplish these goals, each Church focused on the political elite, primarily by forming alliances with conservatives. When liberal parties governed, Catholic prelates tried avoiding conflict for fear of provoking greater attacks on Church prerogatives.

At no time prior to the 1930s did the bishops attempt to gain social influence by building respect and credibility among the majority of their parishioners in the popular classes. Because of their lack of wealth and power, these groups did not contribute many resources to the provision of religious services in their communities. Lacking any viable exit option (i.e., alternative denomination), these parishioners remained nominally Catholic, leading the Church hierarchy to believe they had a firm grasp on religiosity in the country. Predictably, the Church developed into an elite institution uncaring about the poor.

The situation changed beginning in the 1930s. In each country, rival religious organizations were equally free to proselytize for members. Ironically, the country that had legal proscriptions on Protestantism for a longer time—Chile—developed the first significant evangelical population in Spanish America.[34] Evangelical Protestantism and socialism gained substantial momentum in Chile and challenged the Church's (supposed) hegemony over the popular classes, whereas in Argentina these movements languished. The success of Protestantism and socialism among the popular classes alarmed many in the Chilean Church. Reacting to the realization that the Church had failed to evangelize the poor adequately, the Chilean bishops embarked on a series of pastoral reforms that eventually earned them a reputation as Latin America's most progressive and innovative episcopacy. When the military came to power in 1973 and enacted policies injurious to the lower classes, the bishops had to choose between legitimating the military or defending the poor. The former strategy, although it could have resulted in patronage, would have cost the Church dearly in credibility among the very sectors of society in which it was trying to build trust. Opposition to authoritarian rule resulted.

The Argentine Church never confronted a major challenge to its hegemony from below. Although Argentina contained a sizable Protestant population, these Protestants were nonproselytizing; Catholicism's share of the religious market changed little. Socialism never caught fire among workers as it did in Chile, and under Perón the labor movement was coopted from above. Without the presence of alternative religious or ideological movements, the bishops could continue playing an elite-based strategy to improve their legal and financial status. On advice of the Vatican, the Argentine episcopacy promoted Catholic Action programs, but they did not expand them into other programs as in Chile. Elite-based efforts paid dividends in 1943, when the military government reversed many of the anticlerical policies enacted a century earlier. With major gains coming from a policy of elite accommodation and no substantial loss of parishioners to non-Catholic competitors, the episcopacy found no trouble in legitimating the military governments that came to power in the 1960s and 1970s.

# SEVEN

# The Institutional Limits
# of Catholic Progressivism

*When a religion founds its empire only upon the desire of immortality that lives in every human heart, it may aspire to universal dominion; but when it connects itself with a government, it must adopt maxims which are applicable only to certain nations. Thus, in forming an alliance with a political power, religion augments its authority over a few and forfeits the hope of reigning over all.*

Alexis de Tocqueville, *Democracy in America*

From the 1960s to the early 1980s, several national Catholic Churches throughout Latin America gained worldwide attention for their preferential option for the poor and courageous opposition to military dictatorships. The Church's progressive position in these countries surprised many students of Latin American politics, as most Catholic bishops and clergy traditionally were associated with the dominant political and economic elite. Due to their actions on behalf of democracy and human rights, the Catholic clergy regained the respect of the rural and urban poor, a social segment historically ignored by the Church. Although not the principal cause of democratization, the Catholic Church played an important role in mediating the return to civilian rule.[1] Now that democracy (albeit often unstable) has returned to the region, the Church finds itself at a turning point. What will the political role of the Catholic Church be in this new political era?

Early indications suggest the Latin American Church hierarchy is returning to the more conservative strategy of its not too distant past, emphasizing accommodation with the political and economic elite rather than continuing its preferential option for the poor. Why this change in policy now? Some observers have argued that this strategy results from the Catholic hierarchy's increasing lack of concern for issues of social justice (MacEoin 1991). However, given the Church's recent gains in winning back the credibility it had long ago lost among the popular classes, such a strategy appears irrational. Furthermore, the Vatican's emphasis on "new evangelization" as a means of countering Protestant growth in Latin America seems to dictate a greater concern for the poor, as this is where evangelical Protestants have been making substantial gains. Throwing away over three decades of pastoral effort to reach out to the poor would only renew cynicism toward the Catholic Church among the lower classes. In turn, this would lead to further defections from the faith, precisely the outcome Church officials want to avoid.

Is it possible to explain the Church's new strategy of greater accommodation with the political and economic elite while maintaining the assumption that Catholic bishops have a genuine concern for the spiritual and material well-being of the poor? Examining the economic realities surrounding the growth and maintenance of religious organizations may shed light on this issue. Even though the Catholic Church's image among the lower classes has improved dramatically over the past two decades, it still lacks the physical presence among this social sector to stop the exodus to Pentecostalism and other non-Catholic religions. Building a physical presence requires resources, both financial and human. Given the substantial costs of maintaining a highly bureaucratized and priest-centered religious organization, Catholic bishops have been pressured into lobbying for governmental assistance to help the Church compete more effectively with the rising tide of low-cost Pentecostal churches. Such assistance may come in the form of direct cash subsidies to Catholic organizations or as policies that endorse Catholicism over other denominations. This situation compares to noncompetitive domestic industries seeking tariff protection from foreign competitors. When domestic firms find themselves at a competitive disadvantage with more efficient foreign companies, government aid (e.g., tariffs, subsidies) represents a cheaper short-term remedy than does an attempt to restructure the organization for greater efficiency. In addition to the daunting economic costs such an effort would impose, doctrinal (i.e., ideological) considerations make restructuring prohibitive for the Church and increases the necessity of relying on governmental assistance to remain competitive. The irony of this strategy is that state assistance is not as easily achieved as in the past. Politicians, competing for votes in a religiously pluralistic society, are less willing to enact pro-Catholic policies that would isolate Protestant constituencies.

## *From Option for the Poor to New Evangelization*

For most of its five hundred–year history, the Latin American Church operated as an elitist, proauthoritarian institution that largely ignored the needs of the majority of its constituents, specifically the rural and urban poor. Given the monopoly status of Catholicism, Church officials could focus their pastoral energies on servicing the rich and powerful (who contributed most to the maintenance of the institutional Church) without fearing a loss of poor parishioners to other religions. Beginning roughly in the 1950s, a number of national episcopacies traded their elite-based pastoral strategy for a preferential option for the poor as impoverished parishioners increasingly defected to other faiths and ideological movements. Proclaiming itself a voice for the voiceless, the Church engaged in community service projects that cushioned the harsh effects wrought by the military's economic and political policies. For example, the Chilean Church established various organizations to help those adversely affected by the economic policies and repression of the Pinochet regime, including feeding centers, legal services, and health services. It has been estimated that roughly "1 out of every 23 residents" received direct assistance from a Church-sponsored organization (Smith 1990, 331). Given its privileged historical status in society, the Church could undertake a wider range of activity than nonreligious organizations (e.g., labor unions) during this period. In doing so, the Catholic Church recaptured much of the credibility it had previously lost among this sector of the population. Although persecution of Catholic clergy and lay activists occurred, military dictators generally were reluctant to completely shut down Catholic organizations.

Needless to say, the comparatively rapid movement of the Church from a proelite institution to a champion of the poor by the late 1960s drew a great deal of scholarly attention. Much of the scholarship on this subject during the 1970s and early 1980s projected a progressive trajectory for the Catholic Church (see Landsberger 1970; Vallier 1970; Lernoux 1980; Beeson and Pearce 1984). Spurred on by the progressive nature of the regional bishops' conferences in Medellín (1968) and Puebla (1979), it seemed that the Catholic Church would continue moving away from its traditional political strategy of elite accommodation toward greater pastoral activity at the grassroots, with the *comunidades eclesiales de base* (CEBs) representing the model of the future Church.

Lately, however, it appears that the direction of change has been reversed, or at least slowed. A recent edited volume by Cleary and Stewart-Gambino (1992) paints a picture of eroded optimism regarding the role of progressive Catholicism in contemporary Latin America. Within a democratic environment, Church officials appear to be paying less attention to pastoral activity among the poor, instead choosing to devote more time and effort to appeasing the political elite. It is highly unlikely that the Church will return to the days of colonial Christendom; pastoral activity at the base of society continues and the Vatican remains committed to CEBs as a means of reaching the faithful. Nevertheless, the general trend has been toward greater accommodation with the powers that be. Bishops currently devote a greater proportion of their time and energy to securing support from the political and economic elite. In this regard, rather than following the progressive trajectory charted under authoritarian rule, the Catholic Church appears to be experiencing a conservative retrenchment. But, as I will argue below, the terms *progressive* and *conservative* are becoming increasingly anachronistic as bishops pursue a mixed strategy of grassroots activity among the poor concurrent with efforts to court presidents and legislators. The greater devotion paid to the political elite by prelates should not be confused with a lost concern for the poor. Instead, it reflects the economic constraints associated with trying to maintain a religious monopoly in an increasingly pluralistic religious market.

The Catholic Church's new pastoral and consequent political strategy was laid out at the 1992 general meeting of the Latin American bishops held in Santo Domingo, Dominican Republic.[2] In a series of highly secretive meetings, bishops from across Latin America forged a plan for a "new evangelization" of the region. The Catholic left criticized the bishops at this meeting for de-emphasizing the Church's preferential option for the poor in favor of a more politically neutral emphasis on spirituality. The editors at the *National Catholic Reporter* called this approach "sappy, neoliberal religiosity that is all things to all people" (1992, 1). Actually, considering that the Church's universal mission is to evangelize all people (i.e., maximize parishioners), being "all things to all people" is a reasonable strategy, not to mention one of Saint Paul's recommendations. Exclusively favoring one social sector over another will undoubtedly alienate the unfavored group and in the presence of religious pluralism may lead to their conversion away from Catholicism.

Critiques from the left to the contrary, the meeting's final document endorsed "pastoral activity whose starting point is the gospel's preferential option for the poor" (Hennelly 1993, 128). Nevertheless, the general tone of the document sought to dampen the political activity that radical sectors of the Church had become known for during the previous two decades. Although the pontiff urged the clergy to refrain from overt political activity, a constant theme of John Paul II's tenure, this was the time that the Vatican was negotiating friendlier relations with the Mexican government (Tangeman 1995, 74–84). These negotiations, which eventually led to a reform of Mexico's severe anticlerical laws (Gill 1995), were representative of attempts by individual episcopacies across Latin America to seek more favorable (and lucrative) relations with their respective national governments.

The general trend toward elite accommodation became evident in such places as Nicaragua, where Cardinal Miguel Obando y Bravo, who previously warned lower-level clergy against becoming too politically active under the Sandinista regime, energetically endorsed Violeta Chamorro's UNO government. For his support, the government showered the Church with preferential treatment (Dodson 1992, 27–29). Support included partial funding for the construction of a new cathedral in Managua, a donation of public buildings to house a Jesuit university, the use of the Church's catechism in public school textbooks, and a proposed tax on evangelical religious activities (Jeffrey 1992). Beginning in the early 1980s, the Brazilian episcopacy began scaling back its pastoral activity (Della Cava 1989, 153) and continues lobbying for state assistance for a variety of projects (Serbin 1994). In Chile, the Catholic Church has scaled back direct assistance to the poor (Precht, interview) and increased its effort to lobby the government for preferential treatment in such matters as church registration laws and educational subsidies (Chacón, interview). The two most recent archbishops of Santiago—Carlos Oviedo and Juan Francisco Fresno—have adopted a more conciliatory approach when dealing with the country's political elite (both military and civilian), a pattern also apparent in the Chilean episcopal conference as a whole. And in Mexico, the progressive bishop of Chiapas, Samuel Ruíz, faced the possibility of censure at a time when relations between the government and Catholic hierarchy are beginning to thaw after more than a century of animosity (Darling 1993; Tangeman 1995, 15–16). In this last instance, it seems as if the silence of the Church's progressive wing is the price being paid for increased access to state favoritism.[3]

Several factors have influenced this trend toward a more elite-based political strategy on the part of Church officials. On the political side, the often tenuous nature of negotiated transitions to democracy demanded that the Church tone down its criticism of military governments so as not to jeopardize the democratization process. While speaking out vociferously for the rights of the persecuted in the 1970s and early 1980s, the Chilean episcopal conference recently has urged "reconciliation" when it comes to prosecuting the military for human rights violations (*El Mercurio* 1993a, 1993b), a position consistent with former president Patricio Aylwin's decision to keep military trials out of the public eye. For many on the front lines of the battle against tyranny, this apparent retreat from bold proclamations against injustice seemed a betrayal. However, the fragility of the transition process does not adequately account for the continuation of the Church's more conservative posture after the transition has ended and consolidation begun.

A more likely (and widely promulgated) explanation for the reemergence of Catholic "conservatism" can be found within the international Church. The appointment of Pope John Paul II in 1978 ushered in an era of Vatican policy aimed at recovering a substantial portion of pre-Vatican II orthodoxy. Part of John Paul's strategy was to reassert hierarchical control over a Church that had experienced increasing decentralization since Vatican II (Della Cava 1993a). Nowhere was this more evident than in Latin America, where a "parallel church"[4]—composed mostly of lower-level clergy and lay activists—grew ever more autonomous and resisted the directives of the upper hierarchy to scale back radical political action. Furthermore, the presence of Catholic intellectuals proclaiming a new theology of liberation also alarmed the higher echelons of the Church. Thus, both the perceived need to reinstate theological orthodoxy and the desire to recapture hierarchical control over the institution resulted in the appointment of several conservative bishops less amenable (though not necessarily hostile) to the preferential option for the poor promoted at the regional episcopal conferences in Medellín and Puebla.

But are other explanations for this phenomenon possible? Consider a counterfactual.[5] Barring the events above—i.e., the election of a conservative pope and the development of a "renegade" grassroots movement—would the Catholic hierarchy have returned to an elite-based strategy of seeking government accommodation? I argue yes. An extension of the deductive model presented in chapter 3 predicts that given the growth in proselytizing non-Catholic religions and the resource scarcity confronting the Catholic Church, a movement toward elite accommodation would have been likely under democracy despite changes at the Vatican or a split between the upper and lower ranks of the Church hierarchy.

## An Alternative Explanation: The Cost of Competing

The Latin American Catholic Church exists in a rapidly changing environment. Of the utmost concern to Church officials has been the dramatic increase in the number of evangelical Protestants—particularly Pentecostals—who find their most successful recruiting grounds in the poorest barrios. The Protestant challenge has made it clear to bishops and other Catholic officials that they can no longer take the poor for granted and assume they will remain faithful Catholics. Being shielded from the Protestant Reformation for most of its five hundred-year history, and being financially disadvantaged by a bureaucracy that evangelical Protestants do not possess, the Latin American Church finds it difficult to compete with these new religions. This challenge has impacted official Catholic political strategy in such a way as to make elite accommodation the preferable strategy under democracy. Considering the gains in credibility that could be reaped from opposing dictators, the increase in Protestant competition made an antielite strategy attractive under authoritarian rule, but within the confines of a democratic polity the incentives are reversed. Currently, the dominant political strategy for the Catholic episcopacy is to lobby elected government officials for exclusive advantages that would improve the Church's ability to compete with Protestants. The progressive pastoral role of the episcopacy will continue, but it will be tempered more than what one would have expected from the vantage point of the late 1970s.

## Assumptions of the Model Restated

As with almost all other social organizations (be they religious or not), the Roman Catholic Church has an interest in maintaining its membership base at the lowest possible cost. For religious organizations that have an evangelizing mission, the concern with membership is intrinsically built into the purpose of the organization. A stable or increasing membership implies a successful organization, ceteris paribus, while the loss of members indicates failure by the organization's officials to deliver upon the promises made to its constituency. Success or failure, measured in terms of membership, becomes obvious only when meaningful substitutes exist (Hirschman 1970). Although it is generally agreed now that Catholicism was only superficially ingrained in the Latin American population, this did not become apparent until Protestantism offered itself as a viable alternative to religious consumers.

Aside from membership retention (or maximization), organizations have other goals determined by their unique purposes. For churches these goals include promoting justice, maintaining doctrinal purity, etc. As resources (e.g., time, money, effort) must be applied to achieve their other objectives, an organization's leadership has a strong incentive to minimize the cost of maintaining membership in order to devote a greater percentage of resources to those goals. Thus, deductively, we can expect that a basic objective of Catholic officials is to find the least expensive means of maintaining (and perhaps, expanding) its parishioner base.

### The Costs of Religious Competition

If religious organizations concern themselves with maintaining (or augmenting) their parishioner base at the lowest possible cost, how does the Latin American Catholic Church compare with its Protestant rivals? This comparison is important given that organizations that serve adherents at a lower per-member cost can devote more resources to servicing members and will be more successful at expanding or maintaining their parishioner bases, ceteris paribus. Organizations that face higher per-member costs, on the other hand, will be less competitive.

In general, the older and more bureaucratized a religious organization is, the greater its resource expenditure per parishioner.[6] The Roman Catholic Church, having a history longer than any other Christian church in the Western Hemisphere, is by far more bureaucratized than any of its rivals in Latin America. This means that the Catholic Church devotes a higher proportion of resources to maintaining its bureaucracy, relative to servicing its parishioners, than the more decentralized Protestant churches (Stoll 1990, 35). This is not to say that Catholic officials ignore direct parishioner service, but that the indirect (i.e., bureaucratic) costs of parishioner service make up a larger *percentage* of the total Church budget than for its non-Catholic rivals.

Besides the cost of its sizable bureaucracy, the Catholic Church is also disadvantaged by the upkeep of its religious buildings. While Catholics tend, on average, to maintain more sizable and ornate houses of worship, certain Pentecostal churches are often located in more humble surroundings, such as a garage or someone's home.[7] The significance of this cost advantage is not as trivial as it may sound; when discussing the various funding strategies of Protestants, an official Catholic Church publication complained that evangelical Protestants "are not obliged to maintain ancient colonial church buildings, like many Catholic parishes" (Consejo Episcopal Latinoamericano 1984, 35). The Catholic hierarchy is well aware of its cost disadvantage against many Protestant denominations, particularly the Pentecostals. In the final analysis, however, building maintenance and other incidental expenses are only a minor disadvantage for the Catholic Church compared to its most pressing resource problem—personnel costs and the shortage of priests.

One of the most pressing resource concerns for the Catholic Church has been its *crisis sacerdotal* (Poblete 1965). While this has generally been true for *at least* two centuries, the scarcity became glaringly obvious when alternative religions and ideologies started making significant gains by the 1930s in some countries.[8] Prior to that period, nearly everyone was Catholic—at least nominally—and the Church did not have to deploy additional priests to guarantee its parishioner base.[9] Given that population growth continues to outstrip the supply of new seminarians, this problem has only worsened over time. To realize just what a crisis this is for the Catholic Church, compare the number of personnel across denominations. In Brazil, for example, Protestant clergy now outnumber Catholic priests (Stoll 1990, 6) despite a Protestant population approximately one-tenth that of Catholics (Barrett 1982, 186). The situation is similar throughout Latin America, where Protestants typically maintain a higher clergy-to-parishioner ratio than Catholics.

The reason for the scarcity of Catholic priests relative to Protestant ministers lies in the higher cost of being a Catholic priest. Compared to training for Protestant ministers, the Catholic priesthood is a costly endeavor—both for the individual priest and for the Church as an institution. This affects the supply of priests in the region, which in turn reduces the Church's effectiveness in recruiting and retaining devout parishioners. From the institutional side, the Church must devote significant resources to educating priests, which encompasses several years of intellectual and spiritual study in seminaries. Although similar training imposes comparable costs on certain more bureaucratized Protestant denominations (e.g., Anglicans), the primary competitor to the Latin American Catholic Church is Pentecostalism. As the Pentecostal ministry relies more on charisma than dogma and ritual, training time is remarkably short and any cost is usually borne by the prospective ministers themselves.[10] In this light, it is much easier for Pentecostals to place more personnel in the field in a shorter period of time, making parishioner recruitment more cost effective. Moreover, the lack of an overarching bureaucracy aimed at coordinating instruction also reduces the cost of fielding Protestant clergy.

Besides the cost to the organization of training clergy, there are costs borne by priests themselves that make the ministry a more or less attractive career. These costs relate both to the individual's effort invested in becoming a cleric and the cost of continuing such a career. Compared to the Protestant ministry, the Catholic priesthood imposes greater costs on the individual—including longer and more intense training, celibacy, and devotion to a more rigorous dogma—predictably resulting in a lower supply of Catholic priests. For many Protestant denominations, especially Pentecostals, these costs are lower or nonexistent, making it easier to attract ministerial recruits.

Another cost advantage of the Protestant ministry is that some Protestant ministers are allowed to pursue secondary careers to supplement their pastoral incomes. Obviously this reduces the time ministers can devote to their flock and thereby raises the church's per-parishioner cost. Nonetheless, this cost can be ameliorated by reducing the size of the congregation and relying more upon the laity. Indeed, Protestant congregations tend to have significantly smaller memberships than Catholic parishes, a fact that is probably due as much to a conscious decision on the part of Protestants to limit congregation size as to the relative shortage of Catholic priests. Therefore, assuming a Catholic priest is as effective as a Protestant minister in servicing a parishioner base of equal size, the higher cost of becoming a priest (from the perspective of both the individual and institution) results in a lower supply (i.e., scarcity) of priests and makes Catholic pastoral action more costly than Protestant efforts.

Another factor constraining the cost-effectiveness of the Catholic Church is its priest-centeredness. Whereas Protestants rely heavily upon lay involvement in the faith, priests are considered indispensable in Catholicism. The issue of Bible study illustrates this point. Protestant denominations emphasize the ability of the individual to read and interpret the Bible, which permits the laity to organize prayer discussions of their own volition, while the Catholic Church relies more upon priestly mediation. In this manner, the burden placed on a Protestant minister is lower than that placed on a Catholic priest.

Given these structural disadvantages, the Catholic Church has attempted to reduce its costs of parishioner service. To some extent, the base community (CEB) movement has eased personnel costs. By giving the laity a greater role in evangelization and Bible study, the Catholic Church has had to rely less upon priests. Moreover, given the modest venues that CEBs typically meet in, the costs of building maintenance are lowered for each Catholic parishioner reactivated in the faith. Again, this is only a minor consideration compared to personnel costs.

However, regardless of the significant scholarly attention paid to them, CEBs touch only a small percentage of Catholics in Latin America. Furthermore, CEBs, with their potential to promote unauthorized political action, have been greeted with a great deal of caution by many members of the hierarchy. Their continued use as a means of evangelization has been greatly circumscribed. In many respects, CEBs represent the decentralization of the Catholic Church and hence threaten the hierarchical power of bishops, papal nuncios, and other officials. C. René Padilla suggests that CEBs might represent the greatest internal challenge to the authority of the institutional Church since the Protestant Reformation:

> [T]he challenge that the CEBs represent for the Roman Catholic Church can hardly be exaggerated. Would it sound too bold to say that since the Protestant Reformation in the sixteenth century there has been no crisis in this church comparable to the one produced by the CEBs in Latin America? Perhaps. The fact remains, however, that there is plenty of evidence to show the very deep concern that these Catholic communities have been causing to the hierarchy since the Latin American Conference of Bishops (CELAM) in 1968. (Padilla 1985, xiii)

Although endorsing the general evangelizing principles of the CEBs, John Paul II and the Latin American bishops cautioned that they should be under the strict guidance of trained clergy, hardly making the CEBs an effective tool to overcome the scarcity of priests (Hennelly 1993, 92). With this in mind, it is doubtful that CEBs will likely be ardently promoted as the primary means of competing with evangelical Protestants.

With this said, for any given level of parishioner service, the cost per parishioner to the Catholic Church is significantly higher than it is for Protestants. In other words, the Catholic Church must expend more resources to minister to the same amount of parishioners than their nearest rivals. For this reason, the Church competes with Protestants at a disadvantage and should have a more difficult time maintaining its membership base.

## The Cost of Competing and Church Political Strategy

How does the competitive disadvantage of the Catholic Church affect its political strategy? Given limited resources, Catholic officials must choose how to distribute those resources between greater pastoral activity at the grass roots and currying favor with the elite. These activities are not mutually exclusive. In fact, the two could be complementary if lobbying the government yields more resources to be devoted to pastoral activity than is expended on the actual lobbying effort. This is essentially the purpose of lobbying government—to obtain a sizable amount of resources that enables the lobbying organization to better serve its constituents. For a religious organization, this could include preferential tax treatment, getting government to pay the maintenance costs of certain churches deemed historic landmarks, and, most important, subsidies for religious education to build religious capital in a new generation of loyal Catholics. All these activities can help the Church serve its parishioners. However, in the short run, lobbying government requires shifting a significant amount of resources (the time and effort of key personnel) away from bolstering grassroots-level evangelization. Successful lobbying also requires a certain rapport with government. Activities that jeopardize this rapport, such as excessive criticism of government officials or efforts to reorganize the status quo of society, must necessarily be avoided.

It also should be noted that the Church also has greater incentive to cater to the needs of the economic elite than to those of the needy. Prior to the Church's declaration of a preferential option for the poor, the highest concentration of religious personnel was in upper-class neighborhoods. At the time, this made good economic sense (although it was questionable in terms of justice): Since the rich had more money to contribute to the Church, ministering to them would often lead to a net gain in resources. In other words, a preferential option for the rich paid handsomely. On the other hand, the poor had little money to give, which meant a net financial loss. With international humanitarian aid drying up in the late 1980s, it makes sense economically for the Church to try to fill its coffers with donations from the rich. In turn, this implies spending more time listening to and meeting the demands of this social class.

Devoting increased time and effort to lobbying the political and economic elite could potentially appear as a betrayal of pastoral action to pastoral agents working at the base of society. In addition to giving the appearance of betrayal, obtaining state subsidies means appealing to the elite on their terms. Organizations that are overly critical of the government, especially in public, are unlikely to win the favoritism of politicians they attack. For this reason, conciliatory gestures and actions are to be expected from Catholic officials seeking preferential treatment from the government.

The question naturally arises why this same dynamic did not occur under authoritarian governments. Under authoritarianism, the Church, in many but not all cases, publicly opposed military dictators. While this meant loss of access to state patronage (or where it didn't exist, the loss of *potential* access), the moral credibility the Church gained among certain segments of the population was far more valuable in retaining members than any assistance state funds could provide. To look at it another way, the accommodation needed to win state assistance would have made the Church appear as it always had—uncaring of the situation of the poor. Silence and accommodation were unlikely to be successful strategies for keeping (or winning back) parishioners. Because Pentecostalism was largely an indigenous phenomenon and Pentecostals did not threaten the state's national security as socialist organizations did, it was difficult for the Church to persuade the government to eliminate them. The Vatican policy of ecumenism promoted in the late 1950s also constrained the Church from asking the state to take punitive actions against Protestants.

In addition to the loss of credibility that accommodation with military regimes would have brought, an increase in pastoral resources during this period made state assistance less necessary, thereby providing the space that allowed the Church to denounce militarism. Where the Catholic Church was most active in promoting social justice, additional funds flowed in from abroad that allowed the Church to pursue pastoral activity with greater ease (Smith 1979). Furthermore, social activists from domestic secular organizations fleeing repression were sheltered and allowed to continue many of their activities on behalf of the poor under the protective umbrella of the Church. An influx of external resources made reliance upon state assistance less necessary and hence opposition to authoritarianism became a less costly option. By vocally opposing the military regime, the Catholic Church gained credibility for its new preferential option for the poor, while the resources that flowed in during this period were put to use in such a way that gave its commitment substantial credibility.

Despite its enhanced credibility among the sectors it defended, the Church still did not have sufficient personnel to adequately compete with the geometrically expanding Protestant population. Although it is impossible to measure, it is likely that in some cases the Church's pastoral outreach to the poor, and concomitant opposition to the military, slowed the number of defections to Protestantism.[11] As the poor became more involved in Church activity through CEBs and other organizations, or by directly benefiting from humanitarian assistance, they were more likely to gain a new respect for the Church and deepen their ties to Catholicism.

With the rebirth of civilian rule in Latin America, a new situation presented itself. International funds for humanitarian causes dried up. The social activists who sought the Church's protection to continue their work returned to their secular organizations. In essence, the Catholic Church confronted a substantial outflow of human and financial resources. This altered the opportunity costs of criticizing the government and raised the benefits of seeking state aid. Lacking the resources to engage in the pastoral activities that it did under authoritarianism, and with governments and secular organizations taking over control of many of those activities, the Catholic Church has naturally scaled back some of its pastoral activities. In the meantime, to compensate for these lost resources the Church hierarchy began appealing to the state for assistance. To many, this may appear as a conservative retrenchment demonstrating that the Church's commitment to the poor was never really lasting. However, it could be that the Church is still concerned about the poor, but now its ability to conduct the same activities it did under authoritarian rule has been severely curtailed.

In this light, the actions of Cardinal Obando y Bravo in Nicaragua can be partially explained as a response to increase Catholicism's competitive position against Protestants.[12] Similarly, it is understandable, given the less competitive position the Church is currently in in Chile, that Catholic officials are seeking greater access to the public schools and exemptions from certain church registration laws. The hierarchy also retains an interest in obtaining legislative support for Church teachings and policy preferences (e.g., laws regulating marriage, divorce, birth control, the religious persuasion of the country's president, etc.). To the extent these teachings differ from Protestant doctrine, such laws effectively endorse Catholicism as the favored cult.

There is, perhaps, a tragic irony to all of this. Just when the Catholic Church most needs government assistance to enable it to compete effectively with the expanding evangelical population, the government is less likely to provide this type of patronage. The reason for this lies in the fact that democratically elected politicians must compete for votes—both Catholic and Protestant. Explicit favoritism to the Catholic Church might cost a candidate a significant share of the vote, estimated to be over 20 percent in Chile, Brazil, and many parts of Central America (Johnstone 1986; Stoll 1990). Lest one discount the Protestant vote, the unexpected election of Alberto Fujimori in Peru should underscore its significance. The importance of Protestants as an electoral constituency has not been lost on political leaders in Chile either. Recently, then-president Patricio Aylwin and presidential candidate Eduardo Frei appeared at a Te Deum given exclusively by evangelical Protestants as a blessing for the current government (*El Mercurio* 1993c). Not to be outdone, the two other major candidates also attended.

## Conclusion

Unlike domestic business firms that can easily obtain government assistance when faced with international competitors, the Catholic Church will continue to find it harder to attract government aid than in the past. This difficulty arises for two reasons. First, because the Church's competitors are largely domestic, it is difficult for Catholics to argue for the exclusion of Protestants on the grounds that they constitute religious imperialism, the equivalent of a business corporation crying unfair competition. Second, and more important, Protestants are a valuable constituency to elected politicians. Any *national* politician or party that aggressively pursues pro-Catholic policy will likely face stiff opposition from Protestant sectors, thereby jeopardizing chances at electoral victory.

If a strategy of accommodation becomes less viable for the Catholic Church in the long run, the only option to remain competitive in the face of the rising tide of Protestantism is to restructure the way the Church services its parishioners in order to reduce its costs. Given the priest-centered nature of Catholicism, reducing the costs associated with recruiting and training religious personnel will remain of the utmost importance to the Church hierarchy. In order to increase the supply of priests and other personnel the Church must make changes that lower the cost of being a priest. Changes to be considered include permitting married clergy, shorter training time for seminarians, and increasing the discretionary decision-making power of the lower clergy. Even if these reforms should increase the interest young men have in undertaking a religious career, the ratio of priests to parishioners (who, if they are good Catholics, are being fruitful and multiplying) will undoubtedly remain low. To compensate for this the hierarchy should stress greater lay involvement, an increased role for women religious, and a stronger advocacy of base communities. As CEBs come very close to approximating Protestant forms of organization, they may be the most cost-effective way of tending the flock.[13]

However, these reforms impose a significant cost on the Catholic Church in terms of altering centuries-old doctrine and tradition. Bringing back into play the facts that there is a conservative pope in the Vatican and that providing lower-level clergy has often resulted in disastrous schisms within the Church only reminds us of how unlikely it is that these costs will be borne. Thus, the optimal short-term strategy remains accommodating the political and economic elite. Whether this becomes a long-term (and potentially ineffective) strategy will depend upon the willingness of Church officials to undertake major changes aimed at lowering the cost of servicing parishioners. The Latin American Catholic Church is at a critical juncture brought about by an increasingly pluralistic religious landscape; it either engages in radical reforms that democratize the Church from within and makes servicing parishioners more cost-effective, or it continues to lose what has always formed the foundation of the true Church—its parishioners.

# Postscript

A scholarly work should inspire as many questions as it answers, if not more. Because I am a *comparative* political scientist in the fullest sense of that tradition, my primary curiosity lies in how well the theory advanced here can explain phenomena in other parts of the world. These questions are critical since religion is becoming ever more salient in political life in almost every region of the globe. Contrary to secularization theory, issues of church and state will not simply fade into the background. While not proclaiming an expertise in countries outside those covered in detail above, I would like to share some preliminary thoughts on how an economic approach to church-state relations can be helpful in understanding religion and politics in regions beyond Latin America.

As presented in chapter 3, the economic theory of church-state relations is premised on the assumptions that states want to minimize the costs of rule while churches want to maximize parishioners as efficiently as possible. For the most part, these assumptions are transportable. It is hard to imagine a government not interested in bolstering citizen compliance through the most cost-effective means available. Staying in power demands at least minimal, if not constant, attention to this issue. The parishioner maximization assumption may be more difficult to sustain in other regions of the world. Religious traditions such as Judaism and Confucianism are not proselytizing to any significant extent; while they may welcome converts, they do not actively seek them. However, it is possible to relax the parishioner maximization assumption to assert that religious organizations want to retain members. Though spiritual leaders may avoid recruiting new followers, they certainly would raise concern over a mass exodus from their faith.

Based on these assumptions, and further observations about the nature of producing citizen compliance and religious goods, it was reasoned that church-state cooperation should be quite common. Religious officials can provide the state with the legitimation it needs to bolster citizen compliance while politicians can return the favor by providing religious organizations with the material resources and legal assistance they need to serve their members. Conflict between leaders of these two entities should be comparatively rare. Even in countries with a history of *legally* repressing religion (e.g., the Soviet Union, Mexico), modi vivendi are typically reached after a short period of intense conflict. Moreover, the economic model advanced here predicts that states will initiate hostility more frequently than churches. This suggests that the starting point for an examination of church-state relations should be church-state cooperation, a topic that unfortunately has been neglected in the literature. Nonetheless, exceptions to aforementioned tendencies (e.g., the Catholic Church in Poland during the 1980s) offer interesting cases from which to explore and modify the assumptions and underlying logic of this model. Models, by definition, are never perfect representations of the world.

A final, and more subtle, implication of the economic model proposed here is that religious market structure has an important impact on church political strategy. Religious leaders behave differently when they have a guaranteed monopoly from when they face active competition for the souls of the faithful. Monopoly buffers the clergy from taking into account the interests of their parishioners. Churches can then play high politics with reckless abandon, seeking alliances with highly unpopular governments. Under more competitive circumstances, religious leaders must consider their political decisions more carefully in order to avoid alienating large groups of important churchgoers. On top of this, leaders of formerly hegemonic religions can be expected to use the political arena to protect their spiritual territory from aggressive newcomers. Often, these tasks may be at odds with one another: pursuing legal advantages over competitors may mean supporting some slippery political characters. The decision on how to balance these demands is neither easy nor automatic, but that is exactly what makes an analysis of the situation so interesting for scholars.

The former Soviet Union and Eastern Europe offer one of the most promising areas of research into these issues. Within the space of a few years, countries in this region have experienced a dramatic shift in the structure of the religious economy, moving from a situation of strangulating regulation to one of laissez-faire competition. The growth of religious pluralism in this region is perhaps the fastest in recorded history. As expected, recent events in Russia and Eastern Europe bolster the predictions of the economic theory of church-state relations. In Russia, the Orthodox Church is on the defensive. Given its highly bureaucratic structure (similar to that of the Roman Catholic Church) and over seventy years of laws repressing the free exercise of religion, the Orthodox Church is at a competitive disadvantage against the myriad of decentralized Protestant churches that have been flooding the country. Consistent with the assumption of parishioner maximization, Orthodox clergy complain frequently about the presence of foreign religions. The Orthodox Archbishop of Kerch recently commented on this matter.

> The Russian nation has traditionally been Orthodox and considers itself as belonging to the Russian Orthodox Church. . . . The Russian people, spiritually weakened by the seventy-year-long onslaught of atheism, were unexpectedly confronted by numerous missionaries from abroad. . . . Chaos occurs when different preachers—not only Christian—come to Russia with a lot of money and hire stadiums, theaters, or similar facilities suitable for their purposes, and advertise themselves, inviting people to meetings, services, and talks. . . . Of course, it is not just atheists and agnostics who will come to these meetings but mostly traditional Orthodox believers who are not qualified to judge denominational matters. . . .[1] Such baptism into a new faith of people who were traditionally Orthodox believers, who had already been baptized but were theologically ignorant and did not understand what was happening to them, has often taken place. . . . The Russian Church is not against witnessing to Christ by these evangelists from abroad, but we would like them to keep contact with their Orthodox brothers and sisters, so as to witness to Christ among the Orthodox population by leaving these people within their own Orthodox Church, not be leading them through artificial means into a new denomination. . . . Please preach to us and help our people to know Christ—but do leave our people in their own native Orthodox Church! (Kuznetsov 1996, 10–11)

Despite professing an ecumenical spirit publicly, it is clear that the Orthodox Church is acting consistent with the assumption of parishioner maximization.

Ecumenical words to the contrary, the Orthodox clergy have lobbied extensively for legislation that excludes "alien" missionary activity (Stanley 1994). As one Methodist professor has noted,

> [L]eaders of the dominant church . . . ask [politicians] for the curtailment of all activities by groups not their own, because they consider the entire

population, without regard for how nonreligious it had become (in Russia about seventy-five percent of men and forty-five percent of women declare themselves nonreligious), as belonging to their church. . . . They plead that at a minimum such efforts should be suspended until they are sufficiently strengthened so as to be able to stand on their own after years of communist devastation of their cadres and church properties. (Mojzes 1996, 5)[2]

Given that religious pluralism is the natural state of affairs in unregulated markets and that less centralized denominations have a competitive advantage, it is unlikely that requests for state assistance will subside in the near future. Prominent Russian politicians have been more than happy to oblige the Orthodox Church's requests in exchange for support during elections and times of political instability (Open Media Research Institute 1996a, 1996b). In addition to antievangelical legislation, the Orthodox Church secured funds for the construction of a new cathedral in Moscow in exchange for supporting the mayor's bid for political office (*Financial Times* 1995).

Similar patterns of church-state relations have appeared in Eastern Europe. "In Romania, the government of Ion Iliescu announced that the new legislation on religion would be based on the precommunist laws of 1928. . . . [T]hese laws discriminated against neo-Protestant communities and treated the Orthodox Church with special favor" (Ramet 1992, 313). Laws proclaiming religious liberty have been implemented in most countries in Eastern Europe, including Bulgaria, Poland, and Hungary, but this has not prevented the traditionally dominant church in each country from asserting its privileged legal position (Powers 1996). A champion for freedom in the 1980s, the Polish Catholic Church recently threw its weight behind a series of laws that give it preferential access to public schools and other perquisites not enjoyed by other religious denominations (Chrypinski 1990, 139; Bock 1992, 98–99; Pasini 1994; Perlez 1995). However, similar to the situation in Latin America, as religious pluralism continues to grow concurrently with the emergence of functioning democracy, these traditional hegemonic churches will find it difficult to guarantee themselves a privileged status. When non-Catholic or non-Orthodox religions begin to represent a significant electoral constituency, religious regulations will begin to reflect a more equal legal status for these churches (Grzymala-Moszczynska 1996, 39). In the short term, religious liberty and related laws will continue to be contentious issues, and we can expect religion to be a significant political cleavage.

The Middle East and Asia offer more difficult tests for the economic theory of church-state relations advanced here. The structure of religious organizations in these societies—e.g., Buddhism, Confucianism, Islam—are significantly less centralized than denominations found in Christianity. Nonetheless, with a proper specification of the institutional constraints facing religious leaders in these traditions, it should be possible to draw insights into these cases. Unfortunately, few scholars have examined the institutional interrelations between "church" (broadly conceived) and state in these nations. Keshavarzian (1996) successfully applies an economic model similar to the one presented here to examine relations between Islamic ulama and the Iranian state in the mid-twentieth century. He found that "ulama-state" relations were cooperative when the Pahlavi regime was at its weakest in the 1920s. However, conflict occurred as state leaders began consolidating their power and found it beneficial to expropriate numerous tasks previously assigned to religious leaders, including both education and legal arbitration. The gains the state obtained in social control from such expropriations far outweighed the legitimating support they received from Islamic clerics. Moustafa (1996) finds in Egypt that the state sought to control a center of religious learning (al-Azhar) and other religious organizations so as to capture their influence over Egyptian society. In line with predictions about the effects of religious monopoly, these religious organizations lost credibility among the general population, which could only be reclaimed by distancing themselves from the state.

Another profitable application of economic theories to the study of religion and politics involves missionary work in Asia and Africa. How do relative newcomers to the religious landscape approach the political arena in ways that permit them greater freedom of access and movement? Religious regulation has been shown in other contexts to greatly affect the growth of religious denominations (Chaves and Cann 1992; Gill 1995). Understanding what legal, political, and economic variables affect the work of churches will go a long way in explaining why certain regions of the world appear more religious than others. Indeed, exploring the question of religious regulation will surely reveal that "secularization" is not so much a function of the loss of religious *belief* in a society as of the decline in physical participation in religious services due to laws inhibiting the freedom to worship as one chooses.

Overall, an economic theory of church-state relations offers great potential to enhance our knowledge of the interaction of religion and politics.

The approach is still new and many of its assumptions and implications (both explicit and implicit) need to be explored further. Having made a small contribution to this endeavor, I hope that other scholars accept my invitation to discover both the possibilities and limitations of this theoretical model.

# Appendix: Rationality and Religion

*It is not clear that [rational choice] is the best way of theorizing about either utopian or religious groups. . . . Where nonrational or irrational behavior is the basis for a lobby, it would perhaps be better to turn to psychology or social psychology than to economics for a relevant theory.*

Mancur Olson, *The Logic of Collective Action*

Is Olson right? Are rational choice models of human behavior inappropriate for examining the social and political behavior of religious groups and individuals? It is generally taken as given that religious belief is an inherently non-rational form of knowledge; spiritual knowledge relies on faith that something is true rather than cost-benefit calculation, empirical verification, and information updating—the hallmarks of rational decision making. Scholars frequently have made the simple assumption that anyone in a religious context cannot be acting according to the principles of rationality.[1] Consequently, discussion of values, norms, and ethical judgments permeates the research done on religious behavior and institutions. However, over the past decade there has been an increasing interest in studying religious behavior from a rational choice perspective, due largely to the pioneering works of Rod Stark, Larry Iannaccone, and Roger Finke. This research strongly suggests that religious behavior is subject to the principles of economic optimization.

Not surprisingly, the "religious economy" literature, as it has become known, has received a substantial degree of criticism. Chaves (1995) accuses practitioners of the approach of employing weak assumptions and exaggerating the claims of rational choice. Robertson claims that those employing "economic imagery" (1992, 147) to study religion must rely inevitably on subjective psychological assertions and therefore that the approach adds little to previous understanding of religious behavior. In a recent edited work,

Satya Pattnayak argues rational choice theory is ethnocentric and hence inapplicable to the study of Latin America. He claims that

> all the authors [in this volume] categorically reject the rational-actor model of individual behavior. This model . . . has been primarily derived from the experiences of advanced capitalist societies. Since they are not rooted in the specific experiences of the Christian communities of Latin America, it is no surprise that the model seems irrelevant. The community spirit—irrational as it seems—still thrives. (1995, 7)

Scholars like Pattnayak and his collaborators prefer an approach that explains behavior as a function of subjective worldviews, norms, and values. Levine shares this critique.

> A positivist approach brings the observer close to the position of the "village atheist" to the extent that it predisposes one to concentrate on the externals of behavior, fitting these into the observer's own categories of analysis with little or no attention to the meaning or significance of action to those involved. . . . Catholic elites (most notably bishops) simply do not consider issues in strictly social or political terms. Instead, their answers are couched in religious concepts and metaphors, which flow from their understanding of the requirements of religious faith, their view of the Church as an institution, and their conclusions about its proper relation to society at large. (1981, 9–13)

Similarly, Mainwaring contends the "Church's actions reflect value choices" (1986, 5), not instrumental, cost-benefit calculation.

To a large extent, these critiques are based on a misunderstanding of rational choice theory.[2] While rational choice does profess to be a unifying theory of human behavior (Iannaccone 1995a, 86), it has its limitations like all other theoretical perspectives. However, to discard this approach wholesale due to its limitations would eliminate a theoretical tool that has proven highly valuable in explaining many aspects of religious behavior. The goal of this appendix is to introduce rational choice theory for those not familiar with this approach. I briefly cover the basic assumptions of rational choice,[3] reveal some of its limitations,[4] and discuss its applicability to the study of religion.[5]

## Rational Choice: A Brief Primer

Rational choice is a means-based theory; it explains how people make choices to obtain their various objectives in the most efficient, or optimal, manner. The choice process can be broken down into three elements—rational calculation, individual preferences, and exogenous constraints.

choice $= f$(rational calculation, preferences, exogenous constraints)

Here, preferences and rationality are taken as given and assumed to be constant. Analysis of human behavior therefore focuses on environmental constraints that affect the costs and benefits associated with various actions. Exogenous constraints could be anything from technological innovation to the strategic action of other individuals. Rational choice further assumes that this model of choice applies to all human beings and that individuals are the primary unit of analysis. Examination of these various components will reveal more about the power and limitations of the approach.

### Preferences

Rational choice is a theory of means. It has little to say about the content of individual preferences or how preferences are formed. At a very basic level, actors are presumed to desire more of a good than less, ceteris paribus. The ceteris paribus clause is crucial here. If an individual were offered a job with a higher salary but less free time, we could predetermine what that individual's choice would be only if we knew their personal utility functions for income and leisure. This assumption is also part and parcel of utility maximization; people will try to get the most benefit net of cost. If an individual could get more of a good at no cost, there is still an opportunity to maximize their utility. Beyond this, rational choice contains no theory of why people have certain preferences. It is up to the scholar to assume a set of preferences for actors based upon specific knowledge of the actor. In many instances, this is fairly easy to do. We can assume safely that many politicians have a strong preference for remaining in office, because if they were not in office they could not obtain any other of their goals (Mayhew 1974). Leaders of various organizations can be assumed to value the continued strength or growth of their institution. In this study, I assert that the main objective of Catholic bishops is to maximize parishioners since their faith demands that all souls be redeemed. As with any assumption, those about preferences must be carefully justified.

Another condition that rational choice theory imposes on preferences is that they remain stable over time (Stigler and Becker 1977; Iannaccone 1995a, 77), or at least over the period of decision making. This condition is more controversial, but as Geddes explains,

[D]iscussions of the implausibility of unchanging preferences arise from a

confusion between preferences as used in the rational choice idiom—
what I have called "goals" here—and second-order, or strategic, preferences. The first-order preferences, or goals, commonly used in rational
choice arguments are extremely simple and, in fact, are relatively stable
(e.g., people prefer more to less material goods, politicians prefer to continue their careers). Second-order preferences are . . . choices of strategies
for achieving first-order preferences. Politicians' policy preferences (in
everyday language) may alter radically in response to changed circumstances. In the rational choice idiom, however, those everyday-language
preferences are not referred to as "preferences," but instead as "strategies" for achieving actors' goals. (1995, 86)

It may be too restrictive to say that first-order preferences are immune to
change. However, explaining every change in behavior as a shift in preferences raises the age-old social science problem of truly knowing what is hap-
pening in people's minds. It also can lead to tautologous conclusions; every
new choice/action can be explained as a change in preference for that activity.[6] A far better method of explaining social change would be first to assume
stable preferences and see if altered environmental circumstances yielded the
hypothesized behavior. Should such attempts fail, it would be appropriate
*then* to divert attention to explanation based on changing preferences.

On a related subject, rational choice has been criticized (and rightly so)
for ignoring the role of culture—norms, values, tastes, and shared beliefs.
The main alternative to rational choice explanation is to explain behavior as
a function of values, tastes, norms, and ideology. Again, rational choice answers by holding these things constant. Norms and ideology are sometimes
incorporated into rational choice explanations as a means to lower information and transaction costs (e.g., North 1981, 45–58).

With respect to religious studies, it should be noted that rational choice
does not try to explain the content of religious doctrine unless such beliefs are
instrumental in the pursuit of other goals. Consider the reasoning behind
Pascal's wager (Durkin and Greeley 1991). It states that if a person desires to
live forever, it may be rational to believe in God since not believing in a deity
would imply that life ends at death. The belief in God is a means to another
end, eternal life. Nonetheless, rational choice does not speak to the question
of why someone desires eternal life. Hull (1989) shows how the Catholic
doctrines of purgatory and hell evolved to bolster the enforcement of property rights and cooperative behavior among feudal lords during a time when
central political authority was weak and labor scarce.

## Rationality Assumptions

The concept of rationality rests on the assumption that individuals are utility maximizers. In any given situation, people will chose an action that provides them with the most benefits relative to costs. In the (common) event that the outcome of a given action is unknown (e.g., due to limited information), people will maximize their expected utility based upon the logic of probability calculus (Tsebelis 1990, 26–31). For example, my decision to carry an umbrella is based not only upon costs of carrying it and the benefit derived from staying dry in a rainstorm, but also on the probability that it will rain. A further assumption required for rational calculation is that an individual's preferences be transitive. That is, if a person prefers X to Y and Y to Z, she must therefore prefer X to Z.[7] This is not an assumption about preferences per se, but rather an assumption about preferences in relation to the utility maximization requirement. Failing transitivity, preferences become cyclical and choice essentially becomes random, not the most ideal situation under which to maximize utility.[8]

These rationality assumptions have come under fire for being unrealistic. It is argued that people simply do not have the cognitive capacity to make the necessary calculations required for utility maximization. Moreover, information about the probability of events occurring is often so severely limited that maximizing expected utility becomes little more than a craps shoot. Furthermore, Tversky (1969) and Tversky and Kahneman (1981) have demonstrated that the transitivity requirement can be violated when frames of reference shift.

Rational choice theorists typically respond to these critiques in several ways. First, they rely upon "learning curve" and "evolutionary" models. If similar choices are repeated over time, people will learn from past mistakes and compensate accordingly. Alternatively, suboptimal strategies will be eliminated by simple natural selection. For example, Geddes observes that "firm managers do not actually think about profits when they make most decisions. Nevertheless, existing firms behave as though they were profit-maximizers because competition drives out of business those that deviate too far from profit-maximizing behavior" (1995, 89). Second, and more important, rationality assumptions become more realistic as information improves and choices become more salient. When there is a lot on the line, individuals are more careful to gather information and think through the costs and benefits associated with various strategies. Therefore,

[t]he appropriate domain of rational choice arguments thus includes situ-

ations in which outcomes are very important to actors, since that impels gathering knowledge; situations in which the rules governing interactions are clear and precise; and situations that occur repeatedly so that actors can learn, or efficient strategies can evolve even in the absence of conscious learning. Where choices have few consequences (e.g., "cheap talk," such as in survey responses) or little effect on overall outcomes . . . we should expect scant investment in information gathering, and rational choice arguments may not predict actor behavior very well. (Geddes 1995, 89–90)

Keeping this in mind, rational choice is highly applicable to the study of church-state relations. Such relations typically involve highly informed individuals (e.g., bishops, presidents, legislators) engaged in repeated interactions (thereby facilitating learning) playing for high stakes (e.g., access to public schools, tax policy). The fact that the stakes are typically high provides an incentive for all relevant actors to stay well informed. It may be argued that the clergy process information through theological filters, thereby making ideology a critical variable. However, other actors in the political arena rarely rely upon the same filters. Thus, if the clergy want to successfully interact with these individuals, they must calculate their strategies in terms that politicians can understand and respond to. Kalyvas (1996b) demonstrates precisely this point when he shows that shifts in the Vatican's worldview had little impact on episcopal strategy in Belgium during the mid- to late 1800s.

Even under conditions of low salience and poor information—e.g., allocating household resources to worship (see below)—people do behave as if the rationality assumptions are true. Iannaccone (1990, 1995b) offers the most comprehensive and tested research of religious behavior at the individual and household level. His theory relies upon the concept of religious capital wherein religion is not only a consumption good, but individual consumers are also part of the production of religion via their participation at services, practicing prayers, reading the Torah, etc. Religious capital represents all the skills, experiences, and goods that a religious consumer accumulates that helps her both enjoy religiosity more and produce it more efficiently. Iannaccone correctly predicts, based on various data sources, that those lacking large amounts of religious capital are the most likely to convert to other denominations. Those who have spent years learning the tenets of one particular faith will not want to give up their investment, especially considering that such an investment brings increasing returns. This explains why denominational switching is most common among the young and those whose parents did not regularly attend religious services. Not surprisingly, those who do switch denominations will typically choose faiths that most resemble their previous faith.

Life cycle patterns of religious participation are also confirmed by Iannaccone's model: Time and money are valuable commodities that households must allocate. Given that midlife years tend to be the busiest period and one of highest income for individuals, time will be relatively more precious than money. Such individuals will be expected to favor increased financial contributions relative to time spent on religious activities. This hypothesis predicts that older and younger people will engage in more time-intensive participation. Iannaccone's results convincingly show that rationality can apply in scenarios where the rationality assumptions are least likely to hold (see also Iannaccone 1994, 1992). Though many will disagree, the best test of a hypothesis is not the realism of its assumptions, but its ability to predict actual behavior (Friedman 1953).

## Exogenous Constraints

If preferences and rationality are taken as given and held constant, then the primary focus of explaining variations in behavior over either time or space becomes the constraints on actors' behavior. Such constraints—be they budgets, resource endowments, position in the world economy, access to information, or the strategic action of other individuals—alter the relative costs of the strategies (i.e., means) available to individuals. Changes in these constraints affect changes in behavior. These environmental conditions are typically specific to the context of the problem being examined. Contrary to the critique that rational choice is insensitive to historical context, it is precisely the specification of the context that makes most rational choice explanations interesting (Geddes 1995, 90–91).[9]

## Methodological Individualism

Rational choice views the individual as the primary unit of analysis; all social behavior begins with the individual, thus any theory purporting to explain social phenomena requires a model of individual behavior. Structures and systems possess no independent causal weight and are conceived best as behavioral constraints (Cohen 1994, 43). While it is possible to use groups as the unit of analysis (e.g., firms, militaries, churches), the researcher must have ample justification for considering those aggregations as unitary actors since any group will experience the pull of individual interests that makes collective action difficult (Olson 1965); positing groups as individual actors should be viewed as a simplifying assumption, not as a statement of fact. Rare are the instances where some level of internal group tension is not present.

## Universality

Finally, the above assumptions of rationality apply to all persons across time and space. In other words, rationality is not culture bound. This is in direct contrast to claims that rational choice is ethnocentric, biased in favor of Western European thought (e.g., see the earlier comment by Pattnayak). Claims of ethnocentrism are based on the mistaken belief that rational choice is exclusively concerned with the maximization of material self-interest and all forms of cooperation are ruled out.[10] To be ethnocentric, all people in a given, non-Western culture would have to either not want to improve their well-being, be it material or nonmaterial or make choices in a random fashion or without recourse to learning. In many respects, arguing that rational choice does not apply to certain cultures appears the more "politically incorrect" route. Rational choice theory has been applied successfully to explain phenomena in such non-European cultures such as Latin America (Ames 1987; Cohen 1994), Africa (Bates 1981), and Asia (Popkin 1979). Given that this theoretical perspective has demonstrated applicability across world cultures, it would seem reasonable to expect that it also applies across religious traditions. While most research using rational choice to explain religious phenomena has focused on the United States and Europe, some scholars are now successfully applying it outside these areas (Miller 1995; Keshavarzian 1996; Moustafa 1996).

## *Conclusion*

Rational choice is a theoretical perspective that explains human behavior as a function of the pursuit of *interests*. These interests are assumed to be fixed over a given period of time, and exogenous constraints (which condition relative costs and benefits) chiefly determine an individual's actions. Religion, on the other hand, operates in the realm of ideas—norms, values, ideology, and theology—something that rational choice has little to say about (except, perhaps, how given norms and ideologies simplify information and transaction costs). Thus, it is not surprising that scholars of religion and religious institutions have ignored rational choice as a method of analysis.

Using economics to understand religion is definitely a challenging endeavor, but one that offers unique and important insights into human behavior. Stathis Kalyvas summarized this theoretical enterprise best:

> Because of their ideological bias, religious movements are an ideal testing ground for determining if the strategic pursuit of interests is a better predictor of political action that ideology. Furthermore, showing that actors who place an extreme emphasis on doctrine and ideology act strategically on the basis of cost-benefit calculations, even when this means sacrificing their core principles, allows for the exploration of the conditions and the specification of mechanisms through which principles are subverted by "pragmatism." (1996b, 5–6)

If rational choice can predict the behavior of religious actors accurately, this provides strong evidence for a theory that emphasizes the primacy of interests over ideas.

While it is true that religiously motivated individuals have distinct sets of ideas about the world, they also exist in a world of scarcity and must necessarily make choices that optimize a limited set of resources, including time, money, and energy. To the extent that religious individuals—be they parishioners or priests—have a fixed set of objectives and are interested in improving their life situation, much of their behavior can be explained by rational choice theory. Ample justification exists to believe such individuals possess stable goals: Adherents seem to continuously desire spiritual salvation, answers to tough questions, and the fellowship of other members of the congregation; and clergy want to reach as many parishioners as possible while gathering sufficient material resources to meet this goal. Moreover, many religious situations involve highly salient issues with well-informed individuals who engage in repeated actions with one another. These situations only make the use of an economic approach more appropriate. In the case of Latin American episcopacies deciding whether or not to denounce a military regime—with the consequences potentially being the loss of parishioners, government resources, or even the lives of clergy—it seems reasonable to expect that bishops are carefully considering the costs and benefits of their actions.

Rational choice does have its analytical limitations, many of which could be improved by the adoption of insights from cognitive psychology, cultural perspectives, or complexity theory. Ideas do matter, especially in determining how people process information or set their initial preferences. However, the limitations of an economic approach should not exclude it from the arsenal of theoretical tools available to scholars. (Cultural and psychological theories are equally, if not more, limited in their ability to generate testable hypotheses and accurately predict social phenomena.) All said, rational choice offers a powerful tool for understanding behavior wherever religious actors face conditions of scarcity and are making decisions meant to improve their social welfare.

# Notes

## One

1. Obviously, this is not true for all clergy. Many become involved closely with governmental affairs and their image as independent and ethical arbitrators of political life suffers accordingly, especially if they are associated with unpopular politicians or policies. Why religious leaders link themselves to unpopular governments is a major theme of this book and receives greater attention in subsequent chapters.

2. For example, see Wallace 1966 and Berger 1967.

3. Scholarly attempts to rethink, revise, or replace the secularization thesis are numerous. See Hadden 1987 and Warner 1993 for excellent summaries of these efforts. Also noteworthy on this front are works by Stark and Bainbridge (1985, 1987); Finke (1992); Finke and Stark (1992); and Stark and McCann (1993). An edited volume by Steve Bruce (1992) offers a number of opposing positions on the utility of the secularization concept. From another perspective, Cox (1984, 1990) argues that religiosity need not be in conflict with secularization, while Casanova (1994) contends that certain axioms and hypotheses advanced by traditional secularization theorists still hold true even though other assumptions and predictions need to be revised. In this light, Casanova (1994) offers a unique way of revising a mainstay of sociological analysis without entirely abandoning the notion of "secularization" altogether.

4. See Casanova 1994 and Kepel 1994 for references to the renewed interest in religion and politics on the global level. In studies of Latin America, for example, only a handful of serious works existed on the subject of church-state relations prior to 1970. See Holleran 1949, Kennedy 1958, Mecham 1966, Willems 1967, and Vallier 1970 for the most important early contributions. Of these authors, Vallier was the only one who offered a consciously theoretical analysis. Since Vallier's landmark contribution, the field of Latin American religion and politics has burgeoned.

5. Episcopal pressure for democratization is also important for the Catholic Church as an organization per se. Given that the Catholic Church is a rigidly hier-

archical institution, advocacy of democratic norms potentially can lead to conflict over the control of religious authority between the upper and lower echelons of the institution. Indeed, the efforts of Pope John Paul II to contain liberation theology is as much about the proper boundaries of dissent within the Church as it is about the actual theological message. This is no small issue for the Church. Remember, at its root, the Protestant Reformation represented the liberalization of Catholicism via the freedom of individuals to dissent from hierarchical authority.

6. As discussed in chapter 4, two of the anomalous cases for the thesis advanced here—Guatemala and Ecuador—can be explained by moving down a level of abstraction and examining the internal dynamics of the episcopacy.

7. Marxist studies provide a good example of this. Classical Marxism, with class as its primary unit of analysis, could not account for relative lack of revolutionary worker organizations. To help explain this failing, numerous Marxist scholars began looking at the internal dynamics of class formation and general problems of collective action.

8. In strict statistical terms, a sample size of twelve cases would hardly qualify as a "large $n$" study. However, in the field of comparative politics, where the unit of analysis often is an entire country, examining more than a small handful of cases represents a substantial undertaking. Comparative politics remains dominated by the single-case study. When placed in this perspective, "$n = 12$" is large.

9. Refer to chapter 4 for a detailed description of these hypotheses and measures.

### Two

1. Although the term *separation* is often used by both scholars and historical actors when discussing the reduction of the Church's political privileges, the situation was never as simple as this word implies. Politicians advocating separation often hid a strong desire to exercise extensive control over the Church. Likewise, Church leaders who urged the clergy to divorce themselves from politics were frequently guilty of meddling in affairs of the state.

2. Dussel defines *Hispanic Christendom* as "the tendency to unify indissolubly the aims and purposes of the state and of the Church. This tendency can be traced from the Constantinian period through the Visigoths and the Pontifical States. . . . The absolutism of Henry VIII of England and of some of the Danish monarchs was an expression of the same philosophy but was obviously taken to an extreme" (1981, 38). This overstates the actual situation. Relations were not perfectly harmonious during this period. Despite the tendency for Church and state to align their goals with one another, both entities possessed distinct institutional interests. These autonomous interests led to conflict at times, but for the most part Church and state found cooperation the best policy to achieve their respective goals.

3. While the Church in Spain controlled its own tithing procedures, "in America these revenues went to the crown and the Church was . . . supported by royal

appropriations and regular endowments" (Mecham 1966, 15). For a detailed discussion of the *patronato*, see Mecham 1966, 3–37, and Prien 1985, 119–23.

4. "Religious" refers to the priests of the various religious orders (e.g., Jesuits, Dominicans) that owe their allegiance directly to the Vatican. Although they may participate in diocesan activities (and are eligible to become bishops), they are not under the direct control of the diocese's leadership. "Secular" (or diocesan) priests, on the other hand, report directly to the local bishop.

5. Original citation attributed to José Luis Romero, *A History of Argentine Political Thought,* translated by Thomas F. McGann. Stanford: Stanford University Press, 1963, p. 33.

6. Although Enlightenment thought may not have been as prominent in Iberian societies as it was in France or the United States, several incidents gave the appearance that liberalism was rapidly rising in colonial America. Liberal harbingers "surfaced in cities as far apart as Bogotá (New Granada), where Antonio Nariño produced his Spanish translation of the *Declaration of the Rights of Man*, Santiago (Chile), where a 'French conspiracy' was discovered in 1790, [and] Buenos Aires, where French activists appear to have inspired an abortive slave revolt with republican overtones" (Halperín Donghi 1993, 44). These activities were centered primarily in urban areas, the same location as episcopal leaders. That the First Estate did not fare well during the French Revolution only exacerbated the episcopacy's fear of liberalism.

7. This was primarily true of the secular (diocesan) priests. Religious-order clerics generally benefited financially from the colonial system and thus had pro-royalist sentiments (Goodpasture 1989, 139–40).

8. Liberators such as Simón Bolívar and José de San Martín never publicly threatened the Church's status (Mecham 1966, 45, 90). In fact, they saw the Church as a valuable cultural force for unification. As noted earlier, however, the images of the French Revolution were all too vivid in the minds of Church leaders, who feared anyone tampering with the status quo.

9. I owe this insight to Ellis Goldberg, who brought it to my attention in the context of the Middle East.

10. Pius IX promulgated the doctrine of papal infallibility during the first Vatican Council (1869). He also was responsible for the creation of the Colegio Pio Latino-Americano (1859), where all subsequent Latin American bishops would be trained. This schooling provided for a common ideological front against liberalism and other anti-Catholic forces (e.g., Masonry) in the region.

11. The *patronato nacional* lingered for many decades, but the national governments would supply a list of names (usually three) from which the pontiff could select. More often than not, the government merely rubber-stamped the decision made by the pope or his delegates. Such a procedure was much less intrusive than the *patronato real*, wherein the crown (or viceroy) mandated the choice of one candidate.

12. Despite the legal "liberation" of the Church from the state, the former

continued to enjoy substantial support from the latter and retained significant advantages over competing denominations. A classic example is the 1853 Argentine constitution that no longer declared Catholicism the official state religion, but which nonetheless provided for the "support" of the Catholic Church (Kennedy 1958, 14–15).

13. Prior to the resolution of the religious question in the late 1800s, bishops commonly held important government posts and priests would often serve as legislators. This practice generally ended under Liberal governments.

14. The Catholic Church is sometimes given credit for the rise of Christian Democratic parties in places such as Venezuela, Chile, and El Salvador. To some degree this is correct. Church teachings certainly influenced the founders of these parties. Many of them started as leaders in Catholic youth organizations. However, Christian Democracy was principally a lay movement that received little or no official organizational support from the Church hierarchy. True, the bishops sometimes publicly endorsed the objectives of the Christian Democrats, but Vatican prohibitions on direct political involvement in partisan politics limited the support they could give. See Fleet 1985 for a discussion of the Chilean Christian Democrats. Kalyvas (1995, 1996a) outlines how direct involvement in the formation and guidance of political parties in Europe was the least preferred strategy of Church elites; his results bear important insights for the Latin American case.

15. Chile, with its reasonably long history of competitive electoral politics prior to 1973, offers the quintessential example of the Church under democracy at this time. During the 1930s and 1940s, the Church actively supported the Conservative Party. After the Vatican chastised the Chilean hierarchy for its open support of Conservative candidates, the bishops became more circumspect in their endorsements. Slowly, however, as the mood of the electorate shifted leftward, the episcopacy cautiously embraced the reformist Christian Democrats with the hope of forestalling a socialist victory. When Salvador Allende won the presidency in 1970 (contrary to the desire of most bishops), the episcopal conference established cordial relations with his Popular Unity government. Having distanced themselves somewhat from direct involvement in the election, it was possible to do this without appearing opportunistic or hypocritical. See chapter 5 for more on the Chilean case.

16. See chapter 4 for a discussion of Acción Católica.

17. Mainwaring and Wilde describe the progressive Church as having "an emphasis on the small, local religious groups known as ecclesial base communities (CEBs), an adherence to liberation theology, and the belief that the Church must assume a political responsibility to promote social justice" (1989, 5). While acknowledging the importance of the first and third conditions, I disagree on the second. Many bishops and clergy have shown progressive attitudes toward social justice without resorting to the more radical elements of liberation theology for guidance. Many progressive Catholics reject the emphasis liberation theologians place on class struggle as both an analytical tool and means to achieving social justice.

18. Scholarly studies of these two countries are numerous. For the most detailed accounts of the Brazilian Church consult Bruneau 1974 and 1982, Della Cava 1976, Mainwaring 1986, and Hewitt 1991. On Chile, see Smith 1982, Mella 1987, and Stewart-Gambino 1992.

19. The first general conference was held in Rio de Janeiro in 1955.

20. Of all the activities undertaken by progressive Catholics, none have drawn more attention than CEBs. Discussion of these groups can be found throughout the literature. For particularly good analyses of these groups, see Bruneau 1980a and 1980b; Hewitt 1986, 1988, 1989, 1990, and 1991; Adriance 1991; Van Vugt 1991; and Burdick 1993.

21. Because of the widely varying definitions of what constitutes a CEB, it is nearly impossible to estimate with any certainty the number of CEBs in Latin America. Estimates of the number of CEBs operating in Brazil in the late 1970s and early 1980s vary between 40,000 and 150,000. For discussion of the methodological problems surrounding data on CEBs see Hewitt 1991, 9–10.

22. As with the progressive Church in general, analysis of liberation theology spawned innumerable scholarly tomes. The most essential text remains Gutiérrez's *A Theology of Liberation* (1973; originally published in Spanish in 1971), which gave the movement its name. Accessible introductions to the topic include Berryman 1987, Hennelly 1990, and Sigmund 1990. Novak 1986 offers a critique of liberation theology from a neoliberal perspective.

23. Among the well-known dependency theorists cited throughout Gutiérrez 1973 are Fernando Henrique Cardoso, Theotonio Dos Santos, André Gunder Frank, and Osvaldo Sunkel.

24. To illustrate this point, consider a simplified example. Suppose a scholar wishes to study social revolutions and chooses the case of Nicaragua. That person will find poverty, repression, and a weakened state structure, and could logically conclude that all three of these factors contributed to the revolution. However, when other cases are examined, including ones where revolutions occurred and did not occur (e.g., Cuba, El Salvador, Honduras, Paraguay), the researcher may consider that several of these variables were less important in predicting a revolutionary outcome.

25. For an excellent example of how a limited number of cases can be segmented to increase sample size see Levine 1992.

26. For a discussion of the numerous biblical passages that can be translated as advocating a preferential option for the poor see Gutiérrez 1973.

27. Mainwaring includes a number of other factors in his analysis of religious change in Brazil. However, this raises the specification problem discussed above—with only one case and a multitude of explanatory variables, it is difficult to determine which one is most important.

## Three

1. For more rigorous statistical tests of these hypotheses see chapter 4.

2. Explanations of this nature (demand-side) are akin to deprivation theories

of revolution that assert collective dissent is caused by worsening living conditions. While unhappiness is surely a necessary cause of revolution, Lichbach (1995) shows that it is not sufficient. One must consider how general dissatisfaction is transformed effectively into organized rebellion, the "supply side" of revolution.

3. Consider the phenomenon of "folk Catholicism," a popular form of religiosity typically found in areas that receive only sporadic visits from Catholic priests. Even where there is no official, priest-led supply of religious services, consumers would organize their own religious celebrations, usually centered around the Virgin Mary or various Catholic saints. Although superficially Catholic, "folk Catholicism" frequently deviates from the official teachings of the institutional Church. Nonetheless, it does indicate a relatively high demand for religious services independent of the low supply. When Catholic priests or Protestant missionaries come into these areas, practitioners of "folk Catholicism" generally defer to the religious teachings of the pastor.

4. See chapter 7 for discussion of the Catholic Church's political strategy under democracy.

5. Gill 1995 provides a detailed list of legal advantages recently obtained by the Mexican Catholic Church. Serbin 1995 reveals a similar set of financial privileges enjoyed by the Brazilian Church. This partial list implies that religious organizations in the United States are not fully disestablished in that they receive preferential tax treatment relative to other private organizations. What is unusual about the United States, though, is that (almost) all religious denominations are treated equally in these ways. In many cases, and historically in Latin America, religious establishment favors one religion over others.

6. This assumes that no coercion is involved in the bargain. It is possible to consider coercion as a cost to be avoided by entering the bargain. Such an approach, however, devolves rapidly into tautology as every human action can then be conceptualized as mutually beneficial. For example, slavery could be considered mutually beneficial because the slave avoided being killed. With regard to colonial Latin America, the negotiation of *el patronato real* between Spain and the Vatican involved no coercion. In fact, bargaining power was relatively equal (Mecham 1966, 12–20), although once the bargain was struck power shifted in favor of the monarch.

7. Levi argues that the amount of revenue a government can extract from society is determined, in part, by the transaction costs of tax collection (1988, 23–32). Lowering transaction costs includes establishing a relatively obedient population, either via ideological or quasi-voluntary compliance (Levi 1988, 50–67).

8. Taylor uses the terms "threats" (coercion) and "offers" (patronage). He adds a further category called "throffers" that "takes the form of promising a reward if some course of action is chosen and threatening a penalty if it is not" (1982, 12). Taylor contends that "threats" and "offers" both contain elements of coercion, although he concludes a distinction still exists (13–18). Coercion and patronage will be considered here in their common usage as negative and positive inducements respectively.

9. The most obvious manifestation of this investment in trustworthiness is the insistence that communications (e.g., confession of sins) between clergy and parishioners remain confidential. Living a morally upright and austere lifestyle also enhances the trustworthiness of clergy who preach that spiritualism is more important than materialism.

10. To my knowledge, no one has ever tested whether religious endorsements of politicians yield greater support for those politicians. Nonetheless, a number of stylized facts support such a claim. For instance, religiosity tends to be one of the most salient variables in predicting voting behavior even after controlling for other relevant variables (e.g., socioeconomic status, education, gender). In the United States, the Christian Coalition has demonstrated a remarkable ability to rally evangelical Christians around Republican candidates. Additionally, religious leaders have shown considerable ability to motivate followers into collective action against regimes (Stark and Bainbridge 1985, 506–30). It is not much of an analytical leap to expect that religious leaders can likewise create compliance. In any event, even if the ability of religious leaders to create ideological or quasi-voluntary compliance is weak, *politicians act as if such legitimation matters* and actively seek out the endorsement of religious officials. That is sufficient to create cooperative relations between church and state.

11. A question arises as to why all political regimes do not coopt religious authority for their purposes. Where religious authority is legitimating an enemy regime, it makes little sense to use that religion for legitimation purposes unless one can make a valid claim that the religion's clergy are poor representatives of the faith, a strategy Liberals tried in nineteenth-century Latin America. Lacking the opportunity for religious legitimation, political leaders will have to construct or rely upon alternative secular ideologies or religious traditions. The resulting hypothesis is that where a state is legitimated by religious authority, political oppositions will have to create strong secular ideologies to provoke collective action or rely upon dissident religious movements. A similar hypothesis, and anecdotal evidence, is advanced by Stark and Bainbridge 1985, 506–30.

12. In his study of European confessional parties, Kalyvas assumes that churches seek to maximize social influence rather than parishioners (1996a, 35). This assumption should be viewed as consistent with, rather than in contrast to, the assumption of parishioner maximization. After all, influence, whether social or political, helps a church gain resources necessary for gaining and holding on to members. Social influence also implies a degree of charisma and credibility that further bolsters the church's proselytism.

13. The biggest challenge to the parishioner maximization assumption with regard to Christianity is the ecumenical movement. However, even though various Christian denominations cooperate in a variety of religious and public policy dimensions (e.g., promoting Christian values, lobbying against racial discrimination), their respective leaders do not actively encourage their members to defect to other churches. It would be difficult to find a Presbyterian minister counseling someone to become Baptist. For such ecumenical denominations, the "minimiza-

tion of parishioner losses" might be a more appropriate assumption, although I suspect that if the opportunity and resources presented themselves, ecumenical-leaning clergy would want an entire town population to attend *their* Sunday services.

14. A tertiary assumption about the preferences of religious organizations is institutional autonomy. All things being equal, churches will prefer more independence from the state to less (Anderson et al. 1992, 352–53). However, as the previous chapter revealed, the Catholic Church willingly yielded institutional autonomy in exchange for state protection and subsidization.

15. Ekelund, Hébert, and Tollison 1989, Hull 1989, and Anderson et al. 1992 focus on historical periods prior to the development of modern states in Europe. The Catholic Church enjoyed a substantial advantage over all other social organizations in revenue extraction during this period (c. 1000–1300). However, as modern states developed greater organizational and coercive power this comparative advantage shifted towards secular authorities.

16. Secularization could be conceived of as the loss of religion's comparative advantage in the production of these tangible goods. This definition of secularization allows for the waning of church influence in some spheres of society (e.g., social welfare) while preserving religion's ability to remain vigorous in others (e.g., providing supernatural compensators). So long as there is a demand for supernatural compensators, religion will remain an active player in society. Overlooking this simple insight was the critical error most scholars made in assuming religion would eventually become irrelevant in the lives of people.

17. This suggests the possibility of scale economies in religious production. The more believers a denomination has, the more credible those compensators are—e.g., "five hundred million Muslims can't be wrong."

18. This raises the puzzle of why denominational switching is not more pervasive than it is. Iannaccone (1995b) argues that as people build religious capital (i.e., become more educated in the tenets and practices of their faith), there is a cost associated with switching, namely they have to learn new practices and beliefs. This hypothesis correctly predicts that converts will tend to be young and lacking in extensive religious experience. Furthermore, most switching should be between similar faiths; conversions to completely different religions will tend to be too costly to maintain and backsliding will be more prevalent. This fits the evidence in Latin America. Those most likely to convert to Pentecostalism are those who have had the least amount of institutional contact with the Catholic Church. Evangelical Protestant growth rates show slower growth in social sectors where the Catholic Church has been historically more visible—the middle and upper classes. Moreover, conversion is generally from "folk Catholicism" to Pentecostalism. Both share the traits of being highly emotional and emphasizing direct communication with God, very different from the more "formal" and mediated version of Catholicism promoted by the Catholic Church. It is not surprising that establishing a presence in primary education is one of the Catholic Church's principal goals; the

earlier that Catholic beliefs are inculcated in children, and the more exposure those children receive, the less likely they will be to defect. This is true for all religions—education, which builds religious capital and enhances the church's ability to maintain parishioners, is one of the top priorities of all religious organizations.

19. Stark (1992) argues correctly that even with state assistance a religion cannot establish a true monopoly. Although the state can limit active competition, it cannot control passive competition—that is, parishioners who defect to their own private worship. Folk Catholicism is Latin America represented such passive competition; believers still considered themselves Catholic, but developed beliefs and practices radically different than those officially sanctioned by the institutional Church.

20. There are numerous caveats to this observation. First, a religious organization could make salvation (another desired goal) contingent upon active participation. Second, religious adherents may have different consumption demands, making it easy to extract revenue from some but not others. For example, persons wanting only to know the meaning of life will be likely to free ride, while those who also desire fellowship will probably contribute more money and time to their church.

21. This model has yet to be adapted to account for church-state behavior in religiously plural societies. From initial observations, it appears that governments in such societies prefer not to provide establishment to any single denomination. In fact, it is the state's refusal to provide exclusive dominion that leads to religious pluralism in the first place. This is discussed below in the section on church-state conflict; one of the ways states attack religious organizations is to invite in religious competitors (also see Gill 1995). However, politicians are still likely to provide various forms of subsidization in exchange for support. In the United States, where church-state separation is a contentious issue, such support may take the form of certain laws that benefit religious charities, other religious organizations, or specific policy causes. The battle over school vouchers is a case in point. Very few scholars have examined church-state relations in pluralistic societies from an institutional perspective. Most studies involve either normative legal commentary (e.g., "where should the line of separation be drawn?") or examination of how religious beliefs influence voting behavior. Posner (1987) and Finke (1990) present analyses of church-state interaction in the United States from a "new institutionalist" perspective.

22. As with prices in competitive markets, the price one party pays in a bargain should be equal to the value of the compensation it receives in return. Although it would appear that the benefits to the Church in the form of landholdings far outweighed the value of legitimation it provided, remember that land was an abundant asset and hence relatively cheap during the initial period of colonization. Over time, with the growing importance of agricultural production, land became more scarce in relative terms and its value increased. Needless to say, the threat of expropriation grew accordingly.

23. For a comparison of the Brazilian and Argentine cases see Gill 1993.

24. See Keshavarzian 1996 for an application of this point to Iran under Reza Shah.

25. I am thankful to Barbara Geddes for pointing this out.

26. See epigraph to this chapter. Consistent with the earlier discussion of church-state cooperation, Smith also observes that religions will ask for state assistance in ridding the country of competitors.

27. See note 3 to this chapter.

28. Obviously, there are limits to the degree to which religious leadership can ignore extreme human suffering and blatant violations of human rights. In such cases, religious leaders can be expected to condemn the atrociousness of the act, while still accommodating the governing elite. Such was the occasional case in Argentina, Paraguay, and Uruguay.

29. Segundo made a similar observation when discussing Catholic support for dictatorship:

> [T]he tacit and frequent alliances of the Latin American church with centers of political and economic power do not seem to derive from any will to political or financial power. They seem to be based on the principle of choosing the lesser evil. Since Christian majorities are in great danger of falling away from the church in modern society, it seems more prudent to protect their Christianity with the help of outside authorities. (1978, 77–78)

While Segundo seems to be addressing the threat of secularization here, his comments could be generalized to refer to religious competitors. In Latin America, religious competition is a much greater threat to the Catholic Church than secularization.

30. Nicaragua is a recent case in point. By comparative standards, the Nicaraguan episcopacy during the 1970s was quite progressive, embracing the preferential option for the poor and the use of base communities. Catholic bishops also demonstrated vocal opposition to Somoza after 1973 and advocated a democratic form of government. However, although de facto allies in the downfall of the Somoza regime, the Church hierarchy and the Sandinistas quickly parted ways after 1979. Archbishop Miguel Obando y Bravo criticized several priests and nuns for actively participating in the revolutionary government. Soon thereafter, Pope John Paul II publicly chastised Catholic priest Rodolfo Cardenal for his role as the FSLN's minister of culture. As a result, the Catholic hierarchy quickly earned a reputation as a reactionary force. See Dodson and O'Shaughnessy 1990.

31. Ironically, after the Church made a commitment to defend the poor against the dictatorship, indiscriminate government attacks on clergy and lay activists made converting to Protestantism an attractive option for peasants caught in the crossfire (Stoll 1990, 193–203). This is precisely what Church officials wanted to avoid. (Even the best laid plans have unintended consequences.) Nonetheless, identification with the military in these situations would have tarnished the image the poor had of the Church and may have led them to convert to Protestantism anyway.

*Four*

1. To restate an earlier caveat, this is not a study of why Protestantism expanded in some countries but not in others. The growth rate of Protestantism is assumed to be exogenous to this model. That is, evangelical Protestantism grew for reasons unrelated to relations between the Catholic Church and the state. Religious liberty was introduced by liberal governments in the 1800s as a counter to Church power, but Protestants did not use this freedom to their advantage for at least another century.

2. See Consejo Episcopal Latinoamericano 1981 and 1984, Poblete and Galilea 1984, Damen 1988, Sampedro 1989, and Conferencia Episcopal de Chile 1992. These works represent the more scholarly publications issued by the Church. There also exists a huge amount of pamphlet literature on the subject of evangelical movements, oftentimes instructing pastoral agents how to defend against the "invasion of the sects."

3. A partial list includes Paredes-Alfaro 1980; Lalive d'Epinay 1983; Alves 1985; Nuñez and Taylor 1989; Burdick 1990 and 1993; Kanagay 1990; Martin 1990; Stoll 1990; Canales, Palma, and Villela 1991; Goodman 1991; Sweeney 1992a and 1992b; Bastian 1993; and Garrard-Burnett and Stoll 1993. Also see Garrard-Burnett 1992 and Dixon 1995 for reviews of recent scholarship.

4. This fact is reflected both in Church documents and scholarly research. For examples of pre-1980 academic studies focusing exclusively on Latin American Protestantism, see Crivelli 1931, Vergara 1962, Damboriena 1963, Willems 1964 and 1967, Lalive d'Epinay 1969, Lodwick 1969, González 1970, and Pierson 1974. The growth of Protestantism even merited brief mentions in some of the major works on the Catholic Church (Vallier 1970; Turner 1971), but the implications of such growth were never fully elaborated.

5. This follows directly from Iannaccone's theory of religious capital (1990). Those who have developed religious participation skills and fellowship bonds are less likely to convert to other faiths. As the Catholic Church was most active among the middle and upper classes until the mid–twentieth century, these classes accumulated sufficient (Catholic) religious capital to raise significantly the opportunity costs of converting to other faiths.

6. In 1941, Stanley Rycroft also founded the *Latin American News Letter* to report on and promote Protestant activity in the region. However, not all Protestants shared this expansionary zeal. John White, a Protestant himself, argued that the activities of North American missionaries jeopardized the U.S. government's Good Neighbor Policy at a time when the Allied Forces most needed Latin American support (White 1943).

7. Stoll 1993 divides this wave into two separate movements: mainline denominations (e.g., Presbyterians) and "faith missions" (i.e., organizations not directly affiliated with any existing Protestant denomination). From the Catholic point of view, however, a Protestant was a Protestant. As this study examines the Catholic reaction to Protestantism, the Catholic definition will suffice.

8. Burdick (1993) provides an excellent analysis of the interaction between Catholicism, Protestantism, and Spiritism in Brazil.

9. Information for this section comes mostly from personal interviews with Protestant church officials and missionaries connected to, or residing in, Latin America.

10. This abbreviated list was compiled from a number of sources, including numerous interviews with former missionaries. See Rycroft 1946, 315–19 for a typical missionary plan.

11. A number of foreign missionaries I interviewed shared similar stories. People were often afraid to accept Bibles as gifts from missionaries because priests told them the book was forbidden to laity (Perkins, interview). Catholic clergy even took this attitude to the extreme of burning Protestant-imported Bibles (McIntire, interview)!

12. Protestant success in improving the lives of individuals may have been caused by selection bias. Redemption and lift may have worked precisely because those people most motivated to change their lives were attracted to evangelical churches. See Dixon 1992 for a similar argument. This selection bias was of little consolation to Catholic bishops who were losing the best and brightest among their (nominal) flock.

13. This observation was also made by Vallier:

[T]he traditional Catholic system in Latin America has not had to groom the layman as an instrument of religious influence or anchorage since, in fact, the whole Catholic system was sponsored, protected, supported, and cradled by the total society, especially the conservative political system. Why, then, should the grass roots, or the laity, be shaped, organized, and delegated to "win the neighbor"? All the neighbors were baptized Catholics. . . . In short, building up and channeling a membership-based religious enthusiasm were not essential to the operation and viability of the traditional Catholic system. (1970, 69–70)

14. The most famous of these holiday processions is the Brazilian *Carnaval*, which has long since transcended strict religious purposes. In many other places, Catholic holidays become a time for colorful street pageants and bacchanalian behavior (Rosales Nelson 1986). For the majority of those who considered themselves Catholic, this was the extent of their religious involvement.

15. "Laicism" refers here to actions taken by the liberal elite to restrict the legal privileges of the Church.

16. Almost every Protestant missionary I talked with had several personal stories of Catholic intimidation, leading me to believe that such incidents were rather widespread. For a detailed compilation of Catholic harassment, see Goff 1968. Needless to say, there were a good number of Catholic clergy who refused to partake in these activities and were quite willing to learn from their non-Catholic brethren. See also Cavalcanti 1995.

17. Original citation attributed to Alcibiades Delamare, *As Duas Bandeiras: Catholicismo e Brazilidade* (Rio de Janeiro: Editora Centra Dom Vital, 1924),

p. 104. Centra Dom Vital was an official arm of the Catholic Church and books published there can be interpreted reasonably as representing the official views of the episcopacy.

18. As noted in the first chapter, these interviews consisted of open-ended questions and were structured in such a way as to allow the interviewees to elaborate on their personal experiences and impressions of the religious landscape in Latin America. In California, I interviewed former missionaries from mainline Protestant denominations (e.g., Lutherans, Presbyterians) and nondenominational faith missions who were active in Latin America from the 1940s through the 1970s. The areas these missionaries worked in covered a wide range of countries including Guatemala, Ecuador, Brazil, Colombia, Peru, and Cuba. All interviewees were asked to relate personal experiences, dealings with politicians (if any), their techniques of proselytizing, and their relations with the Catholic Church. When I probed their interaction with state officials, the political leanings (e.g., progressive or conservative) usually came out. From these discussions, it became apparent that no one particular political ideology characterized Protestants. The same techniques were used for interviews with active Protestant ministers in Chile. Again, casual discussion throughout each interview generally revealed the political ideology of the interviewee. I found the Protestants I interviewed to be much more politically progressive than I had anticipated. These impressions are consistent with more rigorous research on the political ideologies of Protestants in Latin America (Garrard-Burnett and Stoll 1993).

19. Building a stock of religious capital early in the life cycle is crucial to guaranteeing a large flock over the long term. The more a person is indoctrinated into the faith—i.e., has invested a sizable stock of human capital—the less likely that person is to defect to another faith later in life. "Apostates," with occasional exceptions, are typically those who have not received significant religious training in their childhood years. For a discussion of "religious capital," see Iannaccone 1990 and 1995b. Even before this concept was formalized by Iannaccone, several scholars noted empirical evidence supporting this notion (Mueller 1971; Kluegel 1980).

20. Missionary organizations generally entered the region backed by sizable financial resources. Moreover, once Protestant missions became self-sustaining churches, their costs of operation were significantly lower (on a per-parishioner basis) than the Catholic Church's, giving the Protestants a serious advantage. See chapter 7 for a more detailed discussion of comparative cost advantages.

21. Ecumenical relations, not surprisingly, were best with nonproselytizing denominations and some of the more mainline missionary denominations (e.g., Presbyterians, Methodists). The majority of Pentecostal churches did not participate in organized ecumenism, both because the Catholic Church considered these denominations too aggressive and because the extremely decentralized nature of these denominations made it logistically difficult to engage in cooperative enterprises. For a history of ecumenical relations in Latin America, see Mejía 1966 and 1969.

22. The "social dislocation" hypothesis dominates the major works on

Protestantism in Latin America (Damboriena 1963; Willems 1967; Lalive d'Epinay 1969; Poblete and Galilea 1984; Martin 1990). This is essentially a demand-side explanation: as rural workers are forced to move to the industrialized cities and break old kinship ties, they seek new cultural identities (e.g., Pentecostalism). This theory assumes that prior to cultural change all persons have similar religious preferences (i.e., Catholicism) and this changes only with exposure to some exogenous factor (e.g., industrialization). Although it is very probable that many people do change their spiritual values when faced with traumatic experiences, I find it equally probable that religious preferences are heterogeneous and the growth of Protestantism is a response to an increased supply of religious diversity.

23. Original citation attributed to a special issue of *Misiones Extranjeras* X (January—December 1963), pp. 136–37.

24. Original cite from José Marins, Teolide Maria Trevisan, and Carollee Chanona, 1978, "Participation in an intensive workshop for CEB pastoral leaders at Maryknoll Mission Institute, July 23–28."

25. See chapter 2 for a discussion of these various hypotheses.

26. Religious data for Latin America must be viewed with healthy skepticism (Stoll 1990, 6–7). Along with the usual measurement error, religious organizations sometimes inflate their own membership rolls to appear more successful than they actually are. Of the various sources of region-wide data available (Barrett 1982; Johnstone 1986; Read, Monterroso, and Johnson 1969), Barrett uses the most detailed methodology to control for these problems and arrives at the most conservative estimates. Barrett's estimates of evangelical growth are consistent with other sources that place Brazil and Chile at the high end, and Paraguay and Uruguay at the other extreme. Additionally, unlike other studies that are primarily concerned with Protestantism, Barrett also includes Spiritist groups.

27. PQLI was calculated from the mean of three equally weighted items: life expectancy at age one, infant mortality, and literacy at age 15+ (Wilkie and Reich 1980, 4).

28. Obviously there are limitations on this index. Countries with smaller episcopacies are more likely to have extreme values because of the averaging process. In other words, the appointment of a bishop in a country with a small episcopacy will have a greater impact on the index number than one appointed at the same time in a country with a large episcopacy. However, the bishop in the smaller country is also more likely to make an immediate contribution to his episcopacy's social strategy. Also, like U.S. Supreme Court justices, the "true" ideology of bishops often only becomes apparent after their appointment (which carries lifetime tenure), either because they have concealed their beliefs in the hopes of being selected to the position, or because their attitudes change over time.

29. I have previously reported (Gill 1994) the value for religious competition for Panama as 4.4 percent. Since that time, it has come to my attention that the archdiocese of Panama City includes the Canal Zone. Adjusting for this fact, I have corrected the value for religious competition to 4.8 percent. Although this change affects the numerical values of the coefficients in the subsequent analysis, it does

not alter the earlier conclusions; both numbers provide statistically significant results.

30. Dichotomous dependent variables violate the linear regression assumption of randomly distributed error terms, thus the well-known procedures of ordinary least squares (OLS) and generalized least squares (GLS) cannot be used. For more on probit and other nonlinear models, see Aldrich and Nelson 1984.

31. As Cavalcanti notes, the president was prepared to prohibit all non-Catholic denominations until various Protestant churches "vouched unconditional Protestant support to the Vargas regime" (1995, 300–301).

32. Both Mainwaring and Doimo note that the bishops were concerned about alternative religions and even suggest that competitive pressures may have had something to do with a change in episcopal attitudes toward the poor, but neither develops this observation further.

33. Numerous studies exist on the Brazilian Church. Consult Bruneau 1974 and 1982, Mainwaring 1986, and Hewitt 1991 for the most comprehensive coverage.

34. El Salvador, unlike Brazil and Chile, did not technically experience a military government in the 1970s. It is widely believed that the generals, rather than exercising power directly, indirectly controlled the government. Until it took direct power in 1979, the military frequently interfered in elections and guaranteed the right-wing Party of National Conciliation victory (Skidmore and Smith 1984, 311–12).

35. Pentecostal groups in the 1930s and 1940s originated from earlier faith missions such as the Central American Mission (not related to LAM) and the Assemblies of God. However, "this early manifestation of the Pentecostal spirit was undisciplined" and failed to attract members (Martin 1990, 90).

36. LAM's mobilization for the campaign and follow-up efforts were phenomenal. They involved the use of billboards, bumper stickers, radio, and signs on an estimated ten thousand homes in Nicaragua alone (Rosales 1968). The only Catholic bishops that avoided hearing about this event were probably dead.

37. Compare this situation with that of Mexico. While the Mexican episcopacy has cultivated a conservative image and has sought improved relations with the state throughout the 1970s and '80s (largely to overturn Latin America's most anticlerical laws), many bishops in the southern third of the country became increasingly progressive in their pastoral and political activity. Bishop Ruíz, mentioned above, is the quintessential example. Ruíz's diocese has one of the worst priest/parishioner ratios, and consequently the highest Protestant growth rates, in the country. Elsewhere, especially central Mexico, Protestant growth has been comparatively slow owing to the same anticlerical laws used to punish the Catholic Church. In these areas, Catholicism remains quite traditional and relatively untouched by progressive currents. For more on the Mexican case, see Gill 1995.

38. Monsignor Arzube was one of the participants at this conference. For a description of the events surrounding the detention of the bishops, see Lernoux (1980, 137–42).

39. For example, Acción Católica appeared throughout Latin America, but its impact on Church renewal varied greatly. The Chilean episcopacy vigorously promoted AC, which spawned a number of other social programs, not to mention a political party. But in countries such as Argentina and Uruguay, AC was less innovative.

### Five

1. During the early 1800s, only two bishoprics existed in Chile—Santiago and Concepción.

2. There may have been some enforcement. Protestant missionary David Trumbull complained of legal restrictions on his activities and became a champion of religious liberty (Chacón, interview). Most likely, the government enforced restrictions on missionizing Protestants because they directly threatened Catholic dominance. Ethnic Protestants (e.g., German Lutherans, British Anglicans) avoided converting Catholics and worshipped peacefully with public knowledge. Due to the relative scarcity of evangelicals in Chile until the early 1900s, I am unaware of any documented cases of religious persecution. Even Trumbull's grievances appeared grounded in legal arguments, rather than in complaints of actual harassment (Mackay 1933, 238–39).

3. During colonial times, the *fuero* was one means by which Church leaders could assert control over their institution outside the purview of the state. When this system was abolished, Church personnel became subject to the legal constraints imposed on ordinary citizens and thus accountable to the state.

4. Given that almost all Chileans declared themselves Catholic at this time, it was widely reasoned that the Church had influence over the entire population. No one, not even the Catholic Church, realized how tenuous this influence was. It took successful Protestant expansion to reveal that Chile was not all that Catholic (see discussion below).

5. The alliance was not without problems. During the 1920s, Archbishop Crescente Errázuriz grew concerned that the Conservative party did not have the true interests of the Church at heart. Rather, he felt that the party's leadership was manipulating several clergy for political ends not related to the restoration of Church power. Errázuriz urged clergy to avoid partisan involvement although the majority of Church officials openly associated with the Conservatives (Smith 1982, 73).

6. Original citation from *Informativo Postal N. 38*, Ministerio de Relaciones Exteriores, República de Chile (1925).

7. The terms *communist* and *socialist* will henceforth refer to a broad range of leftist groups, including revolutionary Marxists and more reform-minded socialists. In the eyes of the bishops, these groups were all the same and the terms were used interchangeably in Church documents. The Chilean episcopacy first differentiated between them only in 1971.

8. Smith (1982, 80) also attributes the Vatican's reasoning to its political situation in Europe.

9. Catholic philosophy and social thought were suspicious of both commu-

nism *and* liberal capitalism. Owning substantial assets, the Church naturally favored the right of private property, but capitalism as an ideology was associated with political liberalism and Protestantism. However, communism was a far greater danger in that it promoted atheism, something which liberal capitalism did not. Papal documents such as *Rerum Novarum* could be seen as an effort to promote reform in order to prevent revolution. In this light, the early pastoral efforts of the Chilean episcopacy represented a reaction to communism more than a critique of capitalism.

10. For a discussion of the Church's social policy prior to 1931, see Aliaga Rojas 1989, 170–76.

11. For a flavor of the debate when the Law in Defense of Democracy was implemented, see Centinela 1948 and *Política y Espíritu* 1948. A similar debate followed when the law was repealed in 1958 (Castillo 1958; Prieto 1958).

12. For a discussion of the Chilean Christian Democrats see Fleet 1985. Kalyvas 1996a provides an excellent analysis of the rise of Christian Democrats in Europe and convincingly shows that confessional parties did not arise from direct Church intervention. Rather, they were the unintended consequences of Church social strategy. Kalyvas's model fits the Chilean case quite well. The Chilean bishops never sought to create a Christian Democratic party but their sponsorship of ACC indirectly led to this result.

13. For an argument linking the goal of evangelization (i.e., parishioner maximization) with the credibility of the Church, see Mette 1979.

14. I purposely avoid the term "Chilean Methodist Church" because at the time it was a foreign church, not a truly Chilean entity. In essence, this is what the split was about.

15. *Mensaje* was a Jesuit magazine begun in 1951. Although not directly affiliated with the Catholic hierarchy, it heavily influenced the social thinking of the bishops (Sanders 1972, 111–12). Eventually, in the late 1960s and early '70s, the magazine's editors drifted further to the left than the episcopacy liked, resulting in conflict (*Agencia Informativea Católica Argentina* (AICA) 30 October 1968, 9). *La Revista Católica*, which routinely published statements by the bishops, provided a direct reflection of episcopal thinking.

16. Obviously, they could have pursued both options simultaneously. The question then becomes which strategy received higher priority.

17. This deserves qualification. Pentecostals attracted migrant workers and slum dwellers or, in Marxist terms, the lumpenproletariat (Lalive d'Epinay 1969; Poblete and Galilea 1984; Martin 1990). Marxists concentrated efforts on the industrial proletariat, at least during the 1930s and 40s. It would be interesting to compare what percentage of resources the bishops devoted to each social sector (factory workers vs. the desperately poor) so as to get a rough estimate of which they considered the bigger priority (Marxists or Pentecostals). I am unaware of any published breakdown of Church expenditures along these lines.

18. For a complete survey of his life and work, consult the special edition of *Mensaje*, no. 411 (August 1992).

19. The chapters were: (1) "By Way of Introduction: Catholicism in Our Day"; (2) "The Miseries of Our People"; (3) "Christian Life in Chile"; (4) "The Protestant Campaign in Chile"; (5) "The Most Serious of Problems"; and (6) "The Future of the Chilean Church." The "most serious of problems" identified in chapter 5 was the scarcity of clergy, which aggravated all other problems (e.g., Protestant growth, poor attendance at Mass).

20. Note the use of the word "popular" in the above passage. In Latin America, "popular" (*lo popular*) refers to the lower classes. Hurtado thus indicated that the problem was primarily among the poor.

21. I believe this still holds true. Referring to Padre Hurtado's book I asked several people in Argentina whether their country was a Catholic country. I typically received either puzzled stares or replies to the effect that Argentina has had a long tradition of Catholicism.

22. Many of Vergara's conclusions cited above first appeared in his 1955 article but were repeated more forcefully in his book seven years later.

23. The Spanish word *amenaza* was used throughout the document, which implies a more dangerous threat than the word *desafío*, a softer word indicating "challenge."

24. Ironically, Manuel Ossa, a Jesuit at the time, later would become a Lutheran minister (Ossa, interview), perhaps the ultimate act of ecumenical relations!

25. Despite the progressiveness of the Chilean Church, ecumenism never took root on a wide scale (Chacón, interview; Lagos, interview; Precht, interview). At the Centro Ecuménico Diego de Medellín, an organization established to promote interfaith understanding, I was told that relations were much better at the grass roots, yet still quite limited (Ossa, interview; Ramírez, interview; Rosales, interview).

26. Arturo Chacón brought this connection to my attention.

27. See chapter 4, note 5.

28. *Evangelio, política y socialismos* (1971), in Oviedo 1974, 58–100. Although noteworthy for its acceptance of socialism—broadly conceived as "equality and participation of all" (71)—the text also covered the dangers of "atheistic and scientific Marxism" (73–86). This was the first time the Church differentiated between the various forms of socialism.

29. Allende only received a plurality of the popular vote (36.3 percent); Congress voted to award him the presidency.

30. The Church was having its own internal ideological problems as well. Just prior to the coup, the bishops were about to condemn the activities of Cristianos por el Socialismo (Christians for Socialism). According to many in the episcopacy, this group promoted social unrest with its message of class struggle (Mella 1987, 57).

31. An essential part of the "national security doctrine" is its defense of Christian culture against the advance of atheistic communism. See Comblin 1979, 79–81.

32. By 1975, the Catholic Te Deums stopped blessing the actions of the government and became highly critical in tone. For the history and text of Catholic Te Deums during the military regime, see Cavallo C. 1988.

33. Accounts of these events were taken from Vicaría de la Solidaridad y UNELAM 1978 and various interviews conducted in Santiago.

34. The documents where the antiauthoritarian position of the episcopacy is most explicit are: "*Evangelio y Paz*" (1975), "*Nuestra Convivencia Nacional*" (1977), "*La Iglesia en Chile hoy*" (1977), "*Humanismo Cristiano y Nueva Institucionalidad*" (1978), and "*De Evangelio, Etica y Política*" (1984). All of these can be found in the collection of episcopal documents published by the Conferencia Episcopal de Chile (1982; 1984; 1988). In addition, between 1974 and 1980 there are at least eleven documents that make specific reference to the "detained-disappeared" or government-associated violence.

35. If true, this would indicate that the "doubling rate" of Pentecostalism has slowed somewhat. With current data it is impossible to know if this was due to Catholic efforts or merely a national trend.

## Six

1. There are some indications that this strategy is changing in the 1990s. The Argentine episcopacy recently asked the public to forgive its involvement with the 1976–83 dictatorship and has decried President Carlos Menem's neoliberal economic reforms. However, it is too early to determine whether this is a long-term change or merely a tactical move in response to Menem's attack on the Church's legal status.

2. Sweeney connects these ideas with the Tratado de Comercio, Amistad y Navegación signed in 1825 between Britain and Argentina (1970, 27; 1992a, 213). Nonetheless, it is likely that such ideas predated the 1825 agreement.

3. Most of the land confiscated from the Church was not under productive use; thus expropriation imposed a minimal financial loss. The state, on the other hand, benefited handsomely from both the actual sale of property and the collection of duties once that land was geared toward export agriculture. Under the new Church-state arrangement, the Church prospered to the extent that government revenues expanded, and Argentina fared well economically throughout most of the nineteenth century.

4. This should be differentiated from desired government involvement, e.g., a guaranteed revenue. The hierarchy did not want government to interfere in the internal decisions of the Church (e.g., selection of bishops).

5. Despite the vague wording of this article, sustenance has generally been taken to mean *financial* support. In the early 1990s, such assistance amounted to roughly US$10 million annually, which constitutes only a small percentage of the Church's annual budget (Centeno, interview).

6. Recently, several significant reforms were made to the Constitution of 1853. The only alteration that affected religious matters was the elimination of Ar-

ticle 76, which required both the president and vice president to be Roman Catholics. For the complete text of the constitution, plus a discussion of recent proposed changes, consult Lopresti 1993.

7. Kennedy correctly identifies education as one of the most important policy issues for the Catholic Church. "The Church wants to mold the conscience of the citizen while it is still in the pliable condition of immaturity. To have access to the school children the Church will, it is suggested, make deals with political authorities whenever such deals are feasible." (Kennedy 1958, 186).

8. Chronologically, of course, Grote came before Hurtado, thus it is possible that Padre Hurtado was in reality a "new and improved" version of Padre Grote. However, in terms of lasting influence, Hurtado looms larger over the Church in the Southern Cone, in part because he was a more prolific writer and enjoyed a supportive hierarchy. Besides, Hurtado belonged to the Society of Jesus, whereas Grote was a Redemptorist; anyone familiar with Catholic religious orders knows the Jesuits are the superior spin doctors.

9. Ivereigh (1995, 63–72) presents a good overview of social Catholicism in Argentina at the turn of the century.

10. The UCR represented urban middle-class interests, and its ideology promoted liberal capitalism.

11. Casiello's work, *Iglesia y Estado en la Argentina* (1948), stands out as both a detailed chronology of Church-state relations and a spirited defense of the Church's view of the world. The book's prologue, and glowing endorsement, was written by one of Argentina's most conservative bishops, Antonio Caggiano.

12. UCR president Hipólito Yrigoyen did not extend the liberal reforms of the 1880s. Devout lay Catholics were even instrumental in the Unión Cívica Radical party (Braun, interview).

13. Although an independent entity, the conservative journal *Criterio* closely aligns its views with those of the Argentine Catholic hierarchy. Two former editors—monsignors Gustavo Franchessi and Jorge Mejía—held influential posts in the Church. From this point on, I will consider the views expressed by the editors of *Criterio* to approximate the general thinking of the episcopacy, although I have been told that the episcopacy tends to be slightly more conservative.

14. For a detailed list of the policy benefits received by the Argentine Church, see Lubertino 1987, 37–40.

15. For the most detailed accounts of the Church-state conflict during 1954 and 1955, see Bustos Fierro 1969, 159–91; de Hoyas 1969; and Lubertino 1987.

16. The Argentine Church expanded as an institution quite rapidly during this period. In 1957 alone, twelve new dioceses were created (Galán, interview; Storni, interview).

17. Frondizi's choice of Centeno as subsecretary of religion was probably a strategic move to appease the Church. Centeno was an officer in Acción Católica Argentina during the 1940s.

18. Centeno (interview) and Donini (interview), both close associates of Frondizi, attribute the president's willingness to end the *patronato* to his liberal views on church-state separation. Unlike earlier liberals though, Frondizi truly believed that separation meant separation, not control. However, the president's political savvy prevented him from progressing any further along the lines of separation (e.g., terminating financial support), considering what had happened to the last president who had attempted that. Eliminating the *patronato* was probably the only step towards separation that the Catholic hierarchy would accept. For a full account of the thinking of Centeno and Frondizi, see Centeno 1964.

19. For the text of the final agreement see Donini 1985, 103–5.

20. Presidents Frondizi and Illía were the only two elected executives during this period. José María Guido, who assumed the presidency for the year and a half interim between these two leaders, was a civilian president and legal constitutional successor to Frondizi, but most historians consider him a figurehead for the military. No one I have spoken to has any detailed recollection of what occurred between Church and state during Guido's tenure. Most likely, nothing happened.

21. Sacerdotes para el Tercer Mundo was actually founded in 1965, prior to the coup. For a representative example of the thought of this group, see Mugica 1973. I thank Angel Berlanga for pointing this out.

22. See "Exhortación de Mons. Juan C. Aramburu, referente a un documento de los 'Sacerdotes para el Tercer Mundo'" (*Agencia Informativea Católica Argentina,* 7 July 1969, 21–23); "Declaración del episcopado sobre los 'Sacerdotes del Tercer Mundo'" (*Agencia Informativea Católica Argentina,* 19 August 1970, 2–3).

23. On close inspection of Mignone's book, he actually names five. They were Enrique Angelelli, Jaime de Nevares, Miguel Hesayne, Jorge Novak, and Carlos Ponce de León. The first four are mentioned on page 19, while Ponce de León's case is discussed on pages 145–46.

24. The specific document referenced is "Carta de la comisión ejecutiva de la Conferencia Episcopal Argentina a la Junta Militar, sobre el incalificable asesinato de una comunidad religiosa," 7 July 1976.

25. Monseñor Angelelli, probably the most progressive bishop in Argentina at the time, died in a car "accident" on 4 August 1976 (Mignone 1988, 138–45). Despite the loss of a major Church figure, *AICA* (12 August 1976) released a surprisingly short account of his carreer. No further discussion of this incident appears in official Church publications.

26. Mignone's book is the most cited source on the Argentine Church during the 1976–83 dictatorship since few other works exist. However, a word of caution is in order. Mignone's daughter "disappeared" during the "dirty war." Appeals made to several bishops on her behalf yielded little action. Many people that I talked to while in Argentina believe his intimate involvement with the subject resulted in a harsher critique of the episcopacy than was truly warranted. Nonetheless, they also agreed that the bishops could have handled the situation much better.

27. In the original Spanish, the word used was "moral."

28. The actual document— "Declaración de la comisión permanente llamado a una mayor reconciliación"—was originally released on 14 December 1979.

29. The Witnesses nevertheless continued their activity. In 1977 and 1978, several members of the religious organization were arrested and evicted from the country. See Foreign Broadcast Information Service 1978 and 1979 and *Journal of Church and State* 1978a. It should be noted that the Jehovah's Witnesses and other religious groups (Divine Light Mission and Krishna Consciousness) also evicted did not constitute a major pastoral challenge to the Argentine Church the way Pentecostalism did in Chile. For more discussion on this matter, see the following section.

30. Ligget relates a humorous story of two separate Protestant groups that combined their names and organizations as a result of a bureaucratic mistake. The options before them were to try to correct the mistake and miss the filing deadline, thereby becoming illegal, or merge into one organization. They chose the latter and the organizations remain linked to this day. For a written discussion on the registration laws, see *Journal of Church and State* 1978b and 1980.

31. Barrett (1982, 147, 522) estimates that in 1975 there were approximately 1,050,100 Protestants (affiliated) in Argentina, roughly 4.1 percent of the population. Compare this with Nicaragua with 207,400 Protestants, representing 8.9 percent of the population. Note that these figures are based on Stoll's (1990, 333–34) aggregation of the data in Barrett 1982 and include both proselytizing *and nonproselytizing* denominations. Data presented in chapter 5 only considered proselytizing denominations, as these churches are the direct threat to the Catholic Church.

32. Interestingly enough, even though Italians composed the largest non-Spanish immigrant group, not all of them were Catholic. A sizable number of Protestant Waldensians were among them (Martin 1990, 74).

33. Martin, the one scholar with the insight to compare these two countries side by side, suggests that the "impact of religious or anti-clerical traditions in different regions of Italy" may be one possible explanation, but he fails to develop this hypothesis further (1990, 75).

34. As noted in chapter 5, laws preventing Protestant activities were rarely enforced; the de facto religious liberty of Chile was equivalent to the legal freedom in Argentina.

## Seven

1. Huntington (1991a and 1991b) observes that the "third wave" of global democratization (c. 1973–present) occurred primarily in the predominantly Catholic countries of Southern Europe and Latin America. He attributes this phenomenon to a change in Catholicism brought about by Vatican II (1962–65). However, correlation is not causation. This study indirectly shows that Huntington's observed relationship between religion and democracy is spurious. Democracy returned to, or persisted in, several countries with national Catholic Churches that

were only minimally affected by Vatican II (e.g., Argentina, Uruguay, Paraguay, Colombia) and was comparatively stable prior to 1962 in numerous other countries (e.g., Chile, Costa Rica). Kalyvas (1996b) presents a cogent argument that the connection between democracy and religion is based first and foremost on institutional interests, not theology.

2. This was the fourth in a series of general episcopal conferences in Latin America that also included Rio de Janeiro (1955), Medellín (1968), and Puebla (1979). Consult Hennelly 1993 for a text of the Santo Domingo conference proceedings.

3. Ironically, the 1994 Zapatista revolt in Chiapas breathed new life into Bishop Ruíz's career. As the only person trusted by the Zapatista rebels to negotiate in good faith with the government, the aging bishop's political clout within both the institutional Church and the Mexican polity increased substantially. In 1995, attacks on Ruíz's credibility by wealthy ranchers provoked a defensive response from the Vatican, who had tried forcing him to resign only two years earlier (Gill 1995).

4. Though this term generally refers to the split between base and hierarchy that occurred in Nicaragua shortly after the 1979 revolution, the split has been present in all Latin American countries to some degree.

5. A counterfactual attempts to reconstruct a historical phenomenon as if some event had never taken place. Being largely a thought experiment, using a counterfactual allows the researcher to delve underneath the most apparent (proximate) cause of a phenomenon and search for other underlying variables. For a discussion of this methodology, see Fearon 1991 and Tetlock and Belkin 1996. For Latin Americanists, a familiar example of this technique can be found in Stepan 1978.

6. Although when constructing economic analyses of institutions it is tempting to think of resources solely in terms of money, the definition of resources also includes nonmonetary resources such as time and effort.

7. This is not to say that Catholics do not attend services in humble surroundings. I have seen a number of Catholic churches that are little more than one- or two-room buildings with minimal decoration. However, every national Church in Latin America has more ornate buildings than Pentecostals do.

8. We again can refer to the Chilean Jesuit Alberto Hurtado:

One of the reasons for the success of the Protestant campaign in Chile is the lack of religious cultivation of our people. They are sheep without a pastor. . . . The responsibility for the success of the Protestant campaign in Chile belongs to the Catholics who have not known enough to cultivate their church and all those who have failed to listen to the voice of God. ([1941] 1992, 83)

A recent document addressing the expansion of Protestantism issued by the Chilean episcopacy echoes this critique:

In a number of areas there is a lack of pastoral attention or an absence of true evangelization; our Christian upbringing is poor with regard to filling the Catholic parishioners with the missionary spirit. Who can remain close to the parish without religious attention? (Conferencia Episcopal de Chile 1992, 43)

9. Of course, the Church could have used additional priests to *deepen* the faith of their members, but those in the upper echelons of religious organizations who were divorced from the day-to-day reality at the grassroots were often more concerned with the "numbers game." The prevalence of folk Catholicism at the grass roots indicates that the hierarchy did not know that its flock had strayed from doctrinal purity, or if they did know, they cared little about correcting the situation.

10. Due to their radically decentralized nature, it is impossible to speak of a single Latin American Pentecostal "Church"; rather there are a myriad of Pentecostal churches. Although some institutionalized locations exist for the training of Pentecostal ministers, it is common for a new pastor to emerge from an established congregation and then start his own autonomous ministry. This method of amoebalike expansion accounts for the proliferation of small, autonomous Pentecostal churches.

11. This may not be true in Central America, where Protestant churches were often spared the wrath of military raids aimed at liquidating communist guerrillas and their supposed Catholic sympathizers. Presented with the choice of dying Catholic or living Protestant, many peasants chose the Pentecostal route. Again, the effect of the Church's pastoral effort at slowing the growth of Protestantism is impossible to determine; what is important though is that the bishops believed that their efforts would help stem the tide.

12. One could reasonably inquire then why Obando y Bravo was so hostile to the Sandinista government. This needs to be understood in terms of the Church's other desire: to maintain hierarchically imposed unity. As many CEBs and Delegates of the Word became increasingly involved in the FSLN development program, the cardinal believed that they were less beholden to his directives than to Daniel Ortega's. Since accommodation with the Sandinistas would only have validated what these CEBs were doing, seeking government support would probably—in Obando y Bravo's mind—have further eroded his control over them. When official Catholic support for the FSLN was not forthcoming, President Ortega found Protestants willing to cooperate in exchange for assistance with their proselytizing. This support for Protestants only worsened relations between the cardinal and the revolutionary government.

13. This raises the question of how successful CEBs have been in the past at bringing nominal Catholics into the fold. Without getting into an extensive discussion of the issue, it may well be the case that this question is closely related to problems of collective action. Base communities that provide their members with tangible, exclusive, and ongoing benefits (e.g., self-help groups) tend to endure longer than CEBs that attempt grandiose revolutionary projects aimed at changing the structure of society. The former method—focusing on improving the life of the individual in a real and visible way—is favored by most Protestant groups. The latter, which emphasizes the collectivist attitudes found in the Church's social teach-

ings, is vulnerable to free riding, which means that participation will potentially collapse over time.

## Postscript

1. Note the paternalistic tone of the archbishop's writing. This same attitude was (and in many cases still is) apparent in statements by Latin American Catholic bishops when discussing Protestant encroachment onto their turf.

2. Ironically, the Roman Catholic Church has been one of the more aggressive proselytizing denominations in Russia, has been a firm advocate of religious liberty there, and has drawn the ire of Orthodox leaders. Contrast this with the Catholic Church's position in Latin America and Poland, where bishops lobby intensively for laws restricting freedom of worship (*Latin America Weekly Report* 1991; Perlez 1995). Consistent with the assumption of parishioner maximization, where a church is expanding rapidly it will seek laws that enhance religious liberty. Where that church is on the defensive, its leaders will try to restrict such freedom.

## Appendix

1. See Stark, Iannaccone, and Finke 1995 for discussion of how scientists view religion. They demonstrate that several of the long-standing assumptions about religion—i.e., that "religion must inevitably decline as science and technology advance" and "individuals become less religious and more skeptical of faith-based claims as they acquire more education" (1995, 433)—are refuted by the prevalence of religiosity in their own professions. They cite evidence that religious belief increases with education and scholars engaged in most scientific research (e.g., mathematics, physics, biology) show patterns of religious practice that are consistent with the general population. Only psychologists and anthropologists exhibit low levels of religious belief and practice. Though Stark, Iannaccone, and Finke's data are somewhat limited (e.g., measures of religious belief and practice appear conflated), the available evidence is enough to suggest that one of the central pillars of secularization theory is not true; scientific enlightenment does not lead inevitably to the decline of spiritual faith.

2. Pattnayak, in his claim that his edited volume is "rational choice free," overlooks the chapter by Serbin (1995), who forcefully argues that Brazilian bishops had a primary interest in maintaining high levels of state funding and adjusted their political strategy accordingly. While Serbin avoids the jargon of "rational maximization," his argument can easily be translated into rational choice terms.

3. See Becker 1976; Riker 1990; Tsebelis 1990, 18–51; Cohen 1994, 38–52; and Geddes 1995 for excellent introductions to rational choice.

4. For those interested in a more comprehensive discussion about the limitations of rational choice from the perspective of scholars generally sympathetic to the approach see Elster 1983 and 1984 and Cook and Levi 1990.

5. For more extensive coverage of the debate surrounding religion and rationality, consult Iannaccone and Hull 1991; Robertson 1992; Chaves 1995; Demerath 1995; Ellison 1995; Iannaccone 1995a; Stark, Iannaccone, and Finke (1995).

6. The critique of tautology could also be lodged against rational choice theory when it is used in combination with the utility maximization assumption. If all individuals are assumed to maximize utility, then it could be argued that any observed result is what the individual was trying to maximize. To rectify this situation, rational choice, properly applied, demands that preferences are specified deductively and that the justification for assuming a given set of preferences is independent of observed behavior.

7. As stated here, this is a strong transitivity assumption. A more relaxed version (weak transitivity) states that if $X \geq Y$ (i.e., if a person prefers X to Y or is indifferent when choosing between the two) and $Y \geq Z$, then $X \geq Z$. Weak and strong transitivity are part of the set of consistency requirements for rational choice. Consistency also requires "connectedness"—i.e., individuals must be able to compare all choices in the choice set. The connectedness assumption is trivial here.

8. Tsebelis uses the "money pump" example to further illustrate how intransitive preferences violate the assumption of simple utility maximization.

[S]uppose a person prefers a over b, b over c, and c over a. If she holds a, one could persuade her to exchange it for c provided she pays a fee (say $1). One could also persuade her to exchange c for b for an additional fee (say another dollar). Furthermore, one could persuade her to exchange b for a for an additional fee (say another dollar). Observe that she is in exactly the same situation as before (she holds a); only now she is $3 poorer. (1990, 26)

9. One of the principle criticisms of Green and Shapiro's (1994) attack of rational choice theory is that it avoids any contact with empirical reality. While this approach might be waged against some of the most abstract research in rational choice (e.g., Arrow 1951; Downs 1957; and Schwartz 1986), it ignores a vast rational choice–based literature in comparative politics that is sensitive to empirical reality and historical context. See, for example, Ames 1987, Levi 1988, Tsebelis 1990, Frieden 1991, Cohen 1994, and Geddes 1994. See Friedman 1996 for responses to Green and Shapiro 1994.

10. Pattnayak (1995, 7) appears to assert that cooperative relations cannot come about though rational calculation or self-interest; all collective action must be altruistic in nature. If so, this contradicts the voluminous literature on collective action (see Lichbach 1995). Furthermore, there is nothing in rational choice theory that rules out altruism. A good Samaritan who wants only to help the poor and downtrodden is subject to the same resource constraints as other utility maximizers. If she wants to help as many poor people as possible, she must choose the most efficient means of doing so.

# References

### Books and Periodicals

Acción Católica Chilena
    1946    *Estado de la Iglesia en Chile*. Santiago: Oficina Nacional de Estadistica de la Acción Católica Chilena.

Adriance, Madeleine
    1991    "Agents of Change: The Roles of Priests, Sisters, and Lay Workers in the Grassroots Catholic Church in Brazil." *Journal for the Scientific Study of Religion* 30 (3): 292–305.

Aguilar-Monsalve, Luis
    1988    "Breaking the Bonds of Church and State: The New Religious Freedom in Ecuador." *Thought* 65 (250): 236–49.
    1984    "The Separation of Church and State: The Ecuadorian Case." *Thought* 59 (233): 205–18.

Aldrich, John J., and Forrest D. Nelson
    1984    *Linear Probability, Logit, and Probit Models*. Beverly Hills, Cal.: Sage.

Aliaga, Fernando
    1989    *La Iglesia en Chile: Contexto histórico*. Santiago: Ediciones Paulinas.

Allende, Isabel
    1987    *Eva Luna*. New York: Alfred A. Knopf.

Alves, Ruben
    1985    *Protestantism and Repression: A Brazilian Case Study*. Maryknoll, N.Y.: Orbis Books.

Ames, Barry
    1987    *Political Survival: Politicians and Public Policy in Latin America*. Berkeley and Los Angeles: University of California Press.

Andersen, Martin Edwin
    1993    *Dossier Secreto: Argentina's Desaparecidos and the Myth of the "Dirty War."* Boulder, Colo.: Westview Press.

Anderson, Gary M., Robert B. Ekelund, Jr., Robert F. Hébert,
and Robert D. Tollison
    1992    "An Economic Interpretation of the Medieval Crusades." *Journal
        of European Economic History* 21 (2): 339–63.

Arrow, Kenneth
    1951    *Social Choice and Individual Values*. New Haven: Yale University
        Press.

Asamblea Episcopal del Perú
    1973    "Evangelización: Comentarios y notas a un texto episcopal."
        Working paper. Lima, Peru: Centro de Estudios y Publicaciones.

Auza, Néstor T.
    1962    *Los Católicos argentinos: Su experiencia política y social*. Buenos
        Aires: Ediciones Diagrama.

Barrett, David B., ed.
    1982    *World Christian Encyclopedia*. Nairobi: Oxford University Press.

Barrios, Marciano
    1987    *La Iglesia en Chile*. Santiago: Ediciones Pedagogicas Chilenas.

Bastian, Jean-Pierre
    1993    "The Metamorphosis of Latin American Protestant Groups: A
        Sociohistorical Perspective." *Latin American Research Review* 28
        (2): 33–61.
    1992    "Protestantism in Latin American." In *The Church in Latin
        America, 1492–1991*, edited by Enrique Dussel. Maryknoll, N.Y.:
        Orbis Books.

Bates, Robert
    1981    *Markets and States in Tropical Africa: The Political Basis of
        Agricultural Policies*. Berkeley and Los Angeles: University of
        California Press.

Becker, Gary S.
    1986    "The Economic Approach to Human Behavior." In *Rational
        Choice*, edited by Jon Elster. New York: New York University
        Press.
    1976    *The Economic Approach to Human Behavior*. Chicago:
        University of Chicago Press.

Beeson, Trevor, and Jenny Pearce
    1984    *A Vision of Hope: The Church and Change in Latin America*.
        Philadelphia: Fortress Press.

Beozzo, José Oscar
    1992    "The Church and the Liberal States (1880–1930)." In *The Church
        in Latin America, 1492–1991*, edited by Enrique Dussel.
        Maryknoll, N.Y.: Orbis Books.

Berger, Peter L.
    1967    *The Sacred Canopy*. Garden City: Doubleday and Doubleday.

Berryman, Phillip
1994    "The Coming of Age of Evangelical Protestantism." *NACLA* 27 (6): 6–10.
1987    *Liberation Theology: Essential Facts about the Revolutionary Movement in Latin America and Beyond.* Philadelphia: Temple University Press.
1984    *The Religious Roots of Rebellion.* Maryknoll, N.Y.: Orbis Books.

Bialek, Robert W.
1963    *Catholic Politics: A History Based on Ecuador.* New York: Vantage Press.

Bidegain, Ana María
1992    "The Church in the Emancipation Process." In *The Church in Latin America, 1492–1992,* edited by Enrique Dussel. Maryknoll, N.Y.: Orbis Books.

Blomjous, Joseph
1964    "Ecumenismo y conversiones." *Mensaje* 13 (133): 494–96.

Bock, Paul
1992    "Protestantism in Czechoslovakia and Poland." In *Protestantism and Politics in Eastern Europe and Russia,* edited by Sabrina Petra Ramet. Durham: Duke University Press.

Bruce, Steve
1992    *Religion and Modernization: Sociologists and Historians Debate the Secularization Thesis.* Oxford: Clarendon Press.

Bruneau, Thomas C.
1982    *The Church in Brazil: The Politics of Religion.* Austin: University of Texas Press.
1980a   "The Catholic Church and Development in Latin America: The Role of Basic Christian Communities." *World Development* 8:535–44.
1980b   "Base Christian Communities in Latin America: Their Nature and Significance (Especially in Brazil)." In *Churches and Politics in Latin America,* edited by Daniel H. Levine. Beverly Hills, Cal.: Sage.
1974    *The Political Transformation of the Brazilian Catholic Church.* New York: Cambridge University Press.

Burdick, John
1993    *Looking for God in Brazil: The Progressive Catholic Church in Urban Brazil's Religious Arena.* Berkeley and Los Angeles: University of California Press.
1990    "Gossip and Secrecy: Women's Articulation of Domestic Conflict in Three Religions of Urban Brazil." *Sociological Analysis* 50 (2): 153–70.

Burdick, Michael A.
    1995    *For God and the Fatherland: Religion and Politics in Argentina.*
            New York: State University of New York Press.
Bustos, Raúl
    1969    *Desde Perón hasta Onganía.* Buenos Aires: Ediciones Octubre.
Cáceres Prendes, Jorge
    1989    "Political Radicalization and Popular Pastoral Practices in El
            Salvador, 1969–1985." In *The Progressive Church in Latin
            America*, edited by Scott Mainwaring and Alexander Wilde.
            Notre Dame: University of Notre Dame Press.
Canales, Manuel, Samuel Palma, and Hugo Villela
    1991    *En Tierra Extraña II.* Santiago: SEPADE.
Cardenal, Rodolfo
    1992    "The Church in Central America." In *The Church in Latin
            America 1492–1992*, edited by Enrique Dussel. Maryknoll, N.Y.:
            Orbis Books.
    1990    "The Catholic Church and the Politics of Accommodation in
            Honduras." In *Church and Politics in Latin America*, edited by
            Dermot Keogh. London: Macmillan.
Carnoy, Martin
    1984    *The State and Political Theory.* Princeton: Princeton University
            Press.
Carter, Miguel
    1990    "The Role of the Paraguayan Catholic Church in the Downfall of
            the Stroessner Regime." *Journal of Interamerican Studies and
            World Affairs* 32 (4): 67–121.
Casanova, José
    1994    *Public Religions in the Modern World.* Chicago: University of
            Chicago Press.
Casiello, Juan
    1948    *Iglesia y Estado en la Argentina.* Buenos Aires: Editorial Poblet.
Castillo, Fernando
    1979    "Evangelization in Latin America." *Concilium* 114:85–90.
Castillo, Jaime
    1958    "Respuesta a una acusacíon." *Política y Espíritu* 13 (209):
            11–23.
Cavalcanti, H. B.
    1995    "Unrealistic Expectations: Contesting the Usefulness of Weber's
            Protestant Ethic for the Study of Latin American Protestantism."
            *Journal of Church and State* 37 (2): 289–308.
Cavallo, Ascanio
    1988    *Los Te Deum del Cardenal Silva Henríquez en el régimen militar.*
            Santiago: Ediciones Copygraph.

Centeno, Angel
    1964    *Cuatro años de una política religiosa*. Buenos Aires: Editorial
            Desarrollo.
    1957    "Apologética antiprotestante." *Criterio* 30 (1294): 735–37.
Centinela
    1948    "Democracía y libertad." *Política y Espíritu* 3 (36): 288–91.
Chaves, Mark
    1995    "On the Rational Choice Approach to Religion." *Journal for the
            Scientific Study of Religion* 34 (1): 98–104.
Chaves, Mark, and David E. Cann
    1992    "Regulation, Pluralism, and Religious Market Structure:
            Explaining Religion's Vitality." *Rationality and Society* 4
            (3):272–90.
Chrypinski, Vincent C.
    1990    "The Catholic Church in 1944–1989 Poland." In *Catholicism and
            Politics in Communist Societies*, edited by Pedro Ramet. Durham:
            Duke University Press.
Cleary, Edward L., and Hannah Stewart-Gambino, eds.
    1992    *Conflict and Competition: The Latin American Church in a
            Changing Environment*. Boulder, Colo.: Lynne Rienner Publishers.
Cohen, Youssef
    1994    *Radicals, Reformers, and Reactionaries: The Prisoner's Dilemma
            and the Collapse of Democracy in Latin America*. Chicago:
            University of Chicago Press.
Coleman, William J.
    1958    *Latin American Catholicism: A Self-Evaluation*. Maryknoll, N.Y.:
            Maryknoll Publications.
Comblin, José
    1979    *The Church and the National Security State*. Maryknoll, N.Y.:
            Orbis Books.
Comisión de Estudios de Historia de la Iglesia en Latinoamérica
    1975    *Para una historia de la Iglesia en América Latina*. Barcelona:
            Editorial Nova Terra.
Comisión Nacional sobre la Desaparición de Personas (CONADEP)
    1992    *Nunca más: Informe de la Comisión nacional sobre la
            desaparición de personas*. Buenos Aires: EUDEBA.
Conferencia Episcopal Argentina (CEA)
    1982    *Documentos del episcopado argentino: 1965–1981*. Buenos
            Aires: Editorial Claretiana.
    1981    *Iglesia y Comunidad Nacional*. Buenos Aires: Conferencia
            Episcopal Argentina.
Conferencia Episcopal de Chile (CECH)
    1992    *Evangélicos y sectas: Propuestas pastorales*. Santiago: Cencosep.

1988    *Documentos del Episcopado: Chile 1984–1987.* Santiago:
        Ediciones Mundo.
1984    *Documentos del Episcopado: Chile 1981–1983.* Santiago:
        Ediciones Mundo.
1982    *Documentos del Episcopado: Chile 1974–1980.* Santiago:
        Ediciones Mundo.
1975    "La Iglesia hoy: Orientaciones pastorales para Chile." Santiago:
        Ediciones Mundo.
1971    "Evangelio, política y socialismos." Working document.
        Santiago: Secretario del CECH.
1962    "La Iglesia y el problema del Campesinado Chileno." In
        *Documentados de la Conferencia Episcopal de Chile:
        Introducción y textos, 1952–1977.* Santiago: Equipo de Servicios
        de la Juventuds, n.d.
1960a   "El problema de la Evangelización en nuestro tiempo."
        *Documentados de la Conferencia Episcopal de Chile:
        Introducción y textos, 1952–1977.* Santiago: Equipo de Servicios
        de la Juventuds, n.d.
1960b   "Los deveres de la Hora Presente." *Documentados de la
        Conferencia Episcopal de Chile: Introducción y textos,
        1952–1977.* Santiago: Equipo de Servicios de la Juven-
        tuds, n.d.
1951    "Firmes en la fe: la misonería, el protestantismo, y el comunismo,
        enemigos de los católicos." *Boletín de la Acción Católica Chilena*
        19 (2): 1–3.
Consejo Episcopal Latinoamericano (CELAM)
1984    *Las Sectas en América Latina.* Buenos Aires: Editorial
        Clarentiana.
1981    *Sectas en América Latina.* Bogotá, Colombia: CELAM.
1979    *Hacia un mapa pastoral de América Latina.* Bogotá, Colombia:
        SIDEAT.
Considine, John J., ed.
1966    *The Religious Dimension in the New Latin America.* Notre Dame,
        Ind.: Fides Publishers.
Cook, Guillermo
1985    *The Expectation of the Poor: Latin American Base Ecclesial
        Communities in Protestant Perspective.* American Society of
        Missiology Series, no. 9. Maryknoll, N.Y.: Orbis Books.
Cook, Karen Schweers, and Margaret Levi, eds.
1990    *The Limits of Rationality.* Chicago: University of Chicago Press.
Cox, Harvey
1984    *Religion and the Secular City.* New York: Simon and Schuster.
[1965] 1990    *The Secular City.* New York: Macmillan.

Crahan, Margaret E.
    1975    "Latin American Church: Reluctant Revolution." *America* 135
           (5): 90–91.

Crassweller, Robert D.
    1987    *Perón and the Enigmas of Argentina.* New York: W. W. Norton.

*Criterio*
    1966a    "La Iglesia y el momento político: Declaraciones del arzobispo de
           Córdoba y de los obispos de catamarca y Nueve de Julio." *Criterio*
           39 (1508): 702–4.

    1966b    "Carta del obispo de Nueve de Julio." *Criterio* 39 (1508):
           704.

    1959a    "La penetración comunista en la Argentina." *Criterio* 32 (1330):
           283–86.

    1959b    "Las fuerzas armadas y la política." *Criterio* 32 (1331): 336.

    1958    "El problema político presente." *Criterio* 31 (1301): 363–65.

    1956a    "¿Los protestantes son perseguidos en Columbia?" *Criterio* 29
           (1257): 274.

    1956b    "Ataques de Obispos Episcopalianos Brasileños contra la Iglesia
           Católica." *Criterio* 28 (1252): 74.

    1956c    "Controversia acerca del catolicismo en América Latina."
           *Criterio* 29 (1271): 834.

    1945    "Carta pastoral colectiva." *Criterio* 17 (883): 115–22.

    1944a    "¡No más misioneros!" *Criterio* 16 (832): 128.

    1944b    "La actitud de Chile." *Criterio* 16 (839): 250.

    1944c    "Un peligro grave." *Criterio* 17 (854): 33.

Crivelli, Camilio
    1931    *Los protestantes y la América Latina: Conferencias, acusaciones,*
           *respuestas.* Rome: Publicaciones del Pontificio Colegio Pio
           Latinoamericano.

Damboriena, Prudencio
    1963    *El protestantismo en América Latina.* Fribourg, Switzerland:
           FERES.

Damen, Franz
    1988    "El desafío de las sectas." *Serie Fe y Compromiso,* no. 5. La Paz:
           Secretario Nacional de Ecumenismo.

Darling, Juanita
    1993    "Politically Active Mexican Bishop Faces Threat of Removal by
           Vatican." *Los Angeles Times* (6 November): B10.

Daudelin, Jean, and W. E. Hewitt
    1995    "Latin American Politics: Exit the Catholic Church?" In
           *Organized Religion in the Political Transformation of Latin*
           *America,* edited by Satya R. Pattnayak. Lanham, Md.: University
           Press of America.

Dehainaut, Raymond K.
    1972    *Faith and Ideology in Latin American Perspective.* SONDEOS,
            no. 85. Cuernavaca, Mexico: CIDOC.
de Hoyas, Ruben J.
    1969    "The Fall of the President Juan D. Perón: The Role of the
            Religious Factor in the Revolutionary Process, Argentina
            November 1954–September 1955." Ph.D. diss., New York
            University.
de las Casas, Bartolomé
    1992    *In Defense of the Indians.* Translated by Stafford Poole. DeKalb:
            Northern Illinois University Press.
Della Cava, Ralph
    1993a   "Financing the Faith: The Case of Roman Catholicism." *Journal
            of Church and State* 35 (1): 37–59.
    1993b   "Thinking about Current Vatican Policy in Central and East
            Europe and the Utility of the 'Brazilian Paradigm.'" *Journal of
            Latin American Studies* 25 (2): 257–81.
    1989    "The 'People's Church,' the Vatican and Abertura." In
            *Democratizing Brazil,* edited by Alfred Stepan. New York:
            Oxford University Press.
    1976    "Catholicism and Society in Twentieth Century Brazil." *Latin
            American Research Review* 11:7–50.
Demerath, N. J., III
    1995    "Rational Paradigms, A-Rational Religion, and the Debate Over
            Secularization." *Journal for the Scientific Study of Religion* 34 (1):
            105–12.
de Roux, Rodolfo
    1992    "The Church in Colombia and Venezuela." In *The Church in
            Latin America, 1492–1992,* edited by Enrique Dussel. Maryknoll,
            N.Y.: Orbis Books.
de Tocqueville, Alexis
    1945    *Democracy in America.* New York: Alfred A. Knopf.
Dixon, David E.
    1995    "The New Protestantism in Latin America: Remembering What
            We Already Know, Testing What We have Learned." *Comparative
            Politics* 27 (4): 479–92.
    1992    "Popular Culture, Popular Identity and the Rise of Protestantism
            in Latin America: Voices from Santiago Poblacional." Paper
            presented at the 17th international congress of the Latin America
            Studies Association, Los Angeles.
Dodson, Michael
    1992    "Shifting Patterns of Religious Influence in Central America: The
            Case of Revolutionary Nicaragua." Paper presented at the annual
            meeting of the American Political Science Association, Chicago.

Dodson, Michael, and Laura O'Shaughnessy
    1990    *Nicaragua's Other Revolution: Religious Faith and Political Struggle.* Chapel Hill: University of North Carolina Press.
Doimo, Ana Maria
    1989    "Social Movements and the Catholic Church in Vitória, Brazil." In *The Progressive Church in Latin America*, edited by Scott Mainwaring and Alexander Wilde. Notre Dame: University of Notre Dame Press.
Donini, Antonio O.
    1985    *Religion y Sociedad.* Buenos Aires: Editorial DOCENCIA.
Downs, Anthony
    1957    *An Economic Theory of Democracy.* New York: Harper & Row.
Durán Estragó, Margarita
    1992    "The Reductions." In *The Church in Latin America, 1492–1992*, edited by Enrique Dussel. Maryknoll, N.Y.: Orbis Books.
Durkheim, Emile
    1965    *Elementary Forms of the Religious Life.* New York: Free Press.
    1951    *Suicide.* New York: Free Press.
Durkin, John T., and Andrew M. Greeley
    1991    "A Model of Religious Choice under Uncertainty: On Responding Rationally to the Nonrational." *Rationality and Society* 3 (2): 178–96.
Dussel, Enrique
    1981    *A History of the Church in Latin America: Colonialism to Liberation (1492–1979).* Translated by Alan Neely. Grand Rapids, Mich.: Eerdmans.
    1972    "The Appointment of Bishops in the First Century of 'Patronage' in Latin America (1504–1620)." *Concilium* 77:113–21.
———, ed.
    1992    *The Church in Latin America, 1492–1992.* Maryknoll, N.Y.: Orbis Books.
Einauidi, Luigi, Richard Maullin, Alfred Stepan, and Michael Fleet
    1969    "Latin American Institutional Development: The Changing Catholic Church." Memorandum RM-6136-DOS. Santa Monica, Cal.: RAND Corporation.
Ekelund, Robert B., Jr., Robert F. Hébert, and Robert D. Tollison
    1989    "An Economic Model of the Medieval Church: Usury as a Form of Rent Seeking." *Journal of Law, Economics, and Organization* 5 (2): 305–31.
Ellison, Christopher G.
    1995    "Rational Choice Explanations of Individual Religious Behavior: Notes on the Problem of Social Embeddedness." *Journal for the Scientific Study of Religion* 34 (1): 89–97.

*El Mercurio*
  1993a    "Monseñor Oviedo Exhortó a Mirar con Fe el Porvenir." *El Mercurio*, 16–22 September, 1–2, international edition
  1993b    "Los Obispos Llaman a una Reconciliación sin Exclusiones." *El Mercurio*, 9–15 September, 1–2, international edition
  1993c    "S.E. Asistió a Tedeum Evangélico." *El Mercurio*, 9–15 September, 1, international edition.

Elster, Jon
  1986    *Rational Choice*. New York: New York University Press.
  1984    *Ulysses and the Sirens: Studies in Rationality and Irrationality*. Revised edition. Cambridge: Cambridge University Press.
  1983    *Sour Grapes*. Cambridge: Cambridge University Press.

Escobar, Jaime
  1986    *Persecución a la Iglesia en Chile*. Santiago: Terranova.

Espíndola, Walter Hanish
  1954    "Protestantismo en Chile." *Mensaje* 3 (26): 25.

Farrell, Gerardo T.
  1992    *Iglesia y pueblo en Argentina: Historias de 500 años de evangelización*. Buenos Aires: Editora Patria Grande.

Fearon, James
  1991    "Counterfactuals and Hypothesis Testing in Political Science." *World Politics* 43 (2): 169–95.

*Financial Times*
  1995    "Moscow Puts Its Faith in a Capital Project." *Financial Times*, 24 August, 2.

Finke, Roger
  1992    "An Unsecular America." In *Religion and Modernization: Sociologists and Historians Debate the Secularization Thesis*, edited by Steve Bruce. Oxford: Clarendon Press.
  1990    "Religious Deregulation: Origins and Consequences." *Journal of Church and State* 32 (3): 609-26.

Finke, Roger, and Rodney Stark
  1992    *The Churching of America 1776–1990: Winners and Losers in Our Religious Economy*. New Brunswick: Rutgers University Press.

Fleet, Michael
  1995    "The Chilean Church and the Transition to Democracy." In *Organized Religion in the Political Transformation of Latin America*, edited by Satya R. Pattnayak. Lanham, Md.: University Press of America.
  1985    *The Rise and Fall of the Chilean Christian Democracy*. Princeton: Princeton University Press.

Fontaine, Arturo, and Harald Beyer
  1991    "Retrato del movimiento evangélico a la luz de las encuestas de opinión público." *Estudios Públicos* 44:63–124.

Foreign Broadcast Information Service (FBIS)
    1979    "La Tribuna Discusses Banning of Jehovah's Witnesses." 9
            January, H1.
    1978    "Jehovah's Witnesses Banned." 16 February, B3.

Foroohar, Manzar
    1989    *The Catholic Church and Social Change in Nicaragua*. Albany:
            State University of New York Press.

Franceschi, Gustavo J.
    1944    "Un 'grave problema argentino' imaginario." *Criterio* 16 (830):
            77–84.

Frei, Eduardo
    1964    "Catholic Social Justice, Democracy and Pluralism." In *The
            Conflict between Church and State in Latin America*, edited by
            Frederick B. Pike. New York: Alfred A. Knopf.

Frías, Pedro J.
    1960    "La situación actual del Catolicismo en Argentina." *Criterio* 33
            (1360): 527–30.

Frieden, Jeffry A.
    1991    *Debt, Development, and Democracy: Modern Political Economy
            and Latin America, 1965–1985*. Princeton: Princeton University
            Press.

Friedman, Jeffrey
    1996    *The Rational Choice Controversy: Economic Models of Politics
            Reconsidered*. New Haven: Yale University Press.

Friedman, Milton
    1953    "The Methodology of Positive Economics." In *Essays in Positive
            Economics*, edited by Milton Friedman. Chicago: University of
            Chicago Press.

Fukuyama, Francis
    1995    *Trust*. New York: Free Press.

Gandolfo, Mercedes
    1969    *La Iglesia factor de poder en la Argentina*. Montevideo: Ediciones
            Nuestro Tiempo.

Garrard-Burnett, Virginia
    1992    "Protestantism in Latin America." *Latin American Research
            Review* 27 (1): 218–30.

Garrard-Burnett, Virginia, and David Stoll, eds.
    1993    *Rethinking Protestantism in Latin America*. Philadelphia: Temple
            University Press.

Geddes, Barbara
    1995    "Uses and Limitations of Rational Choice." In *Latin America in
            Comparative Perspective: New Approaches to Methods and
            Analysis*, edited by Peter H. Smith. Boulder, Colo.: Westview
            Press.

1994    *Politician's Dilemma: Building State Capacity in Latin America.*
        Berkeley and Los Angeles: University of California Press.
1990    "How the Cases You Choose Affect the Answers You Get:
        Selection Bias in Comparative Politics." *Political Analysis*
        2:131–52.
Gill, Anthony J.
1995    "The Politics of Religious Regulation in Mexico: Preliminary
        Observations." Paper presented at the 19th international congress
        of the Latin American Studies Association, Washington.
1994    "Rendering unto Caesar?: Religious Competition and Catholic
        Political Strategy in Latin America, 1962–79." *American Journal
        of Political Science* 38 (2): 403–25.
1993    "To Fall from Grace: The Church-State Obsolescing Bargain in
        Latin America." Paper presented at the annual meeting of the
        American Political Science Association, Washington.
Goff, James E.
1968    *The Persecution of Protestant Christians in Colombia,
        1948–1958.* SONDEOS, no. 23. Cuernavaca, Mexico: CIDOC.
González, Justo L.
1970    *Historia de las misiones.* Buenos Aires: La Aurora.
González, Carlos, and Alejandro Goic
1989    "Carta a las Comunidades Eclesiales de Base." Santiago: n.p.
Goodman, Timothy
1991    "Latin America's Reformation." *American Enterprise* 2:40–47.
Goodpasture, H. McKennie
1989    *Cross and Sword: An Eyewitness History of Christianity in Latin
        America.* Maryknoll, N.Y.: Orbis Books.
Greeley, Andrew
1994    "A Religious Revival in Russia?" *Journal for the Scientific Study
        of Religion* 33 (4): 273–72.
Green, Donald P., and Ian Shapiro.
1994    *Pathologies of Rational Choice Theory: A Critique of
        Applications in Political Science.* New Haven: Yale University
        Press.
Grzymala-Moszczynska, Halina
1996    "Established Religion vs. New Religions: Social Perception and
        Legal Consequences." *Religion in Eastern Europe* 16 (2): 36–40.
Gustafson, Lowell S.
1992    "Church and State in Argentina." In *The Religious Challenge to
        the State*, edited by Matthew C. Moen and Lowell S. Gustafson.
        Philadelphia: Temple University Press.
Gutiérrez, Gustavo
1973    *A Theology of Liberation.* Translated by Caridad Inda and John
        Eagleson. Maryknoll, N.Y.: Orbis Books.

Hadden, Jeffrey K.
    1987    "Toward Desacralizing Secularization Theory." *Social Forces* 65
            (3): 587–611.
Halperín Donghi, Tulio
    1993    *The Contemporary History of Latin America.* Translated by John
            Charles Chasteen. Durham: Duke University Press.
Harris, Joseph Claude
    1993    "Pennies for Heaven: Catholic Underachievers." *Commonweal,* 9
            April, 8–9.
*Hechos e Ideas*
[1955] 1964   "Peronism and the Intensified Attack against the Church." In *The
            Conflict between Church and State in Latin America,* edited by
            Frederick B. Pike. New York: Alfred A. Knopf.
Hennelly, Alfred T., ed.
    1993    *Santo Domingo and Beyond: Documents and Commentaries
            from the Historic Meeting of the Latin American Bishops'
            Conference.* Maryknoll, N.Y.: Orbis Books.
    1990    *Liberation Theology: A Documentary History.* Maryknoll, N.Y.:
            Orbis Books.
Hess, David J.
    1994    *Samba in the Night: Spiritism in Brazil.* New York: Columbia
            University Press.
Hewitt, W. E.
    1991    *Base Christian Communities and Social Change in Brazil.*
            Lincoln: University of Nebraska Press.
    1990    "Religion and the Consolidation of Democracy in Brazil: The
            Role of the Comunidades Eclesiais de Base (CEBs)." *Sociological
            Analysis* 50 (2): 139–52.
    1989    "Origins and Prospects of the Option for the Poor in Brazilian
            Catholicism." *Journal for the Scientific Study of Religion* 28 (2):
            120–35.
    1988    "Christian Base Communities: Structure, Orientation and
            Sociopolitical Thrust." *Thought* 63 (249): 162–75.
    1986    "Strategies for Social Change Employed by Comunidades
            Eclesiales de Base (CEBs) in the Archdiocese of São Paulo."
            *Journal for the Scientific Study of Religion* 25 (1): 16–30.
Hirschman, Albert O.
    1970    *Exit, Voice, and Loyalty: Responses to Decline in Firms,
            Organizations, and States.* Cambridge: Harvard University Press.
Holleran, Mary P.
    1949    *Church and State in Guatemala.* New York: Columbia University
            Press.
Howard, George P.
    1951    *We Americans: North and South.* New York: Friendship Press.

1944    *Religious Liberty in Latin America?* Philadelphia: Westminster Press.

Hudson, Rex A., and Dennis M. Hanratty, eds.

1991    *Bolivia: A Country Study.* Area Handbook Series. Washington: Federal Research Division.

Hull, Brooks B.

1989    "Religion, Afterlife, and Property Rights in the High Middle Ages." *Studies in Economic Analysis* 12 (1): 3–21.

Huntington, Samuel P.

1991a   *The Third Wave: Democratization in the Late Twentieth Century.* Norman: University of Oklahoma Press.

1991b   "Religion and the Third Wave." *National Interest* 24:29–42.

Hurtado, Alberto

[1941] 1992   *¿Es Chile un país católico?* Santiago: Editorial Los Andes.

Iannaccone, Laurence R.

1995a   "Voodoo Economics?: Reviewing the Rational Choice Approach to Religion." *Journal for the Scientific Study of Religion* 34:76–88.

1995b   "Household Production, Human Capital, and the Economics of Religion." In *The New Economics of Human Behavior*, edited by Mariano Tommasi and Kathryn Ierulli. Cambridge: Cambridge University Press.

1994    "Why Strict Churches Are Strong." *American Journal of Sociology* 99 (5): 1180–211.

1992    "Sacrifice and Stigma: Reducing Free-Riding in Cults, Communes, and Other Collectives." *Journal of Political Economy* 100:271–91.

1991    "The Consequences of Religious Market Structure: Adam Smith and the Economics of Religion." *Rationality and Society* 3 (2): 156–77.

1990    "Religious Practice: A Human Capital Approach." *Journal for the Scientific Study of Religion* 29 (3): 297–314.

Iannaccone, Laurence R., and Brooks B. Hull

1991    "The Economics of Religion: A Survey of Recent Work." *Bulletin of the Association of Christian Economists.*

Illich, Ivan

1972    "The Seamy Side of Charity." In *The Roman Catholic Church in Modern Latin America*, edited by Karl M. Schmitt. New York: Alfred A. Knopf.

Ivereigh, Austen

1995    *Catholicism and Politics in Argentina, 1810–1916.* New York: St. Martin's Press.

Jeffrey, Paul

1992    "Chamorro-Church Bonds Irk Evangelicals." *National Catholic Reporter* 28 (18 September): 10.

John Paul II
    1994    *Crossing the Threshold of Hope*. Translated by Jenny McPhee and Martha McPhee. New York: Alfred A. Knopf.
Johnstone, Patrick
    1986    *Operation World*. Bromley, England: WEC Publications.
*Journal of Church and State*
    1980    "Notes on Church-State Affairs." *Journal of Church and State* 22 (1): 173.
    1978a    "Notes on Church-State Affairs." *Journal of Church and State* 20 (3): 601.
    1978b    "Notes on Church-State Affairs." *Journal of Church and State* 20 (2): 371.
Kalyvas, Stathis
    1996a    *The Rise of Christian Democracy in Europe*. Ithaca: Cornell University Press.
    1996b    "Democracy and Religious Politics: Evidence from Europe." Paper presented at the annual meeting of the American Political Science Association, San Francisco.
    1995    "Cleavages, Mobilization, and Identity: Theoretical Insights from the Formation of Confessional Parties." Paper presented at the annual meeting of the Midwest Political Science Association, Chicago.
Kanagy, Conrad L.
    1990    "The Formation and Development of a Protestant Conversion Movement among the Highland Quichua of Ecuador." *Sociological Analysis* 50 (2): 205–17.
Kennedy, John J.
    1958    *Catholicism, Nationalism, and Democracy in Argentina*. Notre Dame: University of Notre Dame Press.
Keogh, Dermot, ed.
    1990    *Church and Politics in Latin America*. London: Macmillan.
Kepel, Gilles
    1994    *The Revenge of God: The Resurgence of Islam, Christianity, and Judaism in the Modern World*. Translated by Alan Braley. University Park: Pennsylvania State University Press.
Keshavarzian, Arang
    1996    *From Holy Alliance to Enemy of Islam: A Political Economy Theory of Ulama-State Relations in Iran, 1921–1941*. Master's thesis, University of Washington.
Kirk, John M.
    1992    *Politics and the Catholic Church in Nicaragua*. Gainesville: University Press of Florida.
    1989    *Between God and Party: Religion and Politics in Revolutionary Cuba*. Tampa: University of South Florida Press.

Klaiber, Jeffrey L.
    1970    "Pentecostal Breakthrough." *America* 122 (4): 99–102.
Kluegel, James R.
    1980    "Denominational Mobility: Current Patterns and Recent
            Trends." *Journal for the Scientific Study of Religion* 19 (1): 16–25.
Kuznetsov, Anatoly
    1996    "Ecumenism, Evangelism, and Religious Freedom in Russia and
            the Former Soviet Republics." *Religion in Eastern Europe* 16 (2):
            8–14.
Lalive d'Epinay, Christian
    1983    "Political Regimes and Millenarianism in a Dependent Society:
            Reflections on Pentecostalism in Chile." *Concilium* 161:42–54.
    1969    *Haven of the Masses: A Study of the Pentecostal Movement in
            Chile*. London: Lutterworth Press.
Landsberger, Henry A., ed.
    1970    *The Church and Social Change in Latin America*. Notre Dame:
            University of Notre Dame Press.
*La Revista Católica*
    1973    "Carta pastoral de los obispos de las provincias centrales de
            Chile." *La Revista Católica* 73 (1026): 162–65.
    1971    "Tedeum Ecumenico en Homenaje a la Patria." *La Revista
            Católica* 71:6180–81.
    1957    "Conclusiones de las Conferencias Episcopales de Chile." *La
            Revista Católica* 50 (979): 1871–78.
    1951    "Firmes en la Fe: Exhortación que el episcopado nacional hace a
            los fieles." *La Revista Católica* 44 (956): 119–22.
    1948a   "El frente del amor." *La Revista Católica* 44 (940): 1745–48.
    1948b   "El frente del amor." *La Revista Católica* 44 (941): 1832–34.
    1946    "Deber Social de los Católicos: Llamado que el episcopado
            nacional hace a los fieles." *La Revista Católica* 44 (929):
            808–12.
Larraín, Jorge
    1947    "Pastoral del Excmo. y Rvdmo. Sr. Obispo del Chillán sobre la
            propaganda protestante." *La Revista Católica* 44 (933):
            1116–19.
Larson, Oscar, and Carlos Valenzuela
    1940    *Respuesta a D. Rosenda Vidal G. y D. Carlos Aldunate E.*
            Santiago: Imprenta la Ilustración.
*Latin American Weekly Report*
    1991    "Government Joins 'Anti-sect' Drive." *Latin American Weekly
            Report,* 10 January, 9.
Lee, John
    1907    *Religious Liberty in Latin America*. Cincinnati: Jennings and
            Graham.

Lernoux, Penny
    1980    *Cry of the People: The Struggle for Human Rights in Latin America.* New York: Penguin Books.

Levi, Margaret
    1988    *Of Rule and Revenue.* Berkeley and Los Angeles: University of California Press.

Levine, Daniel H.
    1992    *Popular Voices in Latin American Catholicism.* Princeton: Princeton University Press.
    1990    "How Not to Understand Liberation Theology, Nicaragua or Both." *Journal of Interamerican Studies and World Affairs* 33 (3): 229–45.
    1987    "From Church and State to Religion and Politics and Back Again." *World Affairs* 150 (2): 93–108.
    1984    "Religion and Politics: Dimensions of Renewal." *Thought* 59 (233): 117–35.
    1981    *Religion and Politics in Latin America: The Catholic Church in Venezuela and Colombia.* Princeton: Princeton University Press.
    1974    "Religion and Politics." *Journal of Interamerican Studies and World Affairs* 16 (4): 497–507.

————, ed.
    1986    *Religion and Political Conflict in Latin America.* Chapel Hill: University of North Carolina Press.
    1979    *Churches and Politics in Latin America.* Beverly Hills, Cal.: Sage.

Lichbach, Mark Irving
    1995    *The Rebel's Dilemma.* Ann Arbor: University of Michigan Press.

Lodwick, Robert E.
    1969    *The Significance of the Church-State Relationship to an Evangelical Program in Brazil.* SONDEOS, no. 40. Cuernavaca, Mexico: CIDOC.

López, José Ignacio
    1995    "Los obispos no eludirían reconocer los errores." *La Nación,* 28 April, 7.

Lopresti, Roberto Pedro
    1993    *El poder constituyente.* Buenos Aires: Corregidor.

Lowden, Pamela
    1996    *Moral Opposition to Authoritarian Rule in Chile, 1973–90.* New York: St. Martin's Press.

Lubertino, María J.
    1987    *Perón y la Iglesia (1943–1955).* 2 vols. Buenos Aires: Centro Editor de América Latina.

MacEoin, Gary
    1991    "In Joust for Latin America, Rome Seeks Option for Rich." *National Catholic Reporter* 28 (8 November): 3.

Machiavelli, Niccoló
    1950    *The Prince and the Discourses.* New York: Modern Library.
Mackay, John A.
    1933    *The Other Spanish Christ.* New York: Macmillan.
Mainwaring, Scott
    1986    *The Catholic Church and Politics in Brazil, 1916–1985.* Stanford:
            Stanford University Press.
Mainwaring, Scott, and Alexander Wilde, eds.
    1989    *The Progressive Church in Latin America.* Notre Dame:
            University of Notre Dame Press.
Martin, David
    1990    *Tongues of Fire: The Explosion of Protestantism in Latin
            America.* Cambridge: Basil Blackwell.
Marx, Karl
    1975    "Contribution to the Critique of Hegel's Philosophy of Law." *On
            Religion.* Moscow: Progress Publishers.
Maryknoll Fathers
    1954    Proceedings of the Lima Methods Conference of the Maryknoll
            Fathers. Maryknoll House, Lima, Peru. 23–28 August 1954.
            Maryknoll, N.Y.: Maryknoll Fathers.
Mayhew, David
    1974    *Congress: The Electoral Connection.* New Haven: Yale University
            Press.
Mecham, J. Lloyd
    1966    *Church and State in Latin America: A History of Politico-
            Ecclesiastical Relations.* Chapel Hill: University of North
            Carolina Press.
Mejía, Jorge
    1969    "Latin America." *Concilium* 44 (1969): 143–46.
    1966    "The Growth of Ecumenism in Latin America." In *The Religious
            Dimension in the New Latin America*, edited by John J.
            Considine. Notre Dame, Ind.: Fides Publishers.
Mella, Orlando
    1987    *Religion and Politics in Chile: An Analysis of Religious Models.*
            Stockholm: Almquist and Wiksell International.
*Mensaje*
    1952    "El protestantismo en el Ecuador." *Mensaje* 1 (9): 326–28.
Mette, Norbert
    1979    "Evangelization and the Credibility of the Church." *Concilium*
            114:54–60.
Mignone, Emilio F.
    1990    "The Catholic Church, Human Rights and the 'Dirty War' in
            Argentina." In *Church and Politics in Latin America*, edited by
            Dermot Keogh. London: Macmillan.

1988    *Witness to the Truth: The Complicity of Church and Dictatorship in Argentina, 1976–1983*. Translated by Phillip Berryman. Maryknoll, N.Y.: Orbis Books.

Miliband, Ralph
   1969    *The State in Capitalist Society*. New York: Basic Books.

Miller, Alan S.
   1995    "A Rational Choice Model of Religious Behavior in Japan." *Journal for the Scientific Study of Religion* 34 (2): 234–44.

Millett, Richard
   1973    "The Protestant Role in Twentieth Century Latin American Church-State Relations." *Journal of Church and State* 15 (3): 367–80.

Moen, Matthew C., and Lowell S. Gustafson
   1992    *The Religious Challenge to the State*. Philadelphia: Temple University Press.

Mojzes, Paul
   1996    "Ecumenism, Evangelism, and Religious Liberty." *Religion in Eastern Europe* 16 (2): 1-7.

Montgomery, T. S.
   1979    "Latin American Evangelicals: Oaxtepec and Beyond." In *Churches and Politics in Latin America*, edited by Daniel H. Levine. Beverly Hills, Cal.: Sage.

Moore, Barrington
   1966    *Social Origins of Dictatorship and Democracy*. Boston: Beacon Press.

Moustafa, Tamir
   1996    "Between State and Society: Changing Relations between the Egyptian Government and al-Azhar." Unpublished manuscript. Seattle: University of Washington.

Mueller, Samuel A.
   1971    "Dimensions of Interdenominational Mobility in the United States." *Journal for the Scientific Study of Religion* 10 (2): 76–84.

Mugica, Carlos
   1973    *Peronismo y Cristianismo*. Buenos Aires: Editorial MERLIN.

*National Catholic Reporter*
   1992    "Santo Domingo foreruns church of next millennium." *National Catholic Reporter* 29 (6 November): 1.

Navarro, Julio
   1933    *El problema religioso en la cultura latinoamérica*. Montevideo: Editorial Mundo Nuevo.

Neuhouser, Kevin
   1989    "The Radicalization of the Brazilian Catholic Church in Comparative Perspective." *American Sociological Review* 54:233–44.

North, Douglass C.
    1981    *Structure and Change in Economic History*. New York: W. W.
            Norton.
Novak, Michael
    1986    *Will It Liberate? Questions about Liberation Theology*. Lanham,
            Md.: Madison Books.
Nuñez, Emilio A., and William D. Taylor
    1989    *Crisis in Latin America: An Evangelical Perspective*. Chicago:
            Moody Press.
Obispos y Sacerdotes de Los Angeles, Chillan y Talca
    1975    "Carta a los campesinos cristianos." Santiago: MUNDO.
O'Brien, Andrea
    1990    "The Catholic Church and State Tension in Paraguay." In *Church
            and Politics in Latin America*, edited by Dermot Keogh. New
            York: St. Martin's Press.
O'Dea, Thomas F.
    1972    "Church Reform and Society in Evolutionary Perspective."
            *Concilium* 73:11–23.
Olson, Mancur
    1965    *The Logic of Collective Action*. Cambridge: Harvard University
            Press.
Open Media Research Institute
    1996a   *OMRI Daily Digest*. 1 (149). Internet service OMRI-
            L%UBVM.BITNET @interbit.cren.net (2 August).
    1996b   *OMRI Daily Digest*. 1 (127). Internet service OMRI-
            L%UBVM.BITNET @interbit.cren.net (1 July).
Ossa, Manuel
    1964    "Comentario teológica." *Mensaje* 13 (133): 497–98.
Oviedo, Carlos, ed.
    1974    *Docuementados del episcopado: Chile 1970–1973*. Santiago:
            Ediciones Mundo.
Pacheco, Luis
    1985    *El pensamiento sociopolítico de los obispos chilenos, 1962–1973*.
            Santiago: Editorial Salesiana.
Padilla, C. René
    1985    Foreword to *The Expectation of the Poor: Latin American Base
            Ecclesial Communities in Protestant Perspective,* by Guillermo
            Cook. American Society of Missiology Series, no. 9. Maryknoll,
            N.Y.: Orbis Books.
Pape, Carlos
    1967    "Los evangélicos somos así." *Mensaje* 16 (156): 35–39.
Paredes-Alfaro, Rubén Elías
    1980    "The Protestant Movement in Ecuador and Peru: A Comparative
            Socio-Anthropological Study of the Establishment and Diffusion

of Protestantism in Two Central Highland Regions." Ph.D. diss., University of California, Los Angeles.

Pasini, Rebecca
1994     "The Search for a New Voice: The Role of the Roman Catholic Episcopate in the Political Transition of Poland." Paper presented at the annual meeting of the American Political Science Association, New York.

Pattnayak, Satya R., ed.,
1995     *Organized Religion in the Political Transformation of Latin America.* Lanham, Md.: University Press of America.

Perlez, Jane
1995     "Shrinking Gap between Church and Polish State." *New York Times*, 17 July, A3.

Perón, Juan
[1954] 1964     "A Denunciation of Certain Argentine Churchmen." In *The Conflict between Church and State in Latin America*, edited by Frederick B. Pike. New York: Alfred A. Knopf.

Peruvian Bishops' Commission for Social Action
1970     *Between Honesty and Hope: Documents from and about the Church in Latin America.* Translated by John Drury. Maryknoll Documentation Series. Maryknoll, N.Y.: Maryknoll Publications.

Pierson, Paul Everett
1974     *A Younger Church in Search of Maturity: Presbyterianism in Brazil from 1910 to 1959.* San Antonio: Trinity University Press.

Pike, Frederick B.
1970     "South America's Multifaceted Catholicism: Glimpses of Twentieth-Century Argentina, Chile and Peru." In *The Church and Social Change in Latin America*, edited by Henry A. Landsberger. Notre Dame: University of Notre Dame Press.

———, ed.
1964     *The Conflict between Church and State in Latin America.* New York: Alfred A. Knopf.

Poblete, Renato
1970     "The Church in Latin America: A Historical Survey." In *The Church and Social Change in Latin America,* edited by Henry A. Landsberger. Notre Dame: University of Notre Dame Press.
1965     *Crisis Sacerdotal.* Santiago: Editorial del Pacífico.

Poblete, Renato, and Carmen Galilea
1984     *Movimiento Pentecostal e Iglesia Católica en medios populares.* Santiago: Centro Bellarmino, Departamento de Investigaciones Sociológicas.

*Política y Espíritu*
1948     "El problema conservador." *Política y Espíritu* 3 (35): 258–62.

Popkin, Samuel
    1979    *The Rational Peasant: The Political Economy of Rural Society in Vietnam*. Berkeley and Los Angeles: University of California Press.
Posner, Richard A.
    1987    "The Law and Economics Movement." *American Economic Review* 77 (2): 1–13.
Powers, Gerard F.
    1996    "Religious Liberty: The State Church and Minority Faiths." *Religion in Eastern Europe* 16 (1): 28–33.
Precht, Cristían
    1992    "Del acuerdo a la reconciliación: La Iglesia de Chile y el camino a la democracia." Paper presented at the 17th international congress of the Latin American Studies Association, Los Angeles.
Prien, Hans-Jürgen
    1985    *La Historia del Cristianismo en América Latina*. Salamanca, Spain: Ediciones Sígueme.
Prieto, Jorge
    1958    "Los metodos del partido conservador unido." *Política y Espíritu* 13 (209): 24–32.
Putnam, Robert D.
    1993    *Making Democracy Work: Civic Traditions in Modern Italy*. Princeton: Princeton University Press.
Ramet, Sabrina Petra
    1992    "The New Church-State Configuration in Eastern Europe." In *Protestantism and Politics in Eastern Europe and Russia*, edited by Sabrina Petra Ramet. Durham: Duke University Press.
Read, William R., Victor M. Monterroso, and Harmon A. Johnson
    1969    *Latin American Church Growth*. Grand Rapids, Mich.: Eerdmans.
Riker, William H.
    1990    "Political Science and Rational Choice." In *Perspectives on Positive Political Economy*, edited by James E. Alt and Kenneth A. Shepsle. Cambridge: Cambridge University Press.
Robertson, Roland
    1992    "The Economization of Religion? Reflections on the Promise and Limitations of the Economic Approach." *Social Compass* 39 (1): 147–57.
Rodríguez, Mario A.
    1992    "Invasion and Evangelization in the Sixteenth Century." In *The Church in Latin America, 1492–1992*, edited by Enrique Dussel. Maryknoll, N.Y.: Orbis Books.
Rosales, Ray S.
    1968    *The Evangelism in Depth Program of the Latin American*

*Mission: A Description and Evaluation.* SONDEOS, no. 21.
Cuernavaca, Mexico: CIDOC.

Rosales Nelson, Susan
1986    "Bolivia: Continuity and Conflict in Religious Discourse." In
*Religion and Political Conflict in Latin America,* edited by Daniel
H. Levine. Chapel Hill: University of North Carolina Press.

Rouillon, Jorge
1995    "Los obispos frente a la represión ilegal." *La Nación,* 26 April,
14.

Rudolph, James D., ed.
1984    *Honduras: A Country Study.* Area Handbook Series. Washington:
Department of the Army.

Rueschemeyer, Dietrich, and Peter B. Evans
1985    "The State and Economic Transformation: Toward an Analysis of
the Conditions Underlying Effective Intervention." In *Bringing
the State Back In,* edited by Peter B. Evans, Dietrich
Rueschemeyer, and Theda Skocpol. Cambridge: Cambridge
University Press.

Rycroft, W. Stanley
1961    "A Statistical Study of Latin America." *Office for Research
Bulletin* 1:9. New York: Commission on Ecumenical Mission and
Relations of the United Presbyterian Church.

1946    *Indians of the High Andes: Report of the Commission Appointed
by the Committee on Cooperation in Latin America to Study the
Indians of the Andean Highland, With a View to Establishing a
Cooperative Christian Enterprise.* New York: Committee on
Cooperation in Latin America.

1942    *On This Foundation: The Evangelical Witness in Latin America.*
New York: Friendship Press.

Salinas, Maximiliano
1987    *Historia del pueblo de Dios en Chile.* Santiago: Ediciones Rehue.

Sampedro, Francisco
1989    *Pentecostales, sectas y pastoral.* Santiago: Comisión Nacional de
Ecumenismo Area Eclesial, Conferencia Episcopal de Chile.

Sanders, Thomas G.
1984    "Catholicism and Authoritarianism in Chile." *Thought* 59 (233):
229–43.

1972    "The Chilean Episcopate: An Institution in Transition." In *The
Roman Catholic Church in Modern Latin America,* edited by Karl
M. Schmitt. New York: Alfred A. Knopf.

1969    *Catholic Innovation in a Changing Latin America.* SONDEOS,
no. 41. Cuernavaca, Mexico: CIDOC.

Sanders, Thomas G., and Brian H. Smith
1976    "The Catholic Church under a Military Regime." In *Military*

        *Government and the Movement toward Democracy in South America*, edited by Howard Handelman and Thomas G. Sanders. Bloomington: Indiana University Press.

Santos, José Manuel, and Carlos Oviedo
    1971    "Deseamos mantener los colegios bajo la dependencia de la Iglesia." *La Revista Católica* 71 (1021): 6152.

Schlesinger, Stephen, and Stephen Kinzer
    1982    *Bitter Fruit: The Untold Story of the American Coup in Guatemala.* Garden City, N.Y.: Anchor Books.

Schwartz, Thomas
    1986    *The Logic of Collective Choice.* New York: Columbia University Press.

Segundo, Juan Luis
    1978    *The Hidden Motives of Pastoral Action.* Translated by John Drury. Maryknoll, N.Y.: Orbis Books.

Sepúlveda, Juan
    1987    "El nacimiento y desarrollo de las Iglesias evangélicas." In *Historia del pueblo de Dios en Chile*, edited by Maximiliano Salinas. Santiago: Ediciones Rehue.

Serbin, Kenneth P.
    1995    "Brazil: State Subsidization and the Church since 1930." In *Organized Religion in the Political Transformation of Latin America*, edited by Satya R. Pattnayak. Lanham, Md.: University Press of America.
    1994    "In Search of Refuge: The Post-Santo Domingo Church in Latin America." Paper presented at the 18th international congress of the Latin American Studies Association, Atlanta.

Shepherd, Frederick M.
    1995    "Church and State in Honduras and Nicaragua Prior to 1979." In *Religion and Democracy in Latin America*, edited by William H. Swatos, Jr. New Brunswick, N.J.: Transaction Publishers.

Sigmund, Paul E.
    1990    *Liberation Theology at the Crossroads: Democracy or Revolution?* New York: Oxford University Press.
    1986    "Revolution, Counterrevolution, and the Catholic Church in Chile." *Annals of the American Academy of Political and Social Science* 483:25–35.

Silva, Raúl Cardenal, and Carlos Oviedo
    1973    "Declaración del Comité Permanente del Episcopado de Chile sobre la Escuela Nacional Unificada." *La Revista Católica* 73 (1024): 69–71.

Siwak, Pedro
    1992    *500 años de evangelización americana: Tomo III (1900/1992)*—

*La evangelización argentina en el siglo XX*. Buenos Aires:
Ediciones del Encuentro.

Skidmore, Thomas E., and Peter H. Smith
    1984    *Modern Latin America*. New York: Oxford University Press.

Smith, Adam
    1986    *The Essential Adam Smith*, edited by Robert L. Heilbroner and
            Laurence J. Malone. New York: W.W. Norton.

Smith, Brian H.
    1990    "The Catholic Church and Politics in Chile." In *Church and
            Politics in Latin America*, edited by Dermot Keogh. New York: St.
            Martin's Press.
    1986    "Old Allies, New Opponents: The Church and the Military in
            Chile, 1973–1979." In *Military Rule in Chile: Dictatorship and
            Oppositions*, edited by J. Samuel Valenzuela and Arturo
            Valenzuela. Baltimore: Johns Hopkins University Press.
    1982    *The Church and Politics in Chile: Challenges to Modern
            Catholicism*. Princeton: Princeton University Press.
    1979    "Churches and Human Rights in Latin America: Recent Trends
            on the Subcontinent." In *Churches and Politics in Latin America*,
            edited by Daniel H. Levine. Beverly Hills, Cal.: Sage.

Stanley, Alessandra
    1994    "From Repression to Respect, Russian Church in Comeback."
            *New York Times,* 3 October, A1, A4.

Stark, Rodney
    1992    "Do Catholic Societies Really Exist?" *Rationality and Society* 4
            (3): 261–71.

Stark, Rodney, and William Sims Bainbridge
    1987    *A Theory of Religion*. New York: Peter Lang Publishing.
    1985    *The Future of Religion: Secularization, Revival, and Cult Formation*.
            Berkeley and Los Angeles: University of California Press.

Stark, Rodney, Laurence Iannaccone, and Roger Finke
    1995    "Religion, Science, and Rationality." *American Economic Review*
            74 (2): 433–38.

Stark, Rodney, and James C. McCann
    1993    "Market Forces and Catholic Commitment: Exploring the New
            Paradigm." *Journal for the Scientific Study of Religion* 32 (2):
            111–24.

Stepan, Alfred
    1978    "Political Leadership and Regime Breakdown: Brazil." In *The
            Breakdown of Democratic Regimes*, edited by Juan Linz and
            Alfred Stepan. Baltimore: Johns Hopkins University Press.

Stewart-Gambino, Hannah W.
    1992    *The Church and Politics in the Chilean Countryside*. Boulder,
            Colo.: Westview Press.

Stigler, George J., and Gary S. Becker
    1977    "De Gustibus Non Est Disputandum." *American Economic Review* 67 (2): 76–90.

Stoll, David
    1993    Introduction to *Rethinking Protestantism in Latin America*, edited by Virginia Garrard-Burnett and David Stoll. Philadelphia: Temple University Press.
    1990    *Is Latin America Turning Protestant?* Berkeley and Los Angeles: University of California Press.

Sweeney, Ernest S.
    1992a    "Presencia y poder del protestantismo en América Latina: el caso argentino." *CIAS* 41 (413): 213–28.
    1992b    "Presencia y poder del protestantismo en América Latina: el caso argentino II." *CIAS* 41 (414): 293–305.
    1970    *Foreign Missionaries in Argentina 1938–1962*. SONDEOS no. 68. Cuernavaca, Mexico: CIDOC.

Tagle, Emilio
    1973a    "Declaración del obispado de Valparaiso ante el proyecto de la 'Escuela Nacional Unificada.'" *La Revista Católica* 73 (1024): 75–76.
    1973b    "Declaración del obispo de Valparaiso." *La Revista Católica* 73 (1026): 174–75.

Tangeman, Michael
    1995    *Mexico at the Crossroads: Politics, the Church, and the Poor*. Maryknoll, N.Y.: Orbis Books.

Taylor, Michael
    1982    *Community, Anarchy and Liberty*. Cambridge: Cambridge University Press.

Tessi, Francisco S.
    1944    "La restauración espiritual de la educación argentina." *Criterio* 16 (831): 111–12.

Tetlock, Philip E., and Aaron Belkin, eds.
    1996    *Counterfactual Thought Experiments in World Politics: Logical, Methodological, and Psychological Perspectives*. Princeton: Princeton University Press.

Todaro Williams, Margaret
    1976    "Church and State in Vargas's Brazil: The Politics of Cooperation." *Journal of Church and State* 18 (3): 443–62.

Tsebelis, George.
    1990    *Nested Games: Rational Choice in Comparative Politics*. Berkeley and Los Angeles: University of California Press.

Turner, Frederick C.
    1971    *Catholicism and Political Development in Latin America*. Chapel Hill: University of North Carolina Press.

Turner, Paul R.
    1979    "Religious Conversion and Community Development." *Journal for the Scientific Study of Religion* 18 (3): 252–60.
Tversky, Amos.
    1969    "Intransitivity of Preferences." *Psychological Review* 76:105–10.
Tversky, Amos, and Daniel Kahneman
    1981    "The Framing of Decisions and the Pyschology of Choice." *Science* 211:453–58.
Vallier, Ivan
    1972    "Church 'Development' in Latin America: A Five Country Comparison." In *The Roman Catholic Church in Modern Latin America*, edited by Karl M. Schmitt. New York: Alfred A. Knopf.
    1970    *Catholicism, Social Control, and Modernization in Latin America.* Englewood Cliffs, N.J.: Prentice Hall.
    1963    *Anglican Opportunities in South America.* New York: Bureau of Applied Social Research.
Van Vugt, Johannes P.
    1991    *Democratic Organization for Social Change: Latin American Christian Base Communities and Literacy Campaigns.* New York: Bergin and Garvey.
Vatican City
    1975    *Annuario Pontificio.* Bristol, Pa.: International Publications Service.
Vergara, Ignacio
    1962    *El protestantismo en Chile.* Santiago: Editorial del Pacífico.
    1955    "El protestantismo en Chile" *Mensaje* 4 (41): 257–62.
Vicaría de la Solidaridad y UNELAM
    1978    *La libertad religiosa en Chile, los evangélicos y el gobierno militar.* Santiago, Chile.
Vicuña, Eladio
    1973    "Declaración del obispo de Chillánm Monseñor Eladio Vicuña, sobre la Escuela Nacional Unificada." *La Revista Católica* 73 (1024): 79–81.
Villalpando, Waldo Luis, ed.
    1970    *Las Iglesias del transplantes: Protestantismo de inmigración en la Argentina.* Buenos Aires: Centro de Estudios Cristianos.
Villegas, Sergio
    1963    "Encuentro católico-protestante latinoaméricano." *Mensaje* 12 (188): 189–91.
Vitalis, Helmut Gnadt
    1969    *The Significance of Changes in Latin American Catholicism since Chimbote 1953.* SONDEOS no. 51. Cuernavaca, Mexico: CIDOC.

Wallace, Anthony F. C.
    1966    *Religion: An Anthropological View*. New York: Random House.
Wallis, Roy, and Steve Bruce
    1992    "Secularization: The Orthodox Model." In *Religion and Modernization*, edited by Steve Bruce. Oxford: Clarendon Press.
Warner, R. Stephen
    1993    "Work in Progress toward a New Paradigm for the Sociological Study of Religion in the United States." *American Journal of Sociology*. 98 (5): 1044–93.
White, John W.
    1943    *Our Good Neighbor Hurdle*. Milwaukee: Bruce Publishing.
Whitfield, Teresa
    1995    *Paying the Price: Ignacio Ellacuría and the Murdered Jesuits of El Salvador*. Philadelphia: Temple University Press.
Wilkie, James W., and Peter Reich
    1980    *Statistical Abstract of Latin America*. Vol. 20. Los Angeles: UCLA Latin American Center Publications.
Willems, Emilio
    1967    *Followers of the New Faith: Cultural Change and the Rise of Protestantism in Brazil and Chile*. Nashville: Vanderbilt University Press.
    1964    "Protestantism and Culture Change in Brazil and Chile." In *Religion, Revolution, and Reform: New Forces for Change in Latin America*, edited by William V. D'Antonio and Frederick B. Pike. New York: Frederick A. Praeger.
Williams, Philip J.
    1989    *The Catholic Church and Politics in Nicaragua and Costa Rica*. Pittsburgh: University of Pittsburgh Press.
Wood, James E.
    1966    "Editorial: Church and State in Latin America." *Journal of Church and State* 8 (2): 173–85.
Yañez, Eugenio
    1989    *La Iglesia y el Gobierno Militar*. Santiago: Editorial Andante.

## Interviews

Arzube, Juan
    Auxiliary bishop, Los Angeles; participant in 1976 Riobamba (Ecuador) Conference. 21 February 1992. Irwindale, Cal.
Braun, Rafael
    Editor of *Criterio*. 26 April 1994. Buenos Aires.
Centeno, Angel
    Subsecretary of religion under Arturo Frondizi and Carlos Menem. 27 April 1994. Buenos Aires.

Chacón, Arturo
    Director, Comunidad Teologica Evangélica de Chile. 6 August 1993.
    Santiago.
Donini, Antonio
    Historian. 25 April 1994. Buenos Aires.
Finkenbinder, Paul
    Director, Hermano Pablo Ministries. 16 March 1993. Costa Mesa, Cal.
Galán, Carlos
    Bishop of La Plata, Argentina; former president of Conferencia
    Episcopada Argentina. 25 April 1994. Buenos Aires.
Galilea, Carmen
    Sociologist, Centro Bellarmino. 28 July 1993. Santiago.
Goff, James
    Retired missionary. 18 February 1993. Claremont, Cal.
González, Miguel
    Researcher, Centro de Estudios Públicos. 15 July 1993. Santiago.
Grellert, Manfred
    Vice president, World Vision. 20 April 1992. Pasadena, Cal.
Gutiérrez, Isaias
    Bishop, Iglesia Metodista de Chile. 23 August 1993. Santiago.
Holland, Cliff
    Director, Latin American Region, World Mission. 1 July 1992. Pasadena,
    Cal.
Lagos, Humberto
    Baptist sociologist, SEDEC. 10 August 1993. Santiago.
Ligget, T. J.
    Retired missionary. 26 June 1992. Claremont, Cal.
McIntire, Robert L.
    Retired missionary. 19 March 1993. Duarte, Cal.
Mejía, Jorge
    Vice president, Pontifical Council for Justice and Peace (Vatican); former
    secretary of ecumenical relations, CELAM. 21 March 1992. Anaheim,
    Cal.
Ossa, Manuel
    Minister, Lutheran Church; Centro Ecuménico Diego Medellín. 19 July
    1993. Santiago.
Pérez del Viso, Ignacio
    Jesuit; Centro de Investigación y Acción Social. 20 April 1994. Buenos
    Aires.
Perkins, Rodger
    Retired missionary. 19 March 1992. Duarte, Cal.
Pierson, Paul
    Former missionary; Professor, Fuller Missionary School. 17 June 1992.
    Pasadena, Cal.

Precht, Christian
    Vicario General de Pastoral y de la Juventud del Arzobispado. 3 August
    1993. Santiago.
Ramírez, Dagoberto
    Methodist minister; Centro Ecuménico Diego Medellín. 19 July 1993.
    Santiago.
Rosales, Raúl
    Catholic priest; Centro Ecuménico Diego Medellín. 19 July 1993.
    Santiago.
Storni, Fernando
    Jesuit; Centro de Investigación y Acción Social. 28 April 1994. Buenos
    Aires.
Thorp, Robert
    Retired missionary. 19 March 1992. Pasadena, Cal.
Van Engen, Charles
    Professor, Fuller Missionary School; former missionary. 23 June 1992.
    Pasadena, Cal.
Wallis, Calvin P.
    Retired missionary. 18 March 1993. Duarte, Cal.
Wegmueller, Paul
    Director, World-Wide Missions. 29 May 1992. Pasadena, Cal.

# Index